RETROSPECTIVE
CONVERSION

LIBRARY HI TECH SERIES

pierian press
1984

RETROSPECTIVE CONVERSION:

FROM CARDS TO COMPUTER

Edited by
Anne G. Adler
and
Elizabeth A. Baber

14099

Library of Congress Catalog Card Number 84-81656
ISBN 0-87650-177-3

THE PIERIAN PRESS
P.O. Box 1808
Ann Arbor, MI. 48106

Contents

Introduction

Several years ago, when the Fondren Library of Rice University decided to embark on a retrospective conversion of its card catalog to machine-readable form, I wrote to the Library Information and Technology Association (LITA) of the American Library Association for assistance. I hoped that there was, within the Information Science and Automation Division (ISAS) of LITA, a committee which could help us with advice and which might give us some answers.

Since there was no such committee, I formed a discussion group to help our library and other interested libraries. This group was officially established at the 1980 ALA Meeting in New York City.

Shortly after this, another concerned librarian, faced with a similar prospect in her library, formed another discussion group under the aegis of the Resources and Technical Services Division (RTSD). At the ALA Mid-Winter meeting in Washington, D.C. in 1981, Roberta Kirby and I joined forces to form the LITA-ISAS/RTSD Retrospective Conversion Discussion Group.

We found no shortage of interesting conversions as reported by experienced librarians. There was an even larger number of interested and inexperienced librarians who wanted to attend these meetings.

Many of the chapters in this book are based on presentations made at the discussion group meetings. There are also two speeded-up, streamlined versions of the original projects. I thought they might give some idea of the compromises and trade-offs you may find you have to make.

Several factors can be expected in a retrospective conversion:

1. You will from the beginning probably be under a time and budget constraint imposed by the library administration and any higher authority under which the library operates. It may take a little while to realize this, but, believe me, it will be brought to your attention.

2. You will probably begin by making the perfectly natural mistake of basing your plans and specifications on a card catalog,

while you should be making your assumptions and plans on an online catalog. Since you very well may never have worked with an online catalog, this mistake should not surprise you.

3. You may start by being a perfectionist; but you will come to terms with money, administration, time, and personnel. You will end by becoming a pragmatist; you will cut out here and curtail there. What you will have, I believe, when you finish will be a better basis and blueprint for your new catalog than you would have had, had you not been kept flexible by these demands.

There are, however, off-setting factors, which I feel sure you will find, as we did:

1. The x-factor we initially worried most about — turnover — has not been the problem that we anticipated. It is true that economic conditions have made jobs at odd hours more attractive, but there is, from our experience and uninfluenced by that factor, a pool of people who are willing to work either before or after a regular work day.

2. Librarians are, as I have always found them to be, willing to help and to share specifications, training tools, and their experiences in general.

These essays have been edited by Elizabeth A. Baber, Principal Cataloger at the Fondren Library, and by me. It is our hope that this book of case studies will help others involved in retrospective conversion, as we have been helped ourselves.

I want to express my gratitude and thanks to Dr. Samuel M. Carrington, Director of the Fondren Library here at Rice University, for his backing throughout this project. Without his support during the early stages of the formation of the discussion group and his encouragement as we moved along, our efforts would not have been as rewarding.

Anne G. Adler

RETROSPECTIVE CONVERSION USING OCLC AT TEXAS A&M UNIVERSITY LIBRARY

Nancy E. Douglas

Texax A&M University Library was one of the first large library collections to have a full retrospective conversion done at OCLC by the group which is now known as the Retrospective Conversion Service. OCLC both updated records found in the database and input new records, and upon completion of the project sent A&M computer tapes for some 338,000 OCLC MARC records. The Library shipped its shelf list to OCLC for the conversion, and the primary conversion specification was that the machine-readable records match the shelf list cards exactly. The project took 19 months and was completed by the end of 1980, with all headings in pre-AACR2 forms.

Scope of the Project and Shelf List Description

The earliest decisions the library faced were those involving what part of the collection was to be converted, what information was to be included in each record, and how this information should be coded into machine-readable form. The library administration was committed to a future comprehensive on-line system, including a catalog; so the decision was made to include all information found on existing catalog cards and to convert every title that was part of the cataloged collections. Since the library had been building a database of OCLC records for current cataloging for several years, it was resolved that the converted records should be in the same MARC format.

In order to convey to conversion vendors the full scope of the project, a shelf list description was prepared. The shelf list was measured to obtain an estimate of total titles, then several drawers were carefully studied to provide a sample of the whole. Percentages were determined for records already cataloged by A&M on OCLC, records which would be in the OCLC database and thus simple updates, records requiring new input, and records which were likely to be problems. Excluding the titles previously done by A&M on OCLC,

1

the shelf list was estimated to contain about 399,000 titles, of which 83 % were predicted to have matching OCLC copy, 14 % to require input of new records, and 2 % to be returned as problems.

Conversion Specifications

The primary specification for conversion was that the machine-readable record match the shelf list card exactly. The head of the OCLC retrospective conversion group visited Texas A&M to review the requirements. A fifty-two page document was prepared to explain the idiosyncrasies of local location stamps and their relationship to OCLC holding library codes, the kinds of records the library wanted to review as problems, the degree of MARC fixed field information expected in the records, sample cards, and so on. The A&M project demanded much more bibliographic detail than had previous projects, leading to re-negotiation on some parts of the specifications during the term of the project. The extensive detail also forced a change in OCLC's predicted time frame from 14 to 19 months, even though the staff size of the OCLC team was greatly enlarged during the project.

Choosing a Vendor

When Texas A&M first started looking at vendors in 1978, very few had had experience in converting large bibliographic files to MARC format. The library hoped to find an experienced vendor, in order to reduce training or involvement by library staff to a minimum. Factors considered in evaluating vendors included cost, schedule, library involvement in conversion, amount of data to be converted, experience of agency, training required, and future uses of the data. The chosen vendor, OCLC, had extensive familiarity with the MARC format, agreed to a cost of 66¢ per record including microfilming the shelf list as a backup file, and predicted a conversion period of 14 months. The A&M project was bid and largely completed before OCLC started charging differential rates on prime and non-prime time use of the system for conversion.

Source of Bibliographic Information

The shelf list cards at Texas A&M had almost always been complete bibliographic records, comparable to main entry cards. Even when slightly less complete, they were usually acceptable for K-level input on OCLC. For this reason, the shelf list was chosen as the source of bibliographic information for the project. Since some tracings had been typed on the backs of shelf list cards, it was decided that the shelf list cards, rather than some sort of reproduction, should be sent to OCLC. A microfilming company was hired to come into the library and film the shelf list, creating one copy for use in cataloging and another for reconstruction of the file in case cards were lost in transit.

Shipping Procedures

Shelf list cards were removed from drawers and packed into OCLC card boxes. Several dozen extra card boxes were obtained from OCLC in order to maintain a steady flow of shipments, and an extra 25 hours per week of student help was used for shipping, receiving, and refiling. The OCLC card boxes were packed into larger cartons, with about five or six boxes per carton. Both A&M and OCLC kept records of boxes and call number ranges shipped and received. The U.S. mail and UPS were both used at various times in the project, and no cards were lost or damaged in shipping. An attempt was made to have only about 50 drawers out of the shelf list at any time, but, in a few instances, large shipments were unaccountably detained in both OCLC's shipping area and the A&M campus mail area, requiring telephone calls to track down their location.

Interim Shelf List

Once the microfilming of the shelf list was begun, no new cards could be added to the file, as the intention was that the file could be reproduced from the microfilm. An interim shelf list was begun, into which were filed all new temporary shelf list cards ("temps") and OCLC shelf list cards from current cataloging. When catalogers assigned call numbers, they checked the permanent shelf list and the interim shelf list. If the necessary drawer of the permanent shelf list was in transit, the cataloger checked the microfilm. The thirty-five reels of shelf list microfilm and two film readers were located near the shelf list. As shelf list cards were returned from OCLC, they were put back into their original drawers, and the interim shelf list cards were gradually interfiled. As well as integrating the files, this procedure served as a check for possible filing disorder from the conversion process. The completed, interfiled drawers were labelled, so that the catalogers could tell there was no longer any need to check the interim file.

Quality Control

Procedures for quality control or quality assurance were an important part of the project. In the first step, the microfilming, a large

3

number of the drawers were checked against the film to insure that no cards had been skipped or damaged in filming. Once the conversion project was under way, the library's systems analyst set up an interface program to allow the loading of OCLC tapes on the university's Amdahl computer, obtaining a printout of records done by the conversion team. Project records were distinguished by the letters "rcp" in the 910 field, and every 200th "rcp" record was selected for printing. Catalogers checked these printout records for accuracy against the shelf list cards. The catalogers checked most carefully for typing errors in call numbers, holding library codes, and access points, checked to see that the full shelf list record had been included, and made certain that serials notes involving title changes had been correctly transcribed and coded. In general, tagging, LC card number, notes, and fixed field elements were not as closely checked. Any errors detected were photocopied and returned to OCLC for correction.

Problem Records

OCLC flagged the shelf list cards for certain categories of problem records by clipping brief notes to the cards. When the cards were returned to A&M, a student photocopied all flagged shelf list cards and gave the photocopies to a cataloger for review. In many cases, the solution to the problem or question was determined by the cataloger, and the corrected photocopy was then returned to OCLC for conversion.

One of the largest categories of problem records involved serials which A&M had once cataloged under "latest entry" rules, but which appeared in OCLC only with the newer "successive entry" records. Some of these ended up being recataloged at A&M, but others were done as updates on a selected record in the database.

Another large category of problem was "dash-ons," in which supplements or slightly variant editions had been added to the catalog card for an earlier edition, usually with a different call number. This practice is not allowed on OCLC, and catalogers at A&M had to decide whether to recatalog the title or change the dash-on to some kind of accompanying material note.

A third large category was flagged "previously updated," that is, though the shelf list was not an OCLC card, the A&M symbol was on the OCLC record already. In most cases, this was a result of having updated on OCLC for an added volume or added copy without the need for producing new cards. If the added volume situation did not apply, A&M simply retained the shelf list card for future resolution.

Some records were flagged due to characters, words, or complete records in non-Roman alphabets. A&M had few items in this category;

so it usually romanized the record and returned it to OCLC for input. On all errors and problems, only photocopies were sent to OCLC, rather than shipping the shelf list card again. At the end of the project, OCLC agreed to accept and correct revisions for an additional three months.

Statistics

OCLC was required to supply monthly reports on the progress of the project. The final statistics for the conversion showed 338,203 items processed by the team, of which 84% were matches in the database, 11% were new input, and 5% were problems. OCLC was able to correct many of the problems when A&M provided further information; so only about 2% of the records remained for in-house resolution.

The calculation of percentage of error was an area which caused considerable disagreement between A&M and OCLC, as each institution was using a different formula. OCLC's procedure for calculating error rate was similar to the one used for the OCLC database as a whole; that is, the only errors recognized were those which had been reported. For example, if twenty errors were reported on a tape containing 40,000 records, the error rate was only .05%.

A&M checked the tapes by a sampling procedure, however, and calculated an error rate from the sample. For example, on a tape of 40,000 records, A&M would sample every 200th record, resulting in a sample of 200 records. If 20 errors were detected in those 200 records, an error rate of 10% was assessed for the tape. A&M sampled almost every tape and calculated error rates that ranged from 1% to 15%. Although OCLC did not fully agree with the sampling technique and statistics, the concern over error rate led OCLC to increase the amount of verification done on both new input and updates during the course of the project. A&M estimated the overall rate to be approximately 7%.

Communications

One person at Texas A&M was the designated contact for questions from the OCLC retrospective conversion team. A telephone log was maintained, and questions were routinely followed by written confirmation. Initially, the contact person was the library's systems analyst; later, the contact was the Head of Copy Cataloging, as most questions were bibliographic in nature or related to the use of input stamps.

Communication with the rest of the library outside of cataloging was also considered important. The Reference Department had public OCLC terminals, and librarians and patrons were interested in using them as a sort of on-line catalog as more of the shelf list was loaded. It was important that other library departments understood the reasons for not changing or pulling cards from the shelf list, since otherwise the microfilm copy would lose its capacity for reconstructing the file.

Staff Involvement

Though the project was not actually done in the library, a very large amount of staff time and cataloging expertise was required. The early preparation of estimates and description of the shelf list, specifications for conversion, and computer programs for quality assessment involved the systems analyst, the Head of Cataloging, and the Head of Copy Cataloging. Extra student hours were used in packing, shipping, receiving, unpacking, and refiling shelf list cards, and in photocopying flagged problems and errors. Quality control involved a minimum of four hours per week from a cataloger or copy cataloger in checking printouts against shelf list cards. Problem resolution was largely done by catalogers and the Head of Copy Cataloging, with some legwork by students to retrieve books. The Head of Copy Cataloging or the systems analyst was responsible for answering telephone questions from OCLC and following up with written documentation; when these individuals were absent, and alternate librarian was assigned the responsibility. The Head of Cataloging devoted time to analyzing periodically the results of the quality control efforts, reporting to the University Librarian, and negotiating revisions in the conversion specifications.

Conclusion

Overall, the Texas A&M University Library was well satisfied with the results of the retrospective conversion done by OCLC. The percentages encountered for the records in the database, new input, and problems were very close to the predictions, although A&M over-estimated the total number of records to be converted by about 15%. The error rate was higher than desired or expected, but the library will not really be able to assess the impact of errors until the records are accessible on a local on-line system. Some errors, such as those involving accession numbers, will be completely irrelevant when replaced by bar-codes in future systems. Most important to the library is the fact that essentially the entire cataloged collection now exists in OCLC MARC format records. Library patrons have access to the records through the two OCLC public services terminals, and the tapes will be used in an on-line circulation system; this will eventually lead to a local on-line catalog. The Texas A&M retrospective conversion project also added approximately 42,000 new records to the OCLC union catalog database.

PLANNING FOR RETROSPECTIVE CONVERSION AT RICE UNIVERSITY: VENDOR AND IN-HOUSE ALTERNATIVES

Elizabeth A. Baber

As in many other libraries in the country, a committee to study the future of the card catalog was appointed in Rice University's Fondren Library in December, 1978. In the course of studying the various alternatives to the catalog, the committee recommended, and the administration approved, the hiring of a consultant to advise us on the alternative of an online catalog. The consultant, Jim Thompson (then of Johns Hopkins University, now Associate Director of the Fondren Library) recommended:

1. that we adopt an online catalog when this became technologically and financially feasible;

2. that we maintain our present single card catalog until that time;

3. that we immediately begin retrospective conversion.

After a review of our options, the committee unanimously recommended in March, 1980, that we follow the advice of our consultant in all respects.

Shortly thereafter, our University Librarian, Dr. Samuel M. Carrington, Jr., appointed a committee to find out what a conversion of our entire catalog of approximately 452,000 titles would cost. We were to get bids from three vendors and also to calculate the cost of an in-house conversion.

Committee Begins Work

Since we, at the beginning of this project, had no practical experience in the area of retrospective conversion, we began by reading or re-reading everything we could get our hands on. An excellent overview of the subject, entitled "The Conversion of Manual Catalogs to Collection Data Bases," is given by Brett Butler, Brian Aveney, and William Scholz in *Library Technology Reports*, vol. 14, no. 2, March–April 1978. This article is now somewhat outdated but gives many of the basic concepts and costs to be considered.

As anyone who has worked with computers knows, editing of a pre-existing machine-readable record is much faster and less expensive than inputting a record from scratch. Since ours is a university library with many foreign-language and other unusual materials, we realized that we should consider only vendors with large databases for our conversion, so that the more costly original input of records could be kept to a minimum. We therefore sought bids only from Blackwell/North America, AMIGOS (our regional network), and OCLC. In-house conversion costs were also calculated on the basis of use of the OCLC database.

Conversion Must Be Done from Public Catalog

We had known from the beginning that Rice had a problem many other libraries do not have. Complete information is not given on our shelflist cards, but only on the main cards in our public catalog. This means that it is necessary to go through our public catalog card by card looking for the main cards from which conversion is to be done. Since we could not send the public catalog drawers to a vendor, it would be necessary to find some other means of making our catalog portable.

We briefly considered the possibility of photocopying the main cards. To avoid leafing through the catalog card by card, we thought we could use the shelflist to isolate main cards. This would entail pulling the shelflist cards, making dummies for the main cards, pulling the main cards, photocopying the main cards, and refiling the main cards and shelflist cards. By simulating this procedure, we found that it took about three minutes per main card. Using an estimate of 460,000 titles, 23,000 hours would be required for this task, at a cost of $82,800.00. We calculated that it would take one person 11 years, 11 people one year, or 44 people three months to do this. Needless to say, this idea was abandoned.

Our next idea, which was the one finally adopted, was that of microfilming the entire catalog. Although film would be somewhat harder to work with, it would make the catalog easily portable. We found that our catalog of 2½ million cards could be filmed for about $20,000.00 in two months time during our summer break. Both the front and the back of cards were filmed, since our tracing is sometimes typed on the backs of cards. We filmed at a reduction ratio of 50X and at an actual cost of $8.00 per 1,000 cards, plus $15.00 per roll. An added advantage, besides portability, of the filming of the catalog was the fact that we now had a copy for security purposes.

When we asked vendors for bids, we indicated that we expected all records to be edited to match exactly the cards in our catalog. The vendors with whom we talked told us that extensive editing of records would run up the cost of the conversion, but we felt that exact information was important in a university environment. If we also had, as we suspected, a high percentage of foreign-language and pre-MARC materials requiring original input, that would increase the cost too.

We, therefore, decided to do a sample of our catalog to determine what percentage of our records were exact matches or needed only minor editing, what percentage needed major changes, what percentage had no copy in OCLC, and what percentage were serials. Our sampling procedure was quite simple. We pulled several drawers, went through the cards in each drawer locating main cards, searched each title on OCLC, compared any record found against our card, and kept count of each category into which our titles fell. By doing this, we found that 26% of these titles were exact matches or required only minor changes, 56% required more extensive changes, 17% had no copy in OCLC, and 1% were serials. Of the records found, 15% consisted of member copy.

From the results of this sample, it became clear to us that even with a database as large as that of OCLC (at that time over six million records) a relatively large percentage of our titles would require original input. With these results, we eliminated Blackwell/ North America from serious consideration as a vendor, because of the much smaller size of this company's database. Blackwell/North America had also indicated that its personnel could not work with microfilm.

Conversion Costs

A summary of our sample results, together with a sample of the microfilm of our card catalog, was sent to AMIGOS and OCLC in mid-May. By August we had bids from both AMIGOS and OCLC. AMIGOS' bid was broken down according to the type of activity required for each title. First there was a fee for searching our records against the OCLC database. This fee, of course, would apply to all titles. An additional fee per title was added for an "update," where no editing was involved, while another fee applied when the record already in the database had to be edited. The fees in both of these categories were somewhat larger for serials than for monographs. If original input were required, still another fee applied. To estimate the total cost of the project from this rather complex fee structure, we used the percentages of each type of title gathered from our sample of the card catalog. Since AMIGOS projected that it would take 3½ to 4 years to complete the conversion, we also added a 10% annual inflation rate.

OCLC gave us a flat bid of so much per title. This fee was at the upper range of their cost scale (at that time $.40 to $1.50) because of the large amount of editing that would be required to meet our standards. They projected that it would take one to two years to complete the conversion.

For an in-house conversion, we calculated that it would cost us $1.45 per title or $655,400 for 452,000 titles. As OCLC had by then imposed a large surcharge on conversions done during prime time, we postulated that it would be necessary to hire a special staff to do the conversion during non-prime time. Since we thought it was unlikely that we could get people to work from 6:00 to 8:00 A.M. and since regular staff members work until 5:00 P.M., we found that only 26 hours per week of actual work time were available for retrospective conversion. Postulating four conversion assistants doing 10 titles per hour (a figure derived from actually trying it), we found that we would be able to do 49,920 titles per year. To do 452,000 titles would then take nine years, or, more realistically (allowing for downtime, absenteeism, and turnover), 10 years.

Committee Report

In an August report to the University Librarian we set forth the cost figures derived from the vendors and from our in-house calculations. Since the OCLC bid was substantially lower than that of AMIGOS and somewhat lower than in-house conversion costs would be, we strongly recommended that OCLC be given the retrospective conversion contract. In addition to the cost factor, the fact that OCLC could do the project in about one-half the time projected by AMIGOS and one-fifth the time projected for an in-house conversion weighed the scales heavily in favor of OCLC. We also strongly favored an out-of-house conversion because we felt that the involvement of the regular staff would be minimal. Since we thought it would be difficult for existing staff to absorb new duties, we considered this to be an important consideration in recommending that conversion be done by a vendor.

In order to sell retrospective conversion to the university administration, our librarian requested that we include a section on future savings that could be realized by converting our catalog to machine-readable form. We projected that the salaries of four full-time employees and 20 hours of student time per week could be saved through the elimination of filing and other card-related tasks and through the increased efficiency of an online catalog. We projected salary savings (including benefits) over a 10-year period, adding an 8% inflationary increase each year. Besides salaries, we found that the costs of catalog cards, new catalog units, and the expansion of the card catalog could also be saved. The resulting savings came to $1,140,273.00, well over the amount needed for retrospective conversion. We were careful to point out, however, that savings could not be realized until an online catalog was operational.

Visit to Texas A&M University

Since the library administration was backing the proposed conversion, we were hopeful that the university administration would also accept our recommendations for an out-of-house conversion. However, a time factor built into the contract talks spurred us to begin the next step of planning before administrative approval had been secured. We therefore took a trip to Texas A&M University to talk to the librarians there about the conversion project that OCLC was completing for them. They gave us a lot of helpful pointers, together with a copy of the specifications they had written for OCLC. Upon our return, we immediately began reworking the A&M specifications to fit our situation. We were able to send a draft of the proposed specifications to OCLC by the middle of September.

Closed Catalog versus Conversion

Then began the wait for word from the university administration on our proposal. At the beginning of October our librarian asked us for a memo comparing the options of simply closing the card catalog and beginning an online catalog of new acquisitions versus converting the whole card catalog. We had already considered this question, and we were able to prove to the satisfaction of the library and university administrations that closing the catalog was no less costly than converting it. We found costs associated with a closed catalog to be:

> First, the double look-up that would be necessary for patrons and staff. 20% more reference assistance would be needed, and the work of Acquisitions Department verifiers would be increased.
>
> Second, some maintenance would still be required on a "closed" catalog. Withdrawals, added copies, items transferred from one area of the library to another, and, possibly, errors must still be dealt with. Links between an

old and a new catalog would also need to be created.

Third, there was the problem of open serials. If the catalog were closed, open serials would need to be transferred to the new catalog to accommodate their on-going status. A temporary cataloging position would need to be created to handle this transfer.

Fourth, some of the positions we had projected we could eliminate with an online catalog could not be eliminated, because some maintenance would still be needed and because of the double look-up required with two catalogs.

Fifth, the space taken up by the card catalog could never be freed.

All in all, we figured the cost of keeping a closed catalog to be $629,145.00, a figure comparable to the cost of retrospective conversion.

After a month of increasingly impatient waiting, we got the reply of the university administration to our proposal. It was "no." The administration thought the sum of money involved was simply too large a sum to invest all at once. They did not, however, completely shut the door on the possibility of retrospective conversion.

In-House Plan Reworked

So, at the beginning of December, we once again began figuring the costs of an in-house conversion, this time using six assistants who would work evenings from 4:00 to 9:00 P.M. and all day Saturday. We proposed using two teams and two supervisors, with one team working Monday, Wednesday, and Friday and the other working Tuesday, Thursday, and Saturday, since we were doubtful that we could find people who would want to work all week at those hours. Start-up costs, including salaries, additional terminals, terminal use charges, and OCLC/AMIGOS charges, came to $97,643.50.

Since we were worried about obtaining and keeping a good supervisor for the project, we also devised an alternative plan calling for one full-time supervisor. Under this plan, the supervisor would work froms 1:00 to 9:00 P.M. four days a week and froms 9:00 A.M. to 5:00 P.M. on Saturday. Regular staff members would handle supervisory duties on a rotating basis on the fifth evening of the week. We felt that the advantages of this plan were, first, that a full-time position offering fringe benefits would be more likely to attract and keep the kind of supervisor we needed; second, that one supervisor,

14

rather than two, would feel more responsibility for the end product and be more committed to a high-quality job; and, third, that the overlapping hours would give the supervisor more opportunity for consultation with the regular staff and more of a feeling of being part of that staff. The cost differential between one full-time supervisor and two part-time supervisors was only $1,573.00.

In-House Plan Accepted

This alternative plan was the one accepted by the library administration. Our librarian also suggested that the microfilm copy of the card catalog that had been made could be used by the public, while the conversion assistants worked with the actual catalog drawers. Since we planned to start with "A" and work straight through the alphabet, the film reader could be loaded with successive reels as the project progressed.

In January, 1981, the librarian submitted his in-house conversion proposal to the university administration. He estimated costs using figures of 12 and 15 titles per hour. According to his estimate, start-up costs would be $86,200.00 and total costs would be between $326,211.00 and $466,813.00. His estimated length of the project was between 2¾ and 4 years.

This proposal was approved by the university administration. After approval, the librarian raised the number of conversion assistants from 6 to 8 or 9 in an effort to shorten further the time the conversion would take.

Specifications

We began once more to write specifications for the project, reworking the ones we had done for an out-of-house conversion to fit an in-house situation. We evolved a plan for skipping the more difficult types of material, such as serials, music, maps, non-Roman, and certain types of analytics, in order to get a lot of records input as quickly as possible. These materials were to be flagged with color-coded envelopes so that we could come back to them at the end of the project. With OCLC's price increases occurring at regular intervals, inputting as many records as possible in the early stages of the project would save quite a bit of money.

After discussing the basic premise of the project, our conversion specifications gave instructions on general procedures, such as types of cards to be skipped in the conversion, how to recognize special categories of materials (e.g., serials), and how to choose a matching record. Specific information on the handling of all the different data fields and on problem areas within each field followed. The 049 field was discussed at length, with instructions on and examples of holding library symbols, input stamps, added copy information, and holdings for incomplete sets. Series were also discussed rather extensively, with several pages of examples. Special instructions for serials, music, and maps were given, although the question of what we would do about non-Roman materials and in-analytics had not yet been resolved. As problems were encountered in the conversion and as solutions were found, the document would continue to be updated.

Recruitment and Training of Staff

At the end of March we began recruiting a supervisor. We had thought we might have some difficulty in finding someone who wanted to work evenings and Saturdays, but we had several candidates, and we had completed the hiring process before the middle of June. The supervisor was scheduled to begin work at the beginning of August.

Although we had hoped to have the supervisor early enough so that she could be in on the hiring of the conversion assistants, we had to begin recruitment of the assistants without her. Some of the assistants recruited were graduate students at Rice and other area universities, while others were simply qualified people seeking a part-time job. We were concerned that, because of the hours and the nature of the work, there might be a lot of turnover, which would necessitate continuous training of new personnel.

Since our first conversion assistant was scheduled to begin work the second week in June, we had to go ahead with the planning of training procedures before our supervisor arrived. For suggestions on what to include and how to go about training, we relied heavily on a report by Suzanne Shaw of a conversion project that she had supervised at the University of Florida Libraries. Besides instruction in the parts of a card, we planned search key exercises, call number input exercises, and tagging exercises. Instruction in terminal operation and in searching, editing, and input of new records at the terminal was also included. In addition, new conversion assistants were to save all work for review by the supervisor, while later only records about which a conversion assistant was unsure were to be saved.

We planned to keep various statistics, so that we would know how each conversion assistant was doing and how the project was progressing. The quality of the updates and inputs would also be checked, both directly through the supervisor's monitoring of the project and indirectly through a program to print out records from each tape for visual inspection.

16

Conclusion

Although we set out firmly convinced that the best way to handle retrospective conversion was to farm it out, we are now doing the conversion in-house. Since we are acutely aware of the advantages of shipping out the job, we have tried to pinpoint the advantages of an in-house conversion. They are:

1. You have more control over the project.

2. You can see what areas are causing problems and remedy them immediately.

3. You have an accurate, day-by-day account of your progress.

As we work with retrospective conversion, we find that our viewpoint has gradually changed. At the beginning, we thought we could include all the data we had in our card catalog and even fix things up along the way. We soon came to realize, however, that we did not have time to improve upon past cataloging; we had to concentrate simply on inputting the essential elements of what was already in the catalog. By forcing us to think about what was really necessary for an online catalog, retrospective conversion has become a bridge from our past to our future.

SPECIFICATIONS
FOR
RETROSPECTIVE CONVERSION

Fondren Library
Rice University

May 1981

Table of Contents

SPECIFICATIONS FOR RETROSPECTIVE CONVERSION

I. SCOPE

These specifications cover the retrospective conversion of approximately 452,000 main entry cards contained in the catalog of the Fondren Library of Rice University (RUL). However, all main entry cards produced as a result of Rice's participation in OCLC's On-Line Cataloging System are to be excluded in the conversion. The records to be converted cover all types of materials cataloged by the Library.

The project will result in machine-readable catalog records for all holdings in the card catalog. In addition, the Rice holding symbol (RCE) will appear in OCLC's On-Line Union Catalog for all of Rice's holdings.

II. SOURCE OF CATALOGING DATA

Conversion will be done from main entry cards only. A main entry card is defined as a full catalog entry, usually the author entry, giving all the information necessary to the complete identification of a work. This entry bears also the tracing of all the other headings under which the work in question is entered in the catalog. All main entry cards will be converted except for the ones identified below:

1. Cards originally produced at OCLC, identifiable by the OCLC control number, etc., appearing on the bottom line of a card and by the type face.

2. Information cards, including cards for series classed separately, cards for series not traced, cards referring to special bibliographies, cards referring to technical reports collections, etc. Cards for series classed separately and cards for series not traced should be removed from the catalog when found.

3. Cards for sound recordings encountered in the Main Card Catalog. Sound recordings will be converted from cards in the Music Room Catalog at the end of the project. Sound recordings can be identified by the words "Phonodisc," or "Sound recording" after the uniform or regular title.

4. Human Relations Area File (HRAF) cards.

(For examples, see Appendix A, p. 34-38.)

III. GENERAL PROCEDURES

The basic premise is that OCLC records will be edited to match exactly information found on RUL main entry cards. An exception to this is that, when main entries, added entries, and/or subject headings have been changed in the database to AACR2 form, this form should be used.

Each main entry card to be converted will be searched on the OCLC system to locate a matching record, if it exists.

The record must match our card in all areas itemized below:

1. Bibliographic level (bib lvl)
2. Language
3. Choice of author (Form may differ — Cf. sections on Personal and Corporate Name Access Points)
4. Title
5. Edition
6. Publisher
7. Copyright date or original date of publication
8. Pagination

If more than one matching record is found, a Library of Congress (LC) record should always be used if available. Otherwise, the one which most closely matches RUL's record should be used. If a matching record is found with RUL's holding symbol (RCE) already on it, the entry should be flagged with a red envelope and the problem noted on a slip of paper.

A matching record will be edited, if necessary, to include the call number and holdings information from the card. Other data elements should also be edited to reflect what appears on the card. If no matching record is found, the card will be flagged with a green envelope. During terminal downtime, these cards will be searched through the National Union Catalog to see if LC copy is available. If LC copy is found, a photocopy should be made to compare with RUL's card. Following the guidelines given below, data elements will be edited as necessary, and the record will be tagged for input. All data will be input as it appears on the card, properly tagged.

For each record which is converted, a "1" should be used as the second indicator in the 049 field. This will indicate that the record was processed during the retrospective conversion project.

Problem areas

Non-Roman alphabet cards, serials, scores, maps, in-analytics and other selected analytics will not be converted until the end of the project. (See also Section V for further instructions and Appendix

A, p. 39-42, for examples of these types of materials.) Color-coded envelopes will be placed over the main cards for such items as they are encountered during the course of the conversion. (Cf. Appendix F for color-coding.)

Serials can usually be identified by the presence of a volume or date statement following the title. OCLC records for serials have an "s" in the "bib lvl" field.

Scores are identified by "M" and sometimes "MT" in the call number. "MT" can also identify a monograph, in which case the "type" will be coded "m." OCLC records for sound recordings have "i" or "j" in the "type" field.

Maps can be identified by the word "Map" preceding the call number. Maps are generally classified in the LC classification "G." OCLC records for maps have an "e" in the "type" field.

In-analytics can be identified by a note beginning with the word "In." This note usually comes after the title information.

Other problems will be referred directly to the retrospective conversion supervisor or will be flagged with color-coded envelopes for later handling by the retrospective conversion supervisor.

IV. *NOTES ON DATA FIELDS*

Editing and input of data should follow what is on the main entry card. Typed and handwritten corrections to all cards, including LC printed cards, should be entered as corrected.

Misspellings should be corrected. German nouns should be capitalized on old cards. ISBD punctuation may be retained if the OCLC record has it and the card doesn't. Conversely, if the card has ISBD punctuation and the record does not, ISBD punctuation need not be added to the record.

The tracing appears on the back of some main entry cards. The notation "(over)" appears at the bottom of such cards.

Guidelines for field tagging published by OCLC should be followed. If incorrect tags are discovered in a record, they should be corrected. However, we will not attempt to send error reports on any records used in retrospective conversion.

Fixed Field

For monographs all elements of the fixed field, with the exception of the index field on pre-ISBD cards, can and should be completed using the data available on the card. For serials all elements of the fixed field which can be determined from the card should be filled in. For scores and sound recordings all fixed field elements can be determined from the card and should be completed. Tables in

22

Appendix E, p. 74-82, are guides to the location of data needed to determine the values of fixed field elements.

Library of Congress Card Number (LCCN) – 010

Library of Congress card numbers should be included in the converted record if printed or typed on the main entry card, with the following exceptions:

1. If a "CV" or a "V" follows an LC card number, this card number should not be entered.

2. LC printed cards for a work similar to the one being cataloged were sometimes modified with new values by either erasing and retyping, or by crossing out and typing in new data. If these changes have been made in the descriptive area of the card (i.e., title through collation line), the LCCN on the main entry card is invalid and should not be entered. Such changes are identified by noting differences in type font or type size or by noting crossed-out data.

(Cf. examples in Appendix A, p. 43-44.)

National Bibliography Number – 015

It is not necessary to add an 015 field if it is not on the record.

International Standard Numbers – 020

If an ISBN(s) or an ISSN is present on the main entry card, it should be included in the record used or created for conversion.

Call Numbers

Call numbers should be entered following usual OCLC practice. If NLM classification numbers and Dewey classification numbers appear in a matching record being used, they may be left in the record.

A summary of call number fields which will be used for the different types of material follows. (For examples see Appendix A, p. 45-48.)

1. LC classification.
   a. 050 – If RUL call number matches an LC-assigned call number, any 090 fields already in the record

should be deleted.

b. 090 — If RUL call number does not match an LC-assigned call number, use RUL call number and delete any other 090 fields.

c. RUL numbers for analytics — Analytic call numbers can be identified by a number or volume designation as the last element of the call number. Before joining OCLC, RUL used "s." for series and "v." for volume in call numbers in analytics. In converting analytic records, "s." should be replaced by *ser.* and "v." by *vol.* If the OCLC record has volume designations in any other language, they should be changed to the English equivalent as on RUL cards, e.g., "Bd." to "vol."

2. K Call numbers Derived from the University of Chicago Law Schedule.

   099 — Non-LC K call numbers (i.e., K numbers other than K, KD, KE, and KF) should be entered in an 099 field with each line in an "a" subfield.

3. Superintendent of Documents (SuDoc) classification.

   086 — If RUL has used a SuDoc number, this number should be input in the 086 field if it is not already present. RUL is profiled to have the 086 field override other call number fields if the government document holding library symbol (RCEG) is input in the 049 field.

4. RUL (non-LC) numbers assigned to sound recordings.

   099 — If a local call number begins with the designations "LP," "Tape," or "Cassette" and is in a non-LC format, this RUL call number should be input in the 099 field with each line in an "a" subfield.

Holdings Data — 049

The 049 field should be input following the guidelines in the OCLC tagging manuals.

Holding Library Symbols

The holding library symbol for ≠a of the 049 field is determined by the location stamp on the card, either above or below the call number. If no specific location is present, the main holding library symbol is used. Some of the location stamps on cards to be converted (e.g., "Arch.") are no longer used and should default to the main holding library. For a complete list of holding library symbols, see Appendix B, p. 64-70.

Input Stamps

Occasionally stamps appear on cards in the margin below the call number or elsewhere on the card. These should be input in the 049 field following the holding library symbol or in a note. For a list of stamps and instructions on how and where to input, see Appendix C.

Holdings Information

Multiple Copies — Multiple copies are indicated by a *typed* notation (e.g.,---- Copy 2) on the card. Ignore printed "copy 2" notations at the bottom of LC cards.

a. Both copies in same call number in same holding library. Copy information should be input in ≠c of the 049 field. Also, a 590 note, giving holdings information in capital letters, should be input as the first note. If the added copy varies in some way from the first copy, this variation should be noted in lower-case letters in the 590 field. Also, the holdings of an added copy of a multi-volume set should be indicated in the 590 note.

b. Copies in different call numbers, but in same holding library. Flag with red envelope, unless one call number is an analytic call number. In this case, input as 2 separate records. A "1" should be used in the first indicator position of the 049 field in the second record input. (Analytic call numbers are identified by "v." or "no." as the last element of the call number.)

c. Copies in different holdings libraries. (1) If books are in different holding libraries, but otherwise call number is the same, input the two holding library symbols in the 049 field. (2) If books are in different holding libraries and call numbers are different, input as two separate records. To indicate that the second record input should not bump the first record, a "1" should be added in the first indicator position of the 049 field.

25

d. Two (or more) different editions on same card.

If a DLC record can be located for the dashed-on edition(s), input each edition on a separate record. Check with supervisor to make sure OCLC record for dashed-on entry matches our record. If no DLC record is available for the dashed-on entry but a record exists for the primary work, flag the card with a red envelope and include a slip of paper identifying the problem. If no DLC record is available for either entry, flag with a green envelope.

e. Library has c.2 only.

If such a penciled note appears on card, input this note in capital letters in a 590 field (as the first note). In the 049 field holdings should be: ≠c 2.

(For examples see Appendix A, p. 49-55.)

Holdings for Incomplete Monographic Sets

Holdings are indicated by notes penciled on the main entry card. This note should be input as the first note in the 590 field in capital letters in the form in which it appears on the card. Dates of publication and variations between bibliographical volumes and physical volumes should also be included in the 590 field. In addition, holdings should be input in the 049 field in the appropriate subfields.

(For examples see Appendix A, p. 56-57.)

Personal Name Access Points (Applies to main entries, subject headings and added entries) — 1xx, 6xx, 7xx.

1. Use form of name as it appears on RUL's main entry card, unless this form of name has been converted in the data base to AACR2 form. In this case use AACR2 form. A converted entry can be recognized by a ≠w at the end of the heading and, possibly, an 87x field at the end of the record.

2. British titles should be input in ≠c of the 100, 600, and/or 700 fields regardless of their position on the RUL card.

3. When a maiden name is given in parenthesis on an RUL card and without parenthesis in the record in the data base, the parenthesis may be omitted.

4. Birth and death dates should be input as they appear on RUL cards. An exception to this is that a person's death date should be left on the record if it is a DLC record. When converting a series of records with a personal entry which includes dates, a death date should be added to those records in which it is lacking if it can be easily ascertained from records preceding it in the data base and preceding or *following* it in the catalog.

5. On older LC cards birth and death dates for certain famous people were not given in subject headings with subdivisions. If correct dates appear on the record, they should be left.

6. Penciled parentheses placed around parts of personal names for filing purposes should be ignored, except when an entry has been converted. Converted entries are identified by ≠w following the entry and an 87x field.

Corporate Name Access Points (Applies to main entries, subject headings and added entries) – 1xx, 6xx, 7xx.

1. Use form of name as it appears on RUL's main entry card, unless this form of name has been converted in the data base to AACR2 form. In this case use AACR2 form. A converted entry can be recognized by a ≠w at the end of the heading and, possibly, an 87x field at the end of the record.

2. Spell out "United States," "Great Britain," and "Germany."

Uniform Titles – 240

If RUL's card matches an LC record except for the presence of a uniform title on the LC record, the uniform title should be retained in the record.

Title and Statement of Responsibility – 245

1. The entire title and subtitle should be input as they appear on card, ignoring any penciled parentheses around parts of the title or subtitle.

2. Tag all 245 fields with "1" in the first indicator position if title is distinctive. If entry is under title or title is not distinctive, the first indicator should be "0."

3. Second indicator in 245 field should always be filled in.

4. Add statement of responsibility if on card and not on record. Change fixed field "M/F/B" if necessary.

Edition Statement — 250

The edition statement should always be input as on card.

Imprint — 260

1. In the publisher statement, "Inc.", "Ltd.", "and Co.", "and Sons", "and Bros." may be omitted.

2. "Etc." after place or publisher may be omitted on monographic records.

3. Dates showing that a book is a later printing and copyright dates must be added if not on record.

Collation — 300

1. In collation line, always space before "p.", "v.", and "cm.".

2. 1/2 centimeters should be changed to the next higher whole centimeter on cards for books and scores.

3. Size should be added if not on record.

Price — 350

The 350 field for price on pre-ISBD cards may be omitted. (Pre-ISBD cards are coded "Ø" in the fixed field "Descr".)

Series — 4xx

1. The form of a series statement and the series tracing should conform to what appears on the main entry card, unless heading for personal or corporate author has been converted to AACR2 form. In this case, use AACR2 form. A converted entry can be recognized by a ≠w at the end of the field and, possibly, an 87x field at the end of the record.

2. Check tracing on card to determine correct 4xx tag. On LC cards where a printed parenthesis was used around the series in the tracing, RUL has traced for the series only if the parenthesis has been removed; if the parenthesis has not been removed, the series is

untraced.

3. On some main entry cards the only indication that the series is traced is the fact that the series is underlined in the collation line. In such cases, the series should be tagged 400, 410, 411, or 440 as appropriate.

4. "Half-title", "On Cover", "Added t.p.", and editor should be omitted from series statements in the 4xx field.

5. Care should be taken to add a "≠v" before series numbering if a 490 tag on the record has been changed to a 400, 410, 411, or 440 tag.

6. In the series statement in the collation line or in series added entries, RUL indicated omissions from the LC form of tracing for the series by placing a pencilled parenthesis around that part of the series to be omitted in the added entry. When inputting, we will omit words enclosed in parenthesis except when the name of an issuing body appears after the title in an author/title series added entry. In this case, leave the name of the issuing body as part of the title even when we have parenthesized it out, unless the series is classed together (indicated by "no.", "v.", etc. as the last element of the call number.)

(For examples see Appendix A, p. 58-62.)

Notes

1. Notes should be the same as those on RUL's main entry card. An exception to this is a revised DLC card for the same edition of a work. (A revised DLC card is identified by "//r" following the card number in the 010 field.) If the revised card matches RUL's call number, main entry, and description, notes added to the revised card may be left in the record. Check with the supervisor before updating.

2. When the 590 note is used to show holdings, it should be the first note and be input in capital letters. Otherwise, it should be put in its appropriate place in the prescribed order of notes.

3. The stamped notes "See also following cards" and "For holdings see following cards" should not be entered in any converted records. For other stamped notes, see Appendix C.

4. Notes beginning "Translation of" found at the bottom of some old cards should be put in a 500 note. Check with the supervisor on order of notes.

Subject Headings

1. Subject headings should be edited or input to contain the headings as they appear on the main entry card, except that abbreviations in subject headings should be spelled out. (For example: Gt. Brit. = Great Britain; Hist. & crit. = History and criticism) Cf. Appendix G for a list of abbreviations.

2. NLM subject headings (identified by a "2" in the second indicator position) need not be deleted on DLC records, but on member records only subject headings that appear on RUL main entry cards should be left in the record.

3. Any subject headings other than NLM subject headings which appear in brackets on RUL cards should be ignored.

4. If a revised DLC card (identified by "//r" following the card number in the 010 field) matches RUL's call number, main entry, and description, it is all right if it has additional subject headings or changed subject headings. If record is not a revised or corrected LC card, change subject headings to match RUL card.

5. Subject headings that have been lined out on the RUL card should not be entered in the converted record.

Added Entries

1. Added entries that have been lined out on the RUL card should not be entered in the converted record.

2. Inverted title added entries made up by RUL should be omitted. (For example: Title = Human efficiency; Made-up title added entry = Efficiency, Human)

3. If an added entry lined out on a card is the same as a subject heading on that card, consult the supervisor to see if the added entry should be retained.

Dashed-on Entries (Other than added copies; for added copies cf. Appendix A, p. 49-55.)

Unless a DLC record which clearly matches the dashed-on entry is found in the OCLC On-Line Union Catalog, main entry cards with dash entries will be flagged with red envelopes.

The call number of a separately cataloged dash entry should match that given on the RUL card. If no call number appears by the dash entry on the RUL card, the call number should be that of the primary title plus the generic term of the dashed-on item. (Cf. Appendix A, p. 63 for examples.)

If the dash entry is for a serial, use an orange envelope to flag whole card as serial.

V. *MATERIALS FLAGGED FOR LATER INPUT*

A. *NON-ROMAN*
   (Guidelines not yet written)
B. *IN-ANALYTICS AND OTHER SELECTED ANALYTICS*
   (Guidelines not yet written)
C. *SERIALS*

Matching Criteria

Guidelines for CONSER participants should be followed when matching or inputting serial records. Serials records used for update must match in the 245 and 362 fields and the type of entry (latest or successive). Serials records will be input as successive or latest entries, according to the entry on the card. Whether a record is a successive or a latest entry can be determined from the value of "S/L ent" in the fixed field (the successive/latest entry indicator) or from the presence of a 247, 780, or 785 field(s). The bibliographic level should be "s" for a record to match a serials card, even if other elements match. (This follows current OCLC policy.)

Table 1 of Appendix D contains a list of field tags for fields which may be ignored when determining whether a record matches a main entry card. These fields are nonprinting fields and so would have no corresponding element on the shelflist card.

Field Editing

Notes fields must be tagged correctly with appropriate indicator values. Table 2 of Appendix D provides a list of print constants which may appear on a card. The appropriate tag and indicators are provided for use with the note containing the given print constant.

In 780 and 785 fields used to enter notes which contain a defined print constant, the first indicator should always be coded to print a note. Where the information in a note is too complicated to be handled by the print constants supplied by 780 and 785 fields, the information must be input in a 580 note. In addition, each title involved must be input in an appropriate 780 or 785 field, coded not to print. This must be done so that the titles involved will be indexed.

Certain non-printing fields should also be input for indexing purpose. These are related to specific 5xx notes, which may be interpreted to determine the tag of the indexed field. The fields involved are:

Non-printing, Indexed Field	Interpreted Note Field
770	525
772	580
777	580
787	580

Holding for Serials — No holdings should be input for open serials. For closed serials the beginning and ending volumes and the complete dates should be shown. If RUL does not have a complete run of a closed serial, holdings should also be indicated in the 049 and 590 fields.

D. *MUSIC*

Catalog from which to Convert

Cards for sound recordings will be converted from the Music Catalog. They should be passed over when encountered in the Main Card Catalog, because sound recording cards in the Main Card Catalog did not have to contain complete bibliographic information until 1979.

Score Call Numbers

In formatting call numbers for scores, be careful not to confuse thematic catalog numbers used in the call number with Cutter numbers. (For example: M 178 .M93 K.522 — ".M93" is Cutter number; "K.522" is thematic catalog number.)

For sound recordings the general material designations "Phonodisc" and "Phonotape" should be changed to "Sound Recording", if not already changed in the data base.

E. *MAPS*

Holding Libraries

The holding library for monographic, non-rare maps is RCEA. "[Map]" should be input before the holding library symbol in the 049 field for all maps, and "[Geol.]" (for Geology) should be input after the holding library symbol in the 049 field when it appears on the card. RUL is not profiled to have these notations print as automatic stamps; rather, each stamp must be input.

For maps of a serial nature, the holding library is RCEF. Such maps may frequently be identified by the presence of a volume or date statement following the title and by an "s" following the classification number which precedes the cutter number (e.g., Map G 3701s .C3 var. .U5 Geol.). Input stamps should be added before and after the holding library symbol as indicated above.

The holding library for rare maps is RCEH. Rare maps are identified by the word "Map" and an asterisk preceding the "G" of the call number. The asterisk should be omitted when inputting the call number, but "[Map]" should be input before the holding library symbol in the 049 field.

VI. *MONTHLY PRODUCTION REPORTS*

Monthly reports of work accomplished will include both a summary of records converted for the month and a cumulated summary of records converted since the beginning of the project. A count of records requiring original input will also be kept.

VII. *QUALITY CONTROL*

Rice University Library in its retrospective conversion project will follow quality control methods sufficient to maintain a high degree of accuracy. These methods will include a comprehensive, intensive training program for terminal operators and supervision by a professional cataloger.

RUL has planned a program of local review of records — both updates and inputs. General spot-checking of all records will also be performed.

APPENDIX A. Examples of Main Entry Cards
I. Cards Not to be Converted

```
DF     Frotier de la Coste-Messelière., Pierre.
261       Delphi, Photographien von Georges de
.D35   Mire; Text und Anmerkungen von Pierre
F7     de la Coste-Messelière ... Vorwort von
       Charles Picard ...Übersetzung aus dem
       Französischen von Georges und Vida
       Daux. Paris, Editions Du Chêne [1943].
          335 p., 1 ℓ. incl. front. illus.
       (incl. plans) 249 pl, on 125 ℓ. 32 cm.
          At head of title: École française in
       Athen.

          1. Delphi.  2. Art--Delphi.  I. Daux,
       Georges, 1800-    tr.  II. Daux, Vida,
       Joint tr.  III. Mire, Georges de,
       illus.  IV. École francaise d'Athenes-

TxHR 02 MAR 81      4170111  RCEAsl 46-18884
```

↑ OCLC Control Number

Card Produced at
OCLC – Note
type face.

```
Oxford Shakespeare concordances.  Oxford,
   Clarendon Press, 1969- 73.
      v.  21 cm.  For holdings see following cards.

   No more published?
```

Card for Series
Classed Separately

```
Spitzer, Robert
   ₁Plays in La Petite illustration; revue
hebdomadaire ...  Théâtre₁

   Library has
Si je voulais ... ₁par₁ Paul Géraldy et Robert
   Spitzer. nouv. sér. no.124, 26 juil. 1924.
Son mari ... ₁par₁ Paul Géraldy et Robert
   Spitzer. ₁nouv. sér.₁ no.183, 28 mai 1927.
L'homme de joie ... ₁par₁ Paul Geraldy & Robert
   Spitzer. ₁nouv. sér.₁ no.228, 27 avril 1929.
```

Card for Series
Classed Separately

Card for an Un-
traced Series

Teachers' mathematics reference series.
Englewood Cliffs, N. J., Prentice-Hall.

THE VOLUMES OF THIS SERIES WHICH ARE IN
THE LIBRARY ARE LISTED UNDER THEIR RESPECTIVE
AUTHORS.

Information
Card referring
to special bib-
liography

SOCIALISM

To help locate published information in
this specific field, special bibliographies
are available from the Reference Librarians.

Request Library Pathfinder entitled:
SOCIALIST ECONOMICS

Information
Card referring
to special bib-
liography

POWER RESOURCES

To help locate published information
in this specific field, special bibliographies are available from the Reference
Librarians.

Request Readers advisory service booklist
no. 60; 266.

POWER RESOURCES

   To help locate published information
in this specific field, special bibliographies are available from the Reference
Librarians.

   Request LC Science Tracer Bullet no.: 74-3

Information
Card referring
to special bib-
liography

Rand Corporation.
   [Reports] R—

   The Library's collection of these unclassi-
fied publications is shelved on the 5th floor,

Consult Government Documents Librarian.
SEE ALSO FOLLOWING CARDS FOR SELECTED CATALOGED
   ITEMS.
   I. Rand Corporation. Rand report.

Example of
card referring
to uncataloged
technical reports
collection

Rand Corporation.
   A bibliography of selected Rand publications.
SB—

   The Library's collection of these special
subject bibliographies is shelved in the
reference area. Consult Reference librarians.

Example of
card referring
to uncataloged
technical reports
collection

Houston-Galveston Regional Transportation
    Study Area.

    The library's collection of the reports
of the study is housed in the Government
Documents, Maps & Micromaterials Room (M-17)

    Consult Documents Librarian for use of
these materials.

Example of
card referring to
uncataloged
technical reports
collection

HRAF   Dhaninivat Kromamūn Bidyalabh Bridhyākorn, Prince.
A01   The Khon, by H. H. Prince Dhaninivat Kromamūn
13:     Bidyalabh Bridhyākorn and Dhanit Yupho.   Bangkok,
National Culture Institute, B. E. 2497 [1954]
        15 p.   illus.   (Thailand culture series, no. 11)

        Photo-offset.   New Haven, Human Relations Area
Files, 1955.   13 x 20 cm.

        1. Khon (Dance) 2. Dancing--Thailand.
I. Dhanit Yupho, joint author.   (Series)

                                           CLSU 67

Human Relations
Area File card

Abercrombie, Robert, 1712–1780.
Microprint   Works by this author printed in America before 1801 are available
AS   in this library in the Readex Microprint edition of Early American
36   Imprints published by the American Antiquarian Society.
A47   This collection is arranged according to the numbers in Charles
          Evans' American Bibliography.

        Evans Numbers: 7124, 7826. Request this microprint by
                                   call number and Evans number

    Library of Congress   Information Card

Information
card referring
to a microform
collection

37

SEE   Mozart, (Johann Chrysostom) Wolfgang Amadeus, 1756–1791.
MUSIC   ₍Quartet, strings, K. 499, D major₎ Phonodisc.
ROOM
CATALOG   Quartet no. 20, in D major, K. 499 (Hoffmeister). Quar-
           tet no. 22, in B flat major, K. 589 (2nd Prussian). London
           STS 15116. ₍1971₎
             2 s. 12 in. 33⅓ rpm. stereophonic. (Stereo treasury series)

           Vienna Philharmonic Quartet.
           Duration : 24 min., and 22 min., 55 sec.
           Program notes on slipcase.
           1. String quartets—To 1800.   I. Mozart, Johann Chrysostom
           Wolfgang Amadeus, 1756–1791. Quartet, strings, K. 589, B♭ major.
           Phonodisc. 1971. II. Wiener Philharmonia-Quartett.

           [M452]   72–760899

           Library of Congress   72 ₍2₎   R

Example of
Sound Recording
Card in the Main
Card Catalog —
*Do not convert
from this;*
Convert from the
card in the
Music Catalog

Music
Tape
.H4   Mozart, (Johann Chrysostom) Wolfgang Amadeus,
8   1756–1791.
s   ₍Quartet, strings, K. 458, B♭ major₎
               ₍Sound recording₎
SEE   String quartet in B flat major, K. 458,
MUSIC   "Hunting". Deutsche Grammophon Gesellschaft
ROOM   C 8886. ₍19 ₎
               1/2 reel. 7 1/2 ips. 4-track. stereo.
           7 in.
               With: Haydn, Joseph. Quartet, strings,
           no. 78, op. 76,   no. 3, C major.
LP   Amadeus   Quartet.
                               (over)   R 64–231v

Example of
Sound Recording
Card in the Main
Card Catalog —
*Do not convert
from this*;
Convert from the
card in the
Music Catalog

LP
.H8
8   Hovhaness, Alan, 1911–
s   ₍Symphony, no. 4, band, op. 165₎ Phonodisc.
               Symphony no. 4, op. 165. Mercury SRI 75010. ₍19 ₎
               1 s. 12 in. 33⅓ rpm. microgroove. stereophonic. 12 in.
SEE   Eastman Symphonic Wind Ensemble; Clyde Roller, conductor.
MUSIC   Recorded in the Eastman Theatre, Rochester.
ROOM   Duration : 20 min., 57 sec.
           Program notes by James Ringo and the composer on container.
           With : Giannini, Vittorio. Symphony, no. 3, band.
           1. Symphonies (Band)   2. Eastman Symphonic Wind Ensemble.
           3. Roller, A. Clyde.
                                              R 64–131 rev V

Example of
Sound Recording
Card in the Main
Card Catalog —
*Do not convert
from this;*
Convert from the
card in the
Music Catalog

PG
2131
.L6

Lomtev, Timofeĭ Petrovich.
    (Fonologii͡a sovremennogo russkogo i͡azyka na osnove teorii mnozhestv)
    Фонология современного русского языка на основе теории множеств.   Учеб. пособие для филол. фак. ун-тов. Москва, "Высш. школа," 1972.

      224 p. 22 cm. 0.60rub   USSR 72-VKP
      Includes bibliographical references.

      1. Russian language—Phonology.   I. Title.

TxHR

    PG2131.L6   73–312643

    Library of Congress   73 ₍2₎

Non-Roman Item — Flag with brown envelope

PL
2748
.J98
C49

Chiao, Jyur-Yiin.
   (Ch'ung-Ch'ing Hsiao Yeh-Ch'ü)
   重慶小夜曲　焦菊隱著 〔上海〕
中國文化事業社出版, 1947.
   108 p. 19 cm.

   I. Title.

Non-Roman Item — Flag with brown envelope

QA
23
.S3

Sarfatti, Gad Ben-'Ami.
   מונהי המתמטיקה בספרות המדעית העברית של ימי הביניים.
   מאת גד בן־עמי צרפתי. ירושלים, הוצאת ספרים ע״ש י״ל
כאגנם, האוניברסיטה העברית ₍המכירה הראשית: יבנה, תל־
                      אביב₎ 729 ₍1968₎

      12, 265, xiv p. 25 cm. 12.00
      Added t. p.: Mathematical terminology in Hebrew scientific literature of the Middle Ages.
    "יסוד הספר הזה הוא עבודה לשם קבלת תואר דוקטור לפילוסופיה,
שהוגשה לסינאט של האוניברסיטה העברית בשנת תשכ״ד.
      Contents and summary also in English.
      Bibliography: p. 231–241.
      1. Mathematics, Jewish. 2. Mathematics—Terminology. 3. Hebrew language—Terms and phrases. I. Title.
        Title romanized: Munḥe ha-matematikah ba-sifrut ha-mada'it   ha-'ivrit shel Yeme ha-benayim.
    QA23.S3   77–950789
    Library of Congress   69 ₍2₎   HE

Non-Roman Item — Flag with brown envelope

F
431
.A53

The **American** historical magazine and **Tennessee** historical society quarterly.   v. 1–9;   Jan. 1896–Oct. 1904.   Nashville, Tenn., 1896–1904.

9 v.   illus. (incl. facsims.) plates, ports., maps.   23½ᶜᵐ.

Title varies : 1896–97, The American historical magazine.
1898–Jan. 1902, The American historical magazine, representing the chair of American history in the Peabody normal college.
Apr. 1902–1904, The American historical magazine and Tennessee historical society quarterly.
Editors : 1896–1900, W. R. Garrett.—1901–Jan. 1902, W. R. Garrett, J. M. Bass.—Apr. 1902–1904, A. V. Goodpasture.
Published by the Peabody normal college, 1896–Jan. 1902 ; A. V. and W. H. Goodpasture, Apr. 1902–1904.

(Continued on next card)

5–34792 rev

[r46l2]

Serials — Flag
with orange
envelopes

"Closed" serial

CURRENT NOS. ON PERIODICAL SHELVES

Library has v. 5–date

GC
1
.A47
A233

Oceanology.   v.5–
1965–
Washington, D. C.
     v.   illus.   26 cm.   bimonthly.

Translation of Океанология (transliterated: Okeanologiía) of the Akademiía nauk SSSR.
     "Translated and produced by Scripta technica, inc. for the American Geophysical Union."
     Successor to Soviet oceanography, a translation journal issued 1961-64 by the American Geophysical Union.

(Over)

"Open" serial

Library has v. 1 – date.

AS
221
.B3

Bari (City) Università.   Facoltà di lettere
     e filosofia.
          Annali.   v.1–
1954–
Bari, Grafiche Cressati.
          v.   illus.   25 cm.   annual (irregular)

No volume issued for 1956.
Imprint varies.

"Open" serial

```
M         Weill, Kurt, 1900-1950.
1001          ₍Symphony, no. 2₎
.W399         2. ₍i. e. Zweite₎ Sinfonie (1933).   Mainz, B. Schott's
no.2       Söhne ₍ᶜ1966₎
1966          ₍S₎ p., score (103 p.)   23 cm.   (Edition Schott, 5512)
              Preface in German, French, and English by David Drew.
              Duration: about 28 min.
              1. Symphonies—Scores.
           M1001.W399   no.2  1966
                                           67-41710/M
```

Score – Flag
with black
envelope

```
Map       National Geographic Society, Washington, D. C.   Carto-
G            graphic Section.
5700          Europe and the Near East.  Washington, 1949.
1949          col. map 116 x 130 cm.
.N31          Scale 1 : 4,500,000 or 71 miles to the inch.
              "Chamberlin trimetric projection."
              "Russian and Polish boundaries according to treaties and claims as
           of April 1, 1949."
              Shows "occupation zones in Germany and Austria, World War II."
              "James M. Darley, chief cartographer.  Compilation by H. C. Bryan
           ₍and others₎  Relief by John J. Brehm."
              Enlarged from map issued with the National geographic magazine,
           v. 95, no. 6, June 1949.
              Includes lists of "geographical equivalents" and abbreviations.
              1. Europe—Maps.        2. Near East—Maps.      I. Darley,
           James Morrison.
              G5700 1949.N31                W 544Map 53-1141
              Library of Congress          ₍3₎
```

Map – Flag
with brown
envelope

```
E         Vincent, John Martin, 1857-1939.
172           ... Contributions toward a bibliography of American his-
.A60       tory, 1888-1892, adapted from reports to the "Jahresbericht
1893       der geschichtswissenschaft" of Berlin.  By John Martin Vin-
           cent ...

              (In American historical association.  Annual report ... for the year
           1893.  Washington, 1894. 24½ᶜᵐ. p. 501-572)



              1. U. S.—Hist.—Bibl.  2. America—Hist.—Bibl.  3. U. S.—Biog.—
           Bibl.  I. Series.
                                              C D 17—408
              Library of Congress.        Card div.   E172.A60   1893
                                          ₍a41d1₎             (973.062)
```

Analytics card –
Flag with blue
envelope

"In" analytic

```
FILM
PR      Wedderburn,David,1580-1646.
1105       Abredonia atrata,sub obitum serenissimi ...
.U5     Monarchae,Iacobi VI.pacifici,Britanniae Magnae,
        Galliae,& Hiberniae Regis ... Abredoniae,
        Excudebat E.Rabanus, 1625.
           Signed at end: D.Wedderbvrnvs.
           Short-title catalogue no.25187 (carton 1121)



           1.James I,King of Great Britain,1566-1625--
        Poetry.  I.Title.
                                   MiU F67-488
Request this
film by
call number
and carton
number
```

Analytics cards —
Flag with blue
envelopes

Short Title Cata-
logue analytic

```
                Abendano, Isaac.
    Film          An almanack for the year of Christ,
    PR            1693. [1693]
    1105
    .U51    ENGLISH books, 1641-1700.  Ann Arbor,
    reel       Mich., University Microfilms, 1961-
    162:           reels.  35 mm.
    A1233      Microfilm copy of books included in
            Wing's Short-title catalogue of...
            English books printed...1641-1700.
```

Short Title Cat-
alogue analytic

42

```
E     Coolidge, Mary Elizabeth Burroughs (Roberts)
99       Smith, 1860-
.P9      The rain-makers; Indians of Arizona and New
C75   Mexico.  Boston, Houghton Miflin Co.  [c1929]
         xiii, 326 p.  illus., ports.  23 cm.


         Maps on lining-papers.
         Bibliography: p.[309]-313.


         1. Pueblo Indians.  2. Indians of North
      America--Arizona.  3. Indians of North America
      --New Mexico.  I.     Title.


                                  29-3433 C
```

"C" follows card
number — Input
LC card number.

("C" indicates
that the call
number is the one
used on the
LC card.)

```
E     Fewkes, Jesse Walter, 1850-1930.
99       Ancestor worship of the Hopi Indians.  By
.H7   J. Walter Fewkes.  Washington, Govt. Print.
F32   Off., 1923.
         485-506 p.  illus., plates.  25 cm.
      ([Smithsonian Institution] Publication 2697)

      "From the Smithsonian report for 1921."


         1. Hopi Indians--Religion and mythology.
      I. Title.

                                  24-2417 V
```

"V" follows card
number — Do
not input LC
card number.

("V" indicates
that this card
is a variation of
the LC card.)

```
NA    Kevin Roche, John Dinkeloo and Associates,
737      1962-1975 / vorwort, J. Irwin Miller ; ein-
.K46  leitung, Henry-Russell Hitchcock ; heraus-
K48   gabe und fotografie, Yukio Futagawa ;
      [Französische übersetzung,  Bernard Stephan-
      us ; Deutsche übersetzung, Office du livre].
      -- Stuttgart : Gerd Hatje, 1975.
      255 p. : ill. (some col.) ; 31 x 32 cm.

      English, French, and German.
      Bibliography: p. 253-255.

         1. Architecture, Modern--20th century--
      United States.  I. Roche, Kevin.  II. Dinkeloo,
ixHS  John.  III. Futa     gawa, Yukio, 1932-
                                  77-465470cv
```

"CV" follows card
number — Do *not*
input LC card
number.

("CV" indicates
that this card
is a variation of
the LC card and
the call number
varies from the LC
call number.)

BT   **Kaye-Smith, Sheila.**
309   The mirror of the months, by Sheila Kaye-Smith. Lon-
.K 16   don, Elkin Mathews & Marrot [1930]
1930   3 p. l. 69 p. 1 l. 23^{cm}.

         I. Title.

         Library of Congress   BT309.K16 ✓   26-14697
                                       [2]

Example of LC
printed card
modified by
erasing and typing
in new information
— Do *not* use LC
card number

KB   **Sugden, Edward Burtenshaw,** *1st baron St. Leonards,*
150   1781–1875.
.S94   A practical treatise of powers; by the Right Hon. Sir
1847   Edward Sugden. 2d American, from the 7th London
            ed., with additional references to American cases.
            Philadelphia, T. & J. W. Johnson, 1847.
            2 v. in 1.   24 cm.

         1. Powers (Law)

         Library of Congress   16-5021

Example of LC
printed card
modified by
erasing and typing
in new information
— Do *not* use LC
card number

Sims, Joseph Patterson.
Old Philadelphia colonial details, measvred and drawn by Joseph Patterson Sims ₍and₎ Charles Willing. New York, The Architectvral book pvblishing co., 1914.

NA 707. 2 p. l., 55 pl. 47½ᶜᵐ. $10.00
S. 5   In portfolio.

Architecture

1. Architecture, Colonial. 2. Architecture—Details. 3. Architecture—Philadelphia. i. Willing, Charles, joint author. ii. Title.

Library of Congress   NA707.S5   14—12169
————— Copy 2.   S.5
Copyright A 374627

Example of an LC-like *classification number assigned by RUL*

("Architecture" should be ignored when inputting this number.)

LB   National Society for the Study of Education. *Committee*
5   *on Intelligence: its Nature and Nurture.*
.N25   Intelligence: its nature and nurture. Pt. 1. Comparative
s.2   and critical exposition. Pt. 2. Original studies and experi-
no.39 ments. Prepared by the Society's committee, assisted by
      members of the Society and others. Edited by Guy Montrose
      Whipple. Bloomington, Ill., Public School Pub. Co., 1940.
      2 v. diagrs., tables. 22 cm. (Yearbook of the National Society
      for the Study of Education, 39th, pts. 1–2)
      Includes bibliographies.
      1. Intellect. 2. Heredity. 3. Man—Influence of environment. ₍3.
      Environment₎ 4. Mental tests.   i. Whipple, Guy Montrose, 1876–
      1941, ed.   Series: National Society for the Study of Education.
      Yearbook, 39th, pts. 1–2₎

      LB5.N25 39th,   pt. 1–2   151.082   E 40—580
      U. S. Office of Education.   Library
      for Library of Congress   ₍59r58h²₎†

Example of an *analytic call number*

KJJ   Mélanges Roger Aubenas. — ₍Montpellier₎ : Faculté de droit et des
1122   sciences économiques de Montpellier, 1974.
.M45   818 p., ₍1₎ leaf of plates : port. ; 23 cm. — (Recueil de mémoires et travaux
       publié par la Société d'histoire du droit et des institutions des anciens pays de
       droit écrit ; fasc. 9)   F•••
          At head of title: Université de Montpellier I.
          French, German, Italian, English or Latin.
          Includes bibliographical references.

          1. Law—France—History and criticism—Addresses, essays, lectures. 2.
       Aubenas, Roger.   I. Aubenas, Roger. II. Series: Société d'histoire du droit
       et des institutions des anciens pays de droit écrit. -- Recueil de mémoires et tra-
       vaux ; fasc. 9.

                              340'.0944   75-504344
                                                    MARC
JXHR
          Library of Congress   75

Example of LC-like classification number for law derived from *University of Chicago Law Schedule*

KC
11
.K36

Karst, Kenneth L
    Law and development in Latin America : a case book /
Kenneth L. Karst, Keith S. Rosenn. — Berkeley : University of
California Press, c1975.

    xx, 738 p. ; 26 cm. — (UCLA Latin American studies series ; v. 28)

    Includes bibliographical references and index.
    ISBN 0-520-02955-0

    I. Law—Latin America—Cases.   I. Rosenn, Keith S., joint author. II.
Title. III. Series: California. University. University of Los Angeles. Latin
American Center. { Latin American studies ; v. 28.

                        340'.098   74-30525
                                                    MARC

Library of Congress   76

Example of LC-like classification number for law derived from *University of Chicago Law Schedule*

LC 1.2:P 84/4
Docs.
Dept.

  Posada's Mexico / edited by Ron Tyler.
  -- Washington : Library of Congress :
In cooperation with the Amon Carter
Museum of Western Art, Fort Worth,
Tex. : for sale by the Supt. of
Docs., U.S. Govt. Print. Off., 1979.
xii, 315 p. : ill., facsims., ports.
; 31 cm.
  Catalog of an exhibition held at the
Library of Congress, Washington, D.C.,
Nov. 1, 1979-Jan. 1, 1980, the Amon
Carter Museum of Western Art, Fort
Worth, Tex., Jan. 25-Mar. 9, 1980, and
the Colorado Springs Fine Arts Center,
Colorado Springs, Colo., Apr. 26-June
1, 1980.
    Bibliograph   y: p. 306-309.
    Includes in   dex.

TxHk 09 APR 80   5493257   &CEGsl SEE NEXT CRD

Example of *SuDoc classification* — Input in 086 field

LP   Strauss, Johann, 1825–1899.
.S88   ₍Waltzes, orchestra. Selections₎ Phonodisc.
22   Strauss waltzes.   London SPC 21018.   ₍1967?₎
S   2 s. 12 in. 33⅓ rpm. stereophonic. (Phase 4 stereo concert
R   series)

Examples of local
call number used
for *musical phono-
discs* — Input in
099 field

LP   Graves, Robert, 1895–
.S69   Robert Graves reads from his poetry & from The White
G73   Goddess. ₍Phonodisc₎ Caedmon TC 1066. ₍1957₎
1   2 s. 12 in. 33⅓ rpm. microgroove.

        Title from slipcase.
        Editions recorded: Collected poems (New York, Doubleday, 1955) ;
        The White Goddess (New York, Farrar, Strauss and Cudahy, 1948)
        Biographical note on slipcase.

        1. Poetry. 2. Mythology. 3. Welsh poetry—Hist. & crit.   I. Title.
        II. Title: The White Goddess.

                                                            R 57–999

        Library of Congress   ₍1₎

Music   Respighi. Ottorino, 1579–1936.
Tape   Pini di Roma₎ Phonotape
.R42   Pines of Rome. Fountains of Rome.   RCA Victor FTC
1   2012.   ₍1960 ?₎
S   1 reel. 7 1/2 ips. 4-track. stereo. 7 in.

Tape   Ravel, Maurice, 1875-1937.
.R35   ₍Concerto, piano, G major₎ Phonotape.
1   Piano concerto in G.   Angel YlS-36585.
S   ₍19 ₎
            1 reel (7 in.) 3 3/4 ips. stereophonic.

        Nicole Henriot-Schweitzer, piano; Orchestre
        de Paris; Charles Munch conductor.
        Four-track.
        With: Honegger, Arthur. Symphony, no.2,
        string orchestra.
            1.Concertos (Piano) I. Henriot-Schweitzer,
        Nicole. II. Munch, Charles, 1891-1968.
        III. Orchestre de Paris.   72-750067 V

Examples of local
call number
used for *musical
phono-tapes* —
Input in 099 field.

Cassette
.M9   Mozart, Johann Chrysostom Wolfgang Amadeus,
1   1756-1791.
         [Symphony, K.550, G minor] [Sound recording]
         Symphony no.40 in G minor, K.550. Symphony
         no.41, in C, K.551 (Jupiter). Angel 4XS 36772.
         1 cassette. 4-track. mono.

Music
Cassette Stan Kenton today. [Sound recording] Lon-
.K4   don, Decca LEL 84179. p1972.
1   1 cassette. 4-track. stereo. (Phase 4
S   stereo)

         Stan Kenton and his orchestra.
         Durations listed on cassette.

         1. Dance-orchestra music. I. Kenton, Stan.

Examples of local
call number used
for *musical cas-
settes* — Input
in 099 field

Cassette
MT   Tureck, Rosalyn.
80   The art of embellishment. [Sound recording] Rosalyn
.T87   Tureck compares 19th and 20th century ornamentation.
         Hollywood, Calif., Center for Cassette Studies, 1973. 33354.
            1 cassette. (Tapes of IBS International congresses, ser. A. Em-
         bellishment, 2)

Tape   Sussex tapes. History series II. HA 1-6.
DA   London, Sussex Tapes, 1970.
530   6 reels (5 in.) 3 3/4 ips.
.S88

         Each reel acompanied by 2 booklets giving a
         summary of the discussion on the tape and a
         bibliography relating to the subject discussed.
            Contents.--reel 1. The standard of living
         controversy and the industrial revolution. The
         causes of the industrial revolution.--reel 2.
         Peel and the repeal of the Corn Laws. Peel and

         (Continued on next card)

Examples of LC
classification used
for *non-musical
sound recordings*
Input in 050 or
090 field as
appropriate

NA
2440
.N47
M873
1971

Cooper Union for the Advancement of Science and Art,
New York. School of Art and Architecture.
   Education of an architect: a point of view. An exhibition by the Cooper Union School of Art & Architecture at
the Museum of Modern Art, New York City, November
1971. ₍New York, 1971₎
     323 p. illus. (part col.) 31 cm.
     1. Architecture—Exhibitions. 2. Cooper Union for the Advance-
ment of Science and Art. New York. School of Art and Architecture.
3. Architecture—Study and teaching—New York (City)   I. New
York (City). Museum of Modern Art. II. Title.
   NA2440.N47M873 1971   720′.71′17471   74–184158
                                                           MARC
— ——Copy 2.

049   ≠c 1, 2
590 LIBRARY
HAS C. 1, 2.

ARTS
NA
31
.F55
1966

Fleming, John, 1919–
   The Penguin dictionary of architecture, ₍by₎ John Flem-
ing, Hugh Honour, Nikolaus Pevsner; drawings by David
Etherton. ₍Harmondsworth, Eng., Baltimore, Md.₎
Penguin Books ₍1966₎
     247 p. illus., plans, diagrs. 20 cm. (Penguin reference books,
R13)

   -- ---Copy 2-3.

     1. Architecture — Dictionaries.   I. Honour, Hugh.   II. Pevsner,
Nikolaus, 1902–   III. Title.   IV. Title: Dictionary of architecture.

   NA31.F55 1966a   720.3   66–70279

   Library of Congress   ₍5₎

049   ≠c 1, 2, 3
590 LIBRARY
HAS C. 1, 2, 3.

Bartlett

ML
410
.B4
B2816

Beethoven–Hefte ₍aus der Musik. Berlin,
   Schuster & Loeffler, 1902–27₎
     18 v. illus., facsims., music, ports.
28 cm.

   Imprint varies.
   Made—up collection of assorted issues of
the periodical Die Musik devoted to or
containing articles about Beethoven.

     1. Beethoven, Ludwig van, 1770–1827.
I. Die Musik.
   — ——Copy 2 ₍of v. 16₎

049   ≠c 1
        ≠v 1-18
      ≠c 2 ≠v 16
590 LIBRARY
HAS C. 1, V. 1-18;
    C. 2, V. 16.

NA   Faber, Tobias, 1915–
1223   Arne Jacobsen. ₍Translated by E. Rockwell₎ New
.J3   York, Praeger ₍1964₎
F313   xxiii, 175 p. illus., plans. 26 cm.
           English and German.
           –– ––Copy 2. ₍1966, c1964₎

           1. Jacobsen, Arne, 1902–

           NA1223.J3F313   720.9489   64–16676

           Library of Congress   ₍5₎

049   ≠c 1, 2
590 LIBRARY HAS
C. 1, 2; c. 2 has
imprint date:
1966, c1964.

AXSON Cumberland, Richard, 1732–1811.
PR   The wheel of fortune: a comedy. Performed at the
3392   Theatre-Royal, Drury-Lane. By Richard Cumberland
.W5   ... * London, C. Dilly, 1795.
1795d   79. ₍1₎ p. 22 cm.

           *4th ed.

           –– –––Copy 2.   20 cm.
           i. Title.
                                                26–19617
           Library of Congress   ₍37b1₎
                            ▸PR1241.L6 vol. 231

049   ≠c 1, 2
590   LIBRARY
HAS C. 1, 2;
c. 2 is 20 cm.

AXSON Favart, Charles Simon, 1710–1792.
PQ   The Englishman in Bourdeaux. A comedy. Written in
1983   French, by the celebrated Monsieur Favart. Acted with uni-
.F3   versal applause, at the Theatre-Royal, in Paris ... Translated
A813   by an English lady now residing in Paris. London, G. Kearsly,
1764   1764.
           iv, ₍2₎ 60 ₍2₎ p. 21¼ᶜᵐ.
           ₍Longe, F. Collection of plays. v. 101, no. 6₎·
           –– –––Copy 2.
           Imperfect: all after p. 60 wanting.
           i. Title.
           –– –––Copy 3.   25––6006
           Library of Congress   PR1241.L6 vol. 101
                            ₍42b1₎

049   ≠c 1, 2, 3
590   LIBRARY
HAS C. 1, 2, 3;
c. 2 imperfect:
all after p. 60
wanting.

PQ   Giraudoux, Jean, 1882-
2613   Suzanne et le Pacifique ... Paris,
I74   Émile-Paul frères,1921.
S9   297p. 19cm.
          2 copies.

          I.Title.

          Copy 2 is 1930 issue.

      23-363   W 536 Fr. 1-5-23.

                      c.2 = Gift. French For.
                         Office June, 1938
                            38-2979

049   ≠c 1, 2
590   LIBRARY
       HAS C. 1, 2;
       c. 2 is 1930
          issue.

N   **Kandinsky, Wassily,** 1866–1944.
68   Concerning the spiritual in art, and painting in particu-
.K33 lar. 1912. [A version of the Sadleir translation, with con-
1947 siderable re-translation by Francis Golffing, Michael Harri-
      son and Ferdinand Ostertag] New York, Wittenborn,
      Schultz, 1947.
          95 p. illus., port. 26 cm. (The Documents of modern art [5])
          Bibliography : p. 6.
          "Prose poems (1912–1937)" : p. [79]–91.
      — —Copy 2–3.   93 p.
          1. Aesthetics. 2. Painting.   I. Sadleir, Michael, 1888–   tr.
      II. Golffing, Francis, tr. III. Title. IV. Series .

          N68.K33 1947   701.17   47—12026*

      Library of Congress   [a52x1]

049   ≠c 1, 2, 3
590   LIBRARY
       HAS C. 1, 2, 3;
       c. 2-3 have 93 p.

PQ   Laclos, Pierre Ambroise François Choderlos de,
1993   1741–1803.
.L22   Poésies de Choderlos de Laclos; publiées
A 17 par Arthur Symons et Louis Thomas. Paris,
1908 Chez Dorbon l'aîné, 1908.
          100 p. 21 cm.

          312 copies printed. No.64.
      — ---Copy 2. No.25.
          I. Symons, Arthur, 1865–1945, ed.   II. Thomas,
      Louis, 1885–   jt. ed.

049   ≠c 1, 2
590   LIBRARY
       HAS C. 1, 2;
       c. 2 is no. 25.

51

NA   Banham, Reyner.
680   Theory and design in the first machine age. 2d ed. New
.B25   York, Praeger [1970, c1960]
1967   338 p. illus., plans. 23 cm.
         Bibliographical footnotes.
         1. Architecture, Modern—20th cent.   I. Title.
         NA680.B25 1967   724.9   67–16449

        *"Second edition, 1967. Second printing, 1970."
    -- ---Another issue. 1975, c1960. (Praeger
    University series)

049   ≠c 1, 2
590   LIBRARY
HAS C. 1, 2;
c. 2 is another
issue with imprint
date and series:
1975, c1960.
(Praeger Univer-
sity series)

AXSON [Cumberland, Richard] 1732–1811.
PR   The West Indian: a comedy. As it is performed at the The-
3392 atre Royal in Drury-Lane. By the author of The brothers ...
.W4   London, W. Griffin, 1771.
1771
      3 p. l., 102, [2] p. 21ᶜᵐ.

      Imperfect? Half title wanting?

    — ——Copy 2.
      Part of a collection of early drama formed by John Philip Kemble.
      Text inlaid with Kemble's notes on title page and verso of title
      page.
      I. Title. II. Kemble, John Philip, 1757–1823.

                          24–5987
    Library of Congress   (PR3392.W4 1771

049   ≠c 1, 2
590   LIBRARY
HAS C. 1, 2;
c. 2 is part of a
collection of early
drama formed
by John Philip
Kemble; text inlaid
with Kemble's
notes on title
page and verso of
title page.

---

b. Copies in different call numbers, but in same holding library

NA   Espouy, Hector d', 1854–
351   Fragments d'architecture du moyen âge et de la renaissance
.Es6 d'après les relevés & restaurations des anciens pensionnaires
de l'Académie de France à Rome, publiés sous la direction de
H. d'Espouy ... Paris, C. Schmid; [etc., 1897–] ᶜ1925.
      2 v. in 2 180 pl. (incl. plans) 45½ᶜᵐ.
      Issued in parts (in portfolios)
      The "Table explicative des planches" (v. 1) is by G. Daumet.
      Vol. II has imprint: Paris, C. Massin et cⁱᵉ.
      1. Architecture, Medieval. 2. Architecture, Renaissance.. 3. Archi-
tecture—Italy.   I. Daumet, Georges, 1870–1918. II. Title.

NA   — —Copy 2. (In 2 vols..) [Full name: Marie Désiré Hector Jean Baptiste d'Espouy]
111   — —Copy 3 of v1 only   36–14381 Revised
.E7   Library of Congress (NA1111.E7
                     [r38b2]   720.84

Flag with red
envelope as
problem.

b. Copies in different call numbers, but in same holding library (continued)

PR
1243
.I 4
v.18

Cumberland, Richard, 1732–1811.
    The wheel of fortune; a comedy, in five acts; as performed at the Theatre Royal, Drury-Lane. By Richard Cumberland, esq. ... With remarks by Mrs. Inchbald. London, Longman, Hurst, Rees, Orme, and Brown ₍n. d.₎

    72 p. front. 15ᵐ. (Inchbald, Mrs. Elizabeth. The British theatre ... London, 1808. v. 18 ₍no. 5₎)

    I. Title.

PR
3392
.W5

Library of Congress   (— —Copy 2

₋₋₋₋₋₋ #355 Engl. 7-31-22 82-22116
PR1243.I4 vol.18 22-3811
₍₂₎ 9833 Engl. 10-24-44 44-3341

Input on 2 separate records.

---

c. Copies in different holding libraries
    (1) Call number is same

ML
410
.B4
B96

Burk, John Naglee, 1891–
    The life and works of Beethoven. ₍1st Modern Library ed.₎ New York, Modern Library ₍1946₎, c1943₎

    viii, 483 p. 19 cm. (The Modern library of the world's best books)

    Includes music.
    "Phonograph records": p. 464–478.

Bartlett
ML
410
.B4
B96

-- ---Copy 2.

    1. Beethoven, Ludwig van, 1770–1827.

    [ML410.B4B   ]   (927.8   A 48—6425*
    Yale Univ. Library
    for Library of Congress   ₍60d1₎

Input on same record.
049   RCEA, RCEN

PR
3392
.B7
1770

₍Cumberland, Richard₎ 1732–1811.
    The brothers: a comedy. As it is performed at the Theatre Royal in Covent-Garden. London, W. Griffin, 1770.
    1 p.l.,
    ᴀ v, ₍3₎, 72 p. 21ᶜᵐ.

    ₍Longe, F. Collection of plays. v. 207, no. 5₎
    Engraved t.-p. with vignette.

AXSON
PR
3392
.B7
1770

-- ---Copy 2.

-- ---Another issue.
    Engraved t.-p. with vignette.
    I. Title.

    Library of Congress   (PR1241.L6 vol.207   25—27580
    W11557 Engl. 9-19-49
    ₍3701₎   49-7015

Input on 2 different records.
Record 1 - 049 RCEA
Record 2 - 049 RCEK ≠c 1, 2 590
LIBRARY HAS C. 1, 2; c. 2 is another issue with engraved t. p. with vignette.

APPENDIX A. V. Multiple copies (continued)
c. Copies in different holding libraries
(2) Call number is different

```
⚹PR    Cumberland, Richard, 1732-1811.
1241      The Jew: a comedy. Performed at the Theatre-Royal,
.P48   Drury-Lane. By Richard Cumberland, esq. The 2d ed.
no.3   London, C. Dilly, 1794.

          2 p. l., 75, ₍1₎ p.  20½ᶜᵐ.

AXSCN     ₍Longe, P. Collection of plays. v. 228, no. 4₎
PR        ₍Plays.  1753-1806.  no.3₎
3392   .- ---Copy 2.
.J4

          I. Title.

                                                26—19614

       Library of Congress  (    PR1241.L6  vol. 228
                                 W2994 Engl. 12-17-28
                                 ₍37b1₎    29-137
```

Input as 2 separate records, using 049 1 on second record input.

d. Two different editions on same card

```
JC     Corpus juris civilis. Institutiones.
85        Imperatoris Iustiniani Institutionum libri quattuor, with
.L3    introductions, commentary, and excursus, by J. B. Moyle ...
C623   ₅th ed.₎ Oxford, Clarendon press; London and New York,
       H. Frowde, 1912. 1923.

          vi p., 1 l., 682 p.ₐ 23ᶜᵐ.

       "The text ... followed is that published by Krueger in his and Momm-
       sen's edition of the Corpus juris civilis ₍Berlin, 1877₎"—Pref.


       1. Roman law.    I. Moyle, John Baron, 1852-1930, ed.
            (Continued on next card)
                                                13—25017
                         (    W2487 Anc. Hist. 10-10-27
       Library of Congress       ₍a37d1₎ 27-4623
```

Input on 2 separate records if DLC copy available for dashed-on edition; otherwise, flag with red envelope as problem.

```
JC     Corpus juris civilis.  Institutiones.    Impera-
85        toris Iustiniani Institutionum ...  1923.
.L3       (Card 2)
C623

JC     — —2d ed.  Oxford, Clarendon press, 1890.
85        4 p.l., 683 p.  23ᶜᵐ.  (At head of title:
.L3    Clarendon press series)
C621




                         (    W8274 Hist. 12-27-40
                                41-781
```

54

DG
82
.S8613

Storoni Mazzolani, Lidia.
The idea of the city in Roman thought: from walled city to spiritual commonwealth. Translated by S. O'Donnell. Bloomington, Indiana University Press ₁1970₎

288 p. 23 cm. 6.95 *Library has c. 2 only.*

Translation of L'idea di città nel mondo romano.
Bibliography: p. 281–282.

-- ---Copy 2.

1. Rome—Civilization. 2. Cities and towns, Ancient.   ɪ. Title.

DG82.S8613   913.37′03   79–108947
SBN 253–13980–5   (MARC

Library of Congress   70 ₁4₎

049   ≠c 2
590   LIBRARY
HAS C. 2 ONLY.

JC
85
.L3
S29

Saraiva da Cunha Lobo, Abelardo.
    Curso de direito romano. Historia, sujeito e objecto do direito, instituições juridicas, por Abelardo Saraiva da Cunha Lobo ... prefacio do professor dr. Francisco de Paula Lacerda de Almeida ... Rio de Janeiro, Tip. A. Pinto, 1931–
    3 v. 24ᵐ.   *Library has v. 1–3.*
    "Dedicatoria" signed: Abelardo Lobo.

    1. Roman law—Hist. 2. Roman law—Sources. I. Title.

                                38–36576
                        W7010 Spec. Hist.
Library of Congress   [3] 9-12-38 39-4858-60

Incomplete set
049 ≠v 1-3
    300   v.
590 LIBRARY
HAS VOLS. 1-3

JC
85
.L3
R8

Rudorff, Adolf August Friedrich, 1803–1873.
    Römische rechtsgeschichte. Von Adolf Friedrich Rudorff. Zum akademischen gebrauch ... Leipzig, B. Tauchnitz, 1857–59.
    2 v. 19ᶜᵐ.
    CONTENTS.—1. bd. Rechtsbildung.—2. bd. Rechtspflege.

    1. Roman law—Hist. I. Title.

                  W7326 Hist.   34–7984
                  4-10-39 39-2227-28
Library of Congress   [2]

Complete set
No 049 or 590
field is needed.

JC
85
.L3
S314

Savigny, Friedrich Karl von, 1779–1861.
    Traité de droit romain, par m. F. C. de Savigny ... traduit de l'allemand par m. Ch. Guenoux ... Paris, Firmin Didot frères, 1846–56.
    8 v. 22ᶜᵐ.
    Vols. 1-2 dated 1855; v. 3-4, 2d edition, 1856; v. 5-8, 1846-51.
    CONTENTS.—t. I. Sources du droit romain actuel. Rapports de droit.—t. II. Des personnes considérées comme sujets des rapports de droit.—t. III–IV. De l'origine et de la fin des rapports de droit.—t. V–VII. Violation des droits.—t. VIII. Empire des règles du droit sur les rapports de droits.
    1. Roman law. 2. Roman law—Bibl. 3. Civil law. 4. International law, Private. I. Guenoux, Charles, ed. and tr. II. Title. *Translation of* System des heutigen römischen rechts.

                  W5687 Anc.Hist.1-23-35
                              27—10384
                  35-362-365
Library of Congress   [31b1]

Complete set
No 049 or 590
field is needed.

```
DC    Chantrel, Joseph, 1818-1884.
251       Histoire contemporaine complément de l'His-
.C49  toire de France et du cours d'histoire univer-
      selle, par J. Chantrel.  Paris, Putois-Cretté,
      1864.              Library has v.3 only.
      | 3 v.  19 cm.  (Bibliothèque Saint-Germain.
      2e partie: Éducation et enseignement)
         Bibliographical footnotes.
         Contents.--I. Depuis 1789 jusqu'en 1815.--II.
      Depuis 1815 jusqu'en 1848.--III. Depuis 1848
      jusqu'en 1864.
         1. France--History--1789-1900.  I. Title.
```

049   ≠v 3
300   3 v.
590 LIBRARY HAS
    VOL. 3 ONLY.

```
DC    Histoire socialiste, 1789-1900, sous la direc-
252       tion de Jean Jaurès.  Paris, J. Rouff ₁1901-
.H58     98₃04          Library has v. 1+2 only.
      21?v.  illus., ports., maps, facsims.
      28 cm.

         Contents.--t. 1. La Constituante, 1789-1791,
      par J. Jaurès.--t. 2. La Législative, 1791-
      1792, par J. Jaurès.--t. 3-4. La Convention,
      1792-1794, par J. Jaurès.--t. 5. Thermidor &
      Directoire, 1794-1799, par G. Deville.--t. 6.
      Consulat & Empire, 1799-1815, par P. Brousse &
      H. Turot.
```

049   ≠v 1-2
300   13 v.
590 LIBRARY
HAS VOLS. 1-2,
published 1901-
1904.

LC '50

```
DC    Lavisse, Ernest, 1842-1922 ed.
251       ... Histoire de France contemporaine depuis la révolu-
.L35  tion jusqu'à la paix de 1919; ouvrage illustré de nom-
      breuses gravures hors texte ...  ₁Paris₁ Hachette ₍1920-22₎
         10 v.  n.5. front., illus. (map, plans) plates, ports. 24ᶜᵐ.




         1. France—Hist.—1789-1918.

      Library of Congress          DC251.L35        21-3103
      Copyright  A—Foreign      (   17725
                                     ₍2₎
```

049   ≠v 1-10
300   v.
590 LIBRARY
HAS VOLS.
1-10 (10 v. in 5),
published 1920-
1922.

a. Series is not traced — Note parenthesis around series tracing or lack of series tracing.

PF
3599
.M5
W5
1964

Wiercinski, Dorothea.
    Minne; Herkunft und Anwendungsschichten eines Wortes.
Köln, Böhlau, 1964.
    vi, 106 p. 24 cm. (Niederdeutsche Studien, Bd. 11)
    Issued also as thesis, Münster, under title: Herkunft und An-
wendungsschichten des Wortes Minne.
    Bibliography: p. [101]–106.

    1. Minne (The world)   I. Title.   (Series)

    PF3599.M5W5 1964   66–95599

    Library of Congress   [2]

Series is not traced

PF
3301
.S3

Schipporeit, Luise.
    Tenses and time phrases in modern German.   [1. Aufl.
München] M. Hueber [1971]
    203 p. 21 cm. (Sprachen der Welt)   GDB•••
    Bibliography: p. 199–203.

    1. German language—Tense.   I. Title.

TxHR   PF3301.S3   (438.2'4'21   72–192942
                                                        MARC
       Library of Congress   72 [4]

Series is not traced

PQ
7276
.O68

Orozco, Fernando, comp.
    Cuentos y narraciones de la Ciudad de México / Fer-
nando Orozco. — [México] : Departamento del Distrito
Federal, Secretaría de Obras y Servicíós, 1974.
    111 p. : ill. ; 17 cm. —'(Colección popular Ciudad de México ; 16)
    CONTENTS: Orozco, F. El cuento en México.—Couto, J. B. La
mulata de Córdoba y la historia de un peso.—Riva Palacio, V. Las
mulas de Su Excelencia.—Gutiérrez Nájera, M. La novela del tran-
vía.—Campo, A. del. El jarro.—Estrada, G. El paraíso colonial.—
López Velarde, R. Semana Mayor.—Novo, S. Lota de loco.—Avilés,
R. El hombre del cheque.
    $5.00
    1. Short stories, Mexican. 2. Mexico (City)—Fiction.   I. Title.
(II. Series.)

    PQ7276.O68   (74–235622

TxHR   Library of Congress   74 [2]

Series is not traced

PF
3301
.H3

Hauser-Suida, Ulrike.
Die Vergangenheitstempora in der deutschen geschrie-
benen Sprache der Gegenwart: Untersuchungen an ausgew.
Texten/ Ulrike Hauser-Suida; Gabriel Hoppe-Beugel. —
1. Aufl. — München: Hueber; Düsseldorf: Pädagogischer
Verlag Schwann, 1972.

406 p. ; 21 cm. (Heutiges Deutsch: Reihe 1, Linguistische Grundlagen ; Bd. 4) DM22.00   GDB 73-A4

Bibliography: p. 387-406.

1. German language—Tense.   I. Hoppe-Beugel, Gabriele, joint
author. II. Title. III. Series.

TxHR

PF3301.H3   73-317612

Library of Congress   73 [2]

Series is traced

PQ
1477
.G45
1969

Guernes *de Pont-Sainte-Maxence, 12th cent.*
La vie de saint Thomas le martyr, archevêque de Canterbury [par] Garnier de Pont Sainte Maxence. Publiée et
précédée d'une introd. par C. Hippeau. Genève, Slatkine
Reprints, 1969.

liv, 227 p. 23 cm. (Collection des poètes français du Moyen Age,
2)   Sw***

Reprint of the Paris 1859 ed.
Includes bibliographical references.

1. Thomas à Becket, Saint, Abp. of Canterbury, 1118?-1170—
Poetry.   I. Hippeau, Célestin, 1803-1883, ed. II. Title.   Series

TxER   PQ1477.G45 1969   73-480538

Library of Congress   70 [2]

Series is traced

PF
3599
.L5
S9
1975

Sucharowski, Wolfgang, 1945-
"Liberal" im gegenwärtigen Sprachgebrauch : linguist., psy-
cholinguist. u. semant. Studien zum Jahr 1971 / Wolfgang Sucharowski. — München : Fink, 1975.

409 p. ; 21 cm. — (Münchner Universitäts-Schriften : Philosophische Fakultät) (Münch[e]ner germanistische Beiträge ; Bd. 19)   GFR76-A

A revision of the author's thesis, Munich, 1973.
Bibliography: p. 400-408.
ISBN 3-7705-1169-7 : DM78.00

1. German language—Semantics.   2. Liberal (The German word)   3. German philology—Political aspects.   I. Title.   II. Series: Münchener germanistische Beiträge ; Bd. 19.   III. Series: Münchener Universitäts-Schriften.
Reihe der Philosophischen Fakultät.

PF3599.L5S9 1975   76-459147
                                              MARC

TxHR

Library of Congress   76

Series is traced

59

```
Z       -Cole, George Watson, 1850–
1008      An index to bibliographical papers published by the Biblio-
.B4     graphical society and the Library association, London, 1877–
Reference 1932, by George Watson Cole ... Chicago, Ill., Pub. for the
        Bibliographical society of America at the University of Chi-
        cago press ₍1933₎
           ix, 262 p.  22ᶜᵐ.  ₍Bibliographical society of America. Special pub-
        lication₎
           Author and subject index.
           Indexes also the Library, a quarterly review of bibliography.
           "List of publications indexed": p. vii–ix.
           Reference books consulted cited in "Addenda".
           1. Bibliography—Bibl.  2. Bibliographical society, London—Bibl.  3.
Z       Library association—Bibl.  4. Library science—Bibl.  5. Indexes.    I.
1008    The Library; a quarterly       review of bibliography.  (Indexes)
.B4     II. Title.                         W4566 Gen'1.11–14–33
           Library of Congress            Z1008.B585              33–33065
        ————— Copy 2.                            34–41
        Copyright  A 67127            ₍5₎              016.01
```

Series is traced

Underlining of series heading indicates that a series added entry has been made.

```
LB      Abelson, Paul, 1878–
5           ... The seven liberal arts, a study in mediæval culture.  By
.C8     Paul Abelson ...  New York, Teachers' college, Columbia
no.11   university, 1939.

           x, 150 p.  23₁ cm.  (Columbia university.  Teachers' college.
        Contributions to education, no. 11)

           "Critical bibliography": p. 137–150.


        1. Education  Medieval.    I. Title.

        Library of Congress  (      LA96.A25                7—13492
                                    W12763
                                 ₍51i½₎
```

Series is traced

Underlining of series heading indicates that a series added entry has been made.

```
PQ      Abraham, Claude Kurt, 1931–
1772        Pierre Corneille, by Claude Abraham.  New York, Twayne
.A54    Publishers ₍1972₎
           169 p.   21 cm.  (Twayne's world authors series, (TWAS) 214.
        (France)
           Bibliography: p. 163–166.



        1. Corneille, Pierre, 1606–1684.   Series
        PQ1772.A54          (      842'.4            76–186715
                                                         MARC
        Library of Congress           72 ₍4₎
```

Series is traced

When inputting series in 4xx field, omit part of series that is enclosed in paren- thesis.

Entry for series is: 440 ⊬0 Twayne's world authors series, ⊬v 214

E
540
.I3 A2
v.2

Abel, Annie Heloise, 1873–
    The American Indian as participant in the civil war, by
Annie Heloise Abel ... Cleveland, The Arthur H. Clark company, 1919.

    403 p. incl. front. (facsim.) port., double map, 2 fold. facsim. 24½ᶜᵐ.
(*Her* The slaveholding Indians, vol. II) $5.00

    "Selected bibliography": p. [353]–367.

    1. Indians of North America—Hist.—Civil war. 2. Indian Territory—
Hist.—Civil war. 3. U. S.—Hist.—Civil war—Indian troops.   I. Title.

                                                        19—5303
    Library of Congress   E540.I 3A2

    ————————Copy 2.
    Copyright A 512837   — [2812] W3537 Amer.)Hist. 3-7-30
                                            30-2651

Series is traced

Entry for series
is: 400 11 Her
≠t Slaveholding
Indians; ≠v v. 2

HM
132
.P63

Ponzio, Augusto.
    La relazione interpersonale. Bari, Adriatica, 1967.

    103 p. 22 cm. (Pubblicazioni della Facoltà di lettere e filosofia
della Università degli studi di Bari, 4)   1200   It 68–July

    At head of title: Università degli studi di Bari, Facoltà di lettere
e filosofia.
    Includes bibliographical references.

    1. Interpersonal relations.   I. Title.   Series: Bari (City) Uni-
versità. Facoltà di lettere e filosofia. Pubblicazioni, 4

TxHR   HM132.P63   73–377980

    Library of Congress   69 [11]

Series is traced

Form of series
in collation line
is different from
series tracing.
Series must be
input in both
4xx and 8xx
fields.

c. Omissions from series statements

PT
1703
.A3
Z6

Abraham *a Sancta Clara*, 1644?–1709.
    Etwas für alle. Von Abraham a Santa Clara. Hrsg. und
mit einer einleitung versehen von Richard Zoozmann. [Dres-
den, H. Angermann, 1905]

    xxxv. 488 p. incl. 13 pl., port. 21½ᶜᵐ. (*Added t.-p.*: Angermann's
Bibliothek für bibliophilen ... 3. bd.)

    Illustrated series half-title.
    Extracts from the original, with facsimiles of the engravings and of
the t.-p.: "Etwas für alle, das ist: eine kurtze beschreibung allerley
stands- ambts- und gewerbs-personnen, mit beygeruckter sittlichen lehre
und biblischen concepten, durch welche der fromme mit gebührendem lob

            (Continued on next card)

                                        5–28509 rev.
                    [r33b2]

"Added t. p."
should be omitted
when inputting
series.

61

JA
81
.S3

Sabine, George Holland, 1880–
    A history of political theory, by George H. Sabine ... New York, H. Holt and company [°1937]

    xvi, 797 p. 22ᶜᵐ. (*Half-title:* American political science series; general editor, E. S. Corwin)

    "Selected bibliography" at end of most of the chapters.

    1. Political science—Hist.   ɪ. Title.

Library of Congress   JA81.S3   37–12544
————— Copy 2. —————   W6562 Phil.6-12-37
                            37–4558
Copyright A 107217   [10]   320.9

"Half-title" and "general editor, E. S. Corwin" should be omitted when inputting series.

PQ
7276
.M3

Martínez, José Luis, *comp.*
    Literatura indígena moderna: A. Médiz Bolio, E. Abreu Gómez, A. Henestrosa ... Introducción y selección de José Luis Martínez. México, Ediciones Mensaje, 1942.

    3 p. l., 9–165 p., 1 l. 18ᶜᵐ. (*On cover:* Selecciones hispano americanas)

    "Notas" (bibliographical) : p. 24–25.

    Contents.—Médiz Bolio, Antonio. La tierra del faisán y del venado.—Abreu Gómez, Ermilo. Canek.—Henestrosa, Andrés. Los hombres que dispersó la danza.

    1. Mayas—Fiction.   ɪ. Médiz Bolio, Antonio, 1884–   ɪɪ. Abreu Gómez, Ermilo, 1894–   ɪɪɪ. Henestrosa, Andrés.   ɪᴠ. Title.

                          W27716   A 43–1892
Harvard univ. Library
  for Library of Congress   PQ7276.M3
                        [4]†   860.9

"On cover" should be omitted when inputting series.

VIII. Dashed-on Entries

AI
3
.S85
1966
REF.

Sutton, Roberta (Briggs)
    Speech index; an index to 259 collections of world famous orations and speeches for various occasions. 4th ed., rev. and enl. New York, Scarecrow Press, 1966.

    vii, 947 p. 21 cm.

    "Incorporates all the materials in the three previous Speech Indexes: 1935, 1935–55, and 1956–1961, and augments it [sic] with ... new publications ... through 1965."

—— ———Supplement. 1966-70--   . Metuchen, N. J., Scarecrow Press.
    2 v. 23 cm. *Library has 1966-70-- 1971-75*

                    (Continued on next card)
                [145–2]   [Over]

Dash entry is for a serial – Flag whole card as a serial (with orange envelope)

HG   Donaldson, Elvin Frank, 1903–
173   Personal finance ₍by₎ Elvin F. Donaldson and John K.
.D6   Pfahl. 3d ed. New York, Ronald Press Co. ₍1961₎
1961   717 p. illus. 24 cm.

            Includes bibliography.

            —— ——Instructor's manual. New York, Ronald Press
            Co. ₍1961₎

            96 p. 23 cm.
                                        HG173.D6 1961 Manual ◄————————— Call number for
                                                                                   dash entry
            1. Finance, Personal.   x. Pfahl, John K., joint author.

            HG173.D6 , 1961   ⎛   332.024   61—7071 ‡
                                     ⎝
            Library of Congress   ₍6-r62t3₎

Flag with red envelope unless DLC record is found for the dash entry

---

E   North Carolina. General assembly
573.3 Roster of North Carolina troops in the war
.N87 between the states. Raleigh, Ash & Gatling, state
      printers, 1882.
         4 v. 23 cm.

         ——— ——— Index ₍of names₎ ... filmed from card
FILM index in the North Carolina Department of Ar-
E   chives and History. Raleigh, N. C., 1958.
573.3 15 reels.
.N87
Index   Microfilm copy (16 mm, positive)
         "Compiled by the   W. P. A. Historical Re-
         cords Survey."   ⎛
                          ⎝

Flag with red envelope unless DLC record is found for the dash entry

63

APPENDIX B. Tables of Holding Library Symbols

Call number examples	Holding library symbol	Type of material	How to recognize
DA 3 .M42	RCEA	All monographs not otherwise designated	No additions to call no., or "Arch." in call no.
Ref. Z 7201 .L63 OR Z 7201 .L63 Reference	RCEB	Reference	"Ref.", "REF." or "Reference" appears above or below call no.
Ref. Z 7201 .L63 OR Z 7201 .L63 Reference	RCEC	Reference Serial	"Ref.", "REF." or "Reference" appears above or below call no.; ignore "*" after "Ref." in call no.; card is in serial format
Abstract Z 7201 .L63 OR Z 7201 .L63 Ref. Abstract	RCED	Abstract	"Ref. Abstract" appears below call no. OR "Abstract" appears above call no.
Abstract Z 7201 .L63 OR Z 7201 .L63 Ref. Abstract	RCEE	Abstract Serial	"Ref. Abstract" appears below call no. OR "Abstract" appears above call no.; card is in serial format
DA 3 .M42	RCEF	Serials	No additions to call no.; card is in serial format
C 3.262:979	RCEG	Government document	Superintendent of Documents classification no. has been used.

64

Appendix B continued

Call number examples		Holding library symbol	Type of material	How to recognize
*DA 3 .M42	OR	WRC DA 3 .M42	RCEH	Rare monographs	An "*" precedes first letter of call no., OR WRC appears above call no. (The "*" should be omitted when inputting number.)
*DA 3 .M42	OR	WRC DA 3 .M42	RCEI	Rare serials	An "*" precedes first letter of call no., OR WRC appears above call no.; card is in serial format
*Z 6519 .W55 Ref.	OR	WRC Ref. Z 6519 .W55	RCEJ	Rare reference	An "*" precedes first letter of call no. and "Reference" appears below call no., OR "WRC Ref." appears above call no.
Axson PR 3316 .B25 C4	OR	WRC Axson PR 3316 .B25 C4	RCEK	Axson collection	"Axson" OR "WRC Axson", appears above call no.
Masterson F 389 .R75	OR	WRC Masterson F 389 .R75	RCEL	Masterson collection — Monograph	"Masterson" OR "WRC Masterson" appears above call no.

Appendix B continued

Call number examples	Holding library symbol	Type of material	How to recognize
Masterson F 389 .R75 OR WRC Masterson F 389 .R75	RCEM	Masterson collection — Serial	"Masterson" OR "WRC" appears above call no.; "Masterson" card is in serial format
Bartlett ML 410 .B4 L2 OR WRC Bartlett ML 410 .B4 L2	RCEN	Bartlett collection — Monograph	"Bartlett" OR "WRC" appears above call no. "Bartlett"
Bartlett ML 410 .B4 L2 OR WRC Bartlett ML 410 .B4 L2	RCEO	Bartlett collection — Serial	"Bartlett" OR "WRC" appears above call no.; "Bartlett" card is in serial format
Watson PR 5740 .E7 OR WRC Watson PR 5740 .E7	RCEP	Watson collection	"Watson" or "WRC" appears above call no. "Watson"
Film DA 3 .M42 OR Microfilm DA 3 .M42	RCEQ	Microfilm — Monograph	"Film" OR "Microfilm" appears above call no.

Appendix B continued

Call number examples	Holding library symbol	Type of material	How to recognize
Film DA 3 .M42 OR Microfilm DA 3 .M42	RCER	Microfilm — Serial	"Film" OR "Microfilm" appears above call no.; card is in serial format
Microcard DA 3 .M42	RCES	Microcard — Monograph	"Microcard" appears above call no.
Microcard DA 3 .M42	RCET	Microcard — Serial	"Microcard" appears above call no.; card is in serial format
Microfiche DA 3 .M42	RCEU	Microfiche — Monograph	"Microfiche" appears above call no.
Microfiche DA 3 .M42	RCEV	Microfiche — Serial	"Microfiche" appears above call no.; card is in serial format
Microprint DA 3 .M42	RCEW	Microprint — Monograph	"Microprint" appears above call no.

Appendix B continued

Call number examples	Holding library symbol	Type of material	How to recognize
Microprint DA 3 .M42	RCEX	Microprint – Serial	"Microprint" appears above call no.; card is in serial format
ARTS Art N N 362 OR 362 .A29 .A29	RCEY	Art monographs	"ARTS" OR "Art" appears above call no.
ARTS Art *N Rare 362 OR N .A29 362 .A29	RCEZ	Art rare	"ARTS" appears above call no. in combination with an "*" before first letter of call no. OR "Art Rare" appears above call no.
ARTS Art N Ref. 362 OR N .A29 362 Ref. .A29	RCE1	Art reference – Monograph	"ARTS" appears above call no. in combination with "Ref." below call no. OR "Art Ref." appears above call no.
ARTS Art N Ref. 362 OR N .A29 362 Ref. .A29	RCE2	Art reference – Serial	"ARTS" appears above call no. in combination with "Ref." below call no. OR "Art Ref." appears above call no.; card is in serial format
ARTS Art N N 362 OR 362 .A29 .A29	RCE3	Art serials	"ARTS" OR "Art" appears above call no.; card is in serial format

Appendix B continued

Call number examples		Holding library symbol	Type of material	How to recognize
LP .T3 2	OR Music LP .T3 2	RCE4	Phonodiscs	Call no. begins with "LP" OR "Music LP" and is a local call no.
Tape .B4 28	OR Music Tape .B4 28	RCE5	Phonotapes – Music	Call no. begins with "Tape" OR "Music Tape" and is a local call no.; contents are music
Cassette .M6 22 S	OR Music Cassette .M6 22 S	RCE6	Cassettes – Music	Call no. begins with "Cassette" OR "Music Cassette" and is a local call no.; contents are music
Tape DA 35 .M9	OR Music Tape DA 35 .M9	RCE7	Phonotapes – Non-musical	Call no. begins with "Tape" OR "Music Tape" and consists of an *LC classification no.*; contents are of a non-musical nature
Cassette DA 35 .M9	OR Music Cassette DA 35 .M9	RCE8	Cassettes – Non-musical	Call no. begins with "Cassette" OR "Music Cassette" and consists of an *LC classification no.*; contents are of a non-musical nature
Z 1223 .A 18 Reference Docs.	OR Docs. Ref. Z 1223 .A 18	RCE9	Documents reference – Monographs	"Reference appears below call no. Docs." OR "Docs. Ref." appears above call no.

Appendix B continued

Call number examples	Holding library symbol	Type of material	How to recognize
Z Docs. 1223 Ref. .A18 OR Z Reference 1223 Docs. .A18	RCE+	Documents reference – Serials	"Reference Docs." appears below call no. OR "Docs. Ref." appears above call no.; card is in serial format
M ML MT 25 OR 1209 OR 114 .T6 .L43 .B5	RCE%	Music monographs and scores	Call no. begins with "M", "ML", OR "MT"
ML Music 1209 Ref. .L43 OR ML Ref. 1209 .L43	RCE$	Music reference – Monographs	Call no. begins with "M", "ML", OR "MT" and has "Ref." below call no. OR "Music Ref." appears above call no.
ML Music 1209 Ref. .L43 OR ML Ref. 1209 .L43	RCE#	Music reference – Serials	Call no. begins with "M", "ML", OR "MT" and has "Ref." below call no. OR "Music Ref." appears above call no.; card is in serial format
M ML MT 25 OR 1209 OR 114 .T6 .L43 .B5	RCE*	Music serials	Call no. begins with "M", "ML", OR "MT"; card is in serial format

APPENDIX C

HANDLING OF STAMPS ON CARDS

Stamp	*Handling*
See also following cards	Disregard
For holdings see following cards	Disregard
Score catalog	Disregard. Appears in music catalog on scores. Scores are to be converted from main card catalog.
See music room catalog	Disregard. Appears on sound recording cards in main card catalog. Cards for sound recordings are to be converted from cards in the music catalog.
Parts bound separately	Input in uppercase letters in the 590 field as the first note or as second note if holdings note required. Appears only on cards for scores.
Shelved in micromaterials room	Input in ǂa of the 049 field in brackets as follows: [Shelved] [in Micro] [Material] [Room]
Shelved in technical services area	Input in ǂa of the 049 field in brackets as follows: [Shelved] [in Tech.] [Services] [Area]
Shelved in public services area	Input in ǂa of the 049 field in brackets as follows: [Shelved] [in Pub.] [Services] [Area]
Request this film by call number and carton number	Input in ǂa of the 049 field in brackets as follows: [Request] [film by] [call no.] [& carton] [number]
*Latest ed. only marked Ref.	Appears in lower left corner on serials cards. Input in ǂa of the 049 field in brackets as follows: [Latest] [ed. only] [Ref.]
*Latest ed. only marked Ref. Others restricted.	Variation of above. Disregard "Others restricted" and input exactly as above
*Latest two eds. only Ref.	Variation of above. Input in 049 field as follows: [Latest] [two eds.] [only Ref]
Current nos. on periodical shelves	Appears on some serial cards. Input in uppercase letters in 590 field as the first note.
Imprint varies	Appears on some serial cards. Input as note in 590 field.
Frequency varies	Appears on some serials cards. Input as note in 590 field.
For holdings see ARTS LIBRARY CATALOG	Appears on some Art serials cards. Art Library Catalog will have to be checked for holdings.

APPENDIX D

Tables of Non-Printed Fields and Print Constants Used in Serials Records

Table 1

List of fields which may be ignored when matching serials records
with main entry cards or entering serials records into data base

012	210	752	870
015	265	765	871
019	310	775	872
025	321	776	873
035	350	777	
043		787	
045			
061			
070			
071			
072			
073			
074			
080			

Table 2

Print constants and corresponding field tags and indicator values
for use in serials records (Print constant is *not* input.)

Print Constant in Note	*Tag*	*Indicator 1*	*Indicator 2*
Absorbed:	780	0	5
Absorbed by:	785	0	4
Absorbed in part:	780	0	6
Absorbed in part by:	785	0	5
Added title page title: (note, without corresponding tracing)	246	0	5
Added title page title: (note, with 'Title: __ ' in tracing)	246	1	5
Caption title: (note, without corresponding tracing	246	0	6
Caption title: (note, with 'Title: __ ' in tracing)	246	1	6
Change back to:	785	0	8
Continued by:	785	0	0
Continued in part by:	785	0	1
Continues:	780	0	0

72

Appendix D, table 2 continued

Print Constant in Note	Tag	Indicator 1	Indicator 2
Continues in part:	780	0	1
Cover title: (note, without corresponding tracing)	246	0	4
Cover title: (note, with 'Title: ___ ' in tracing)	246	1	4
Distinctive title: (note, without corresponding tracing)	246	0	2
Distinctive title: (note, with 'Title: ___ ' in tracing)	246	1	2
Formed by the union of , ___ and: ___ *	780	0	4
Merged with: ___ to form: ___ *	785	0	7
Other title: (note, without corresponding tracing)	246	0	3
Other title: (note, with 'Title: ___ ' in tracing)	246	1	3
Running title: (note, without corresponding tracing)	246	0	7
Running title: (note, with 'Title: ___ ' in tracing)	246	1	7
Spine title: (note, without corresponding tracing)	246	0	8
Spine title: (note, with 'Title: ___ ' in tracing)	246	1	8
Split into: ___ and: ___ *	785	0	6
Superseded by:	785	0	2
Superseded in part by:	785	0	3
Supersedes:	780	0	2
Supersedes in part:	780	0	3
Title: (in tracing, no corresponding note)	246	3	0, 1 or 9
Title varies: (note, without corresponding tracing)	247	0	0
Title varies: (note, with 'Title: ___ ' in tracing)**	247	1	0

*Two consecutive 78x fields must be entered to fill in the blanks of the print constants.

**Separate 247 fields are required for each individual title listed on the card after 'Title varies'. Trace only for those earlier titles which appear in tracing on main card.

ELEMENTS OF THE FIXED FIELD

Table 1. Elements of the Fixed Field for Monographs

Mnemonic in Screen Display	Name of Data Element	Identification of Value Using Main Entry Card
OCLC	OCLC control number	System supplied
Rec stat	Record status	System supplied
Entrd	Date entered on file	System supplied
Used	Date of last use	System supplied
Type	Type of record	Always 'a'
Bib lvl	Bibliographic level	Always 'm'
Govt pub	Government publication indicator	Look at publisher (260 ≠b)
Lang	Language of text	Look at title, language notes, and imprint (245, 500, and 260 fields)
Source	Cataloging source	From kind of card in hand (LC-printed, typed, etc.) See also section on LC cd. no.
Illus	Illustration codes	Match codes with contents of illustration statement (300 ≠b)
Repr	Form of reproduction	Look for note about microform
Enc lvl	Encoding level	Generally level I
Conf pub	Conference publication indicator	Look at main entry, title, or subject headings (111, 245, or 6xx field)

Mnemonic in Screen Display	Name of Data Element	Identification of Value Using Main Entry Card
Ctry	Country of publication	Derive from place of publication (260 ǂa)
Dat tp	Type of publication date code	Determined from combination of publication date in imprint (260 ǂc) and notes (5xx fields)
M/F/B	Main entry in body of entry indicator	Look at title statement (all of 245 field)
	Fiction indicator	Look for a P classification no., generally PQ, PR, PS, PT (050, 09C field) with only a title added entry or with 'Fiction' subdivision in subject headings.
	Biography code	Look for person's name in title or subject headings (245 or 6xx fields); in an existing record, the second indicator of a 100 field may indicate that the main entry is also a subject.
Indx	Index indicator	Look for index note on cards, principally ISBD (500 or 504 fields)
Mod rec	Modified record code	'ƀ' (blank) or 'r' for romanized records
Festschr	Festschrift indicator	Look for the word 'Festschrift' in title statement (245 field)
Cont	Form of content codes	Look for specific words in the title statement (245 field), subject headings (e.g. 650 ǂx Dictionaries), or note about bibliography (504 field)
Desc	Descriptive cataloging form	Inspect data on card; quick check of imprint (260 field) or collation (300 field) for type of punctuation.
Int lvl	Intellectual level	Always 'ƀ'
Dates	Publication dates	Imprint (260 ǂc) and notes (5xx field)

Appendix E continued

Table 2. Elements of the Fixed Field for Serials

Mnemonic in Screen Display	Name of Data Element	Identification of Value Using Main Entry Card
OCLC	OCLC control number	System supplied
Rec stat	Record status	System supplied
Entrd	Date entered on file	System supplied
Used	Date of last use	System supplied
Type	Type of record	Always 'a'
Bib lvl	Bibliographic level	Always 's'
Govt pub	Government publication indicator	Look at publisher (260 ≠b)
Lang	Language of text	Look at title, language notes, and imprint (245, 500 and 260 fields)
Source	Cataloging source	From kind of card in hand (LC-printed, typed, etc.)
S/L ent	Successive/latest entry designator	Look at notes for words like 'continued by: — ', etc., for successive entry; or words like 'Title varies: — ' for latest entry
Repr	Form of reproduction	Look for note about microform
Enc lvl	Encoding level	For input, depends on completeness of data on the card
Conf pub	Conference publication indicator	Look at main entry, title, or subject headings (111, 245, or 6xx field)
Ctry	Country of publication	Derive from place of publication (260 ≠a)

Appendix E, table 2 continued

Mnemonic in Screen Display	Name of Data Element	Identification of Value Using Main Entry Card
Ser tp	Type of serial designator	Look at end of collation (300 field) or in a note (5xx fields)
Alphabt	Original alphabet of title	Look at Key title (222 field), regular title (245 field), or notes (5xx field)
Indx	Index Availability code	Always 'u', unless already filled in
Mod rec	Modified record code	'ƀ' (blank) or 'r' for romanized records
Phys med	Physical medium designator	Look in collation (300 field) and in notes (5xx fields)
Cont	Nature of contents codes	Look for specific words in title (245 field), subject headings (e.g., 650 ≠x Dictionaries), or note about bibliography (504 field)
Frequn	Frequency code	At end of collation or in notes on card or default value
Pub st	Publication status code	Look for open dates (= current), closed dates (= dead), or "Superseded by: —" (= dead) (362 field or note fields)
Desc	Descriptive cataloging form	Always 'ƀ' (blank)
Cum ind	Cumulative index availability code	Look in notes (5xx field); otherwise 'u', unless already filled in
Titl pag	Title page availability code	Always 'u', unless already in record
ISDS	ISDS center code	Always 'ƀ' (blank), unless already in record
Regulr	Regularity	Look in collation (300 field) and in notes (5xx field) or default to 'u'
Dates	Beginning date of publication, ending date of publication	Look at dates following title (362 field)

77

Appendix E continued

Table 3. Elements of the Fixed Field and Some Variable Fields

A. SCORES

Mnemonic in Screen Display	Name of Data Element	Identification of Value Using Main Entry Card
OCLC	OCLC control number	System supplied
Rec stat	Record status	System supplied
Entrd	Date entered on file	System supplied
Used	Date of last use	System supplied
Type	Type of record	Always 'c'
Bib lvl	Bibliographic level	Always 'm'
Lang	Language of text	If instrumental music, 'N/A'; if vocal music, look at uniform title, title, language notes, and imprint (240 ≠1, 245, 5xx, and 260 fields)
Source	Cataloging source	From kind of card in hand (LC-printed, typed, etc.) See also section on LC card no.
Text	Accompanying textual matter	Look at notes; if specific kinds of information are indicated (e.g. bibliographies, biographies), code accordingly; if not (e.g., note about preface), code 'i'; if note about performance instructions is present, code 'h'. Leave in any other values present in record.
Repr	Form of reproduction	Look for note about microform.
Enc lvl	Encoding level	Generally level I
Ctry	Country of publication	Derive from place of publication (260 ≠a)

78

Appendix E, Table 3A continued

Mnemonic in Screen Display	Name of Data Element	Identification of Value Using Main Entry Card
Dat tp	Type of publication date code	Determined from combination of publication date in imprint (260 ≠c) and notes (5xx)
MEBE	Main entry in body of entry indicator	Look at title statement (all of 245)
Mod rec	Modified record code	'♭' or 'r' for romanized records
Comp	Form of composition	Derive from subject headings (650) or title (245)
Format	Format of score	Determine from collation (300 ≠a), uniform title (240 ≠s), or notes (5xx; look for phrase such as "Acc. arr. for piano" or "Acc. originally for orchestra", in which case use value 'c')
Prts	Existence of parts	Determine from collation (300 ≠a)
Desc	Descriptive cataloging form	Inspect data on card; quick check of imprint (260) or collation (300) for type of punctuation
Int lvl	Intellectual level	Always '♭'
LTxt	Literary text indicator (Recordings)	Always 'n'
Dates	Publication dates	Look at imprint (260 ≠c) and notes (5xx)
028	Publisher's number for music	Determine from imprint (260 ≠d) or notes (500)
041	Languages	If value in fixed field 'Lang' is other than 'N/A', look at uniform title (240 ≠1), title (245 ≠c), and language notes (5xx)
044	Country of producer	Derive from imprint (260 ≠a)

Appendix E, Table 3A continued

Mnemonic in Screen Display	Name of Data Element	Identification of Value Using Main Entry Card
045	Chronological code	Derive from dates of composition stated in title (245), contents, or other notes (505, 5xx)
047	Form of composition	See under fixed field 'Comp'
048	Number of instruments or voices	Derive from uniform title (240 ≠m), title (245), notes (5xx), or subject headings (650)

B. SOUND RECORDINGS

Mnemonic in Screen Display	Name of Data Element	Identification of Value Using Main Entry Card
OCLC	OCLC control number	System supplied
Rec stat	Record status	System supplied
Entrd	Date entered on file	System supplied
Used	Date of last use	System supplied
Type	Type of record	Determine from title (245), notes (5xx), or subject headings (6xx)
Bib lvl	Bibliographic level	Always 'm'
Lang	Language of text	Same as for scores
Source	Cataloging source	Same as for scores
Text	Accompanying textual matter	Same as for scores
Repr	Form of reproduction	Always 'ϕ'

Appendix E, Table 3B continued

Mnemonic in Screen Display	Name of Data Element	Identification of Value Using Main Entry Card
Enc lvl	Encoding level	Generally level I
Ctry	Country where recording company is located	Determine from imprint (262 ≠a); if no information given, use 'xx⌀'
Dat tp	Type of publication date code	Determine from imprint (262 ≠d) or notes (5xx)
MEBE	Main entry in body of entry indicator	Same as for scores
Mod rec	Modified record code	Same as for scores
Comp	Form of composition	Same as for scores
Format	Format of score	Always 'n'
Prts	Existence of parts (Scores)	Always 'n'
Desc	Descriptive cataloging form	Always '⌀'
Int lvl	Intellectual level	Always '⌀'
LTxt	Literary text indicator	If fixed field is type 'j', use value '⌀'; if fixed field is type 'i', determine from title (245), notes (5xx), or subject headings (6xx)
Dates	Publication dates	Determine from imprint (262 ≠d) and notes (5XX); if no information available, use 1900, [current date]
007	Physical description fixed field	Determine from collation (305)

81

Appendix E, Table 3B continued

Mnemonic in Screen Display	Name of Data Element	Identification of Value Using Main Entry Card
028	Publisher's number for music	Determine from imprint (262 ‡c)
041	Languages	Same as for scores
043	Geographic area code	Derive from subject headings (6xx) containing a geographic term
044	Country of producer	Same as for scores
045	Chronological code	Same as for scores
047	Form of composition	Same as for scores
048	Number of instruments or voices	Same as for scores

APPENDIX F

COLOR-CODED ENVELOPES TO BE USED
IN FLAGGING PROBLEMS

1. Orange   —   Use for serials

2. Black   —   Use for Scores (Plain M's and some MT's; do not use for ML's)

3. Brown   —   Use for Maps and Non-Roman cards

4. Blue   —   In-analytics, Short Title Catalog analytics, Wright's American fiction analytics

5. Yellow   —   Lost Cause Press analytics

6. Green   —   Record requires original input; no matching record found in OCLC

7. Red   —   Other Problems to be checked by Supervisor

When a red envelope is used, a slip of paper with a brief notation as to the nature of the problem should be inserted behind the card and within the envelope.

APPENDIX G

ABBREVIATIONS USED IN SUBJECT HEADINGS

These abbreviations which were previously used in subject heading tracings must now be spelled in full:

Antiq.	Antiquities
Bibl	Bibliography
Bio-bibl	Bio-bibliography
Biog.	Biography
Bound	Boundaries
Cent	Century
Co	County
Comm	Commerce
Condit.	Conditions
Descr.	Description
Descr. & trav	Description and travel
Dict.	Dictionaries
Dict. & encyc	Dictionaries and encyclopedias
Direct	Directories
Disc. & explor	Discovery and exploration
Econ. condit	Economic conditions
Emig. & immig	Emigration and immigration
For. rel	Foreign relations
Geneal.	Genealogy
Gt. Brit	Great Britain
Hist	History
Hist. & crit	History and criticism
Indus.	Industries
Manuf	Manufactures
Period	Periodicals
Pol. & govt	Politics and government
Pt	Point
Sanit. affairs	Sanitary affairs
Soc. condit	Social conditions
Soc. life & cust	Social life and customs
Stat	Statistics
Terr.	Territory
U.S.	United States

RICE UNIVERSITY SPEEDS UP ITS CONVERSION PROJECT

Kathleen L. Jackson

Once it had been decided not to send the Fondren Library Retrospective Conversion Project to an outside agency, specifications were drawn up for an in-house project utilizing card catalog main entry cards and the OCLC database, and I was hired as supervisor. Even before I began work in August 1981, the first four Recon Assistants were hired and had begun an intensive training program devised by members of the Bibliographic Processing Department.

Original Conversion Plan

Very explicit specifications for retrospective conversion had been drawn up by members of the Bibliographic Processing Department. Work would be done from 4:00 P.M. to 9:00 P.M. on week-nights and from 8:30 A.M. to 5:00 P.M. on Saturdays, with staff gradually being built up to use eight terminals during all of those hours. Approximately 452,000 main entry cards from the card catalog were to be searched on OCLC, matching records found and edited, and the library's archival tape updated. All types of materials cataloged by the library would be converted, but, to begin with, we would only convert records for monographs; cards for serials, maps, scores, and some analytics would be flagged with color-coded envelopes for later conversion. Non-Roman alphabet cards would likewise be flagged to be converted at the end of the project. Sound recordings would be skipped when encountered in the main catalog, as their conversion was to be effected by using the separate Music Library Catalog.

The idea was to start with the monographs, which are the simplest, most straightforward records, so as to work quickly and get a good chunk of the project done right away. In so doing, we could gain the confidence of the administration and save money on the overall project. (OCLC's charge per update rises at regular, *frequent* intervals.)

Original Specifications Reworked

While the scope of the project has remained the same, the specifications have been changed many times in the past year. The original specifications were very detailed and called for editing of OCLC records to match Fondren Library main entry cards exactly — down to the last punctuation mark. Following those specifications, Recon Assistants, when trained and up to full speed, were able to average three records edited per hour. Since at this rate the project would have been finished in about forty to fifty years, and four to five years was the original projection, something had to be done.

I met with the Head of the Bibliographic Processing Department, the Principal Cataloger, and the Catalog Maintenance Librarian to pare down the specifications to a more realistic level. The first thing that went was capitalization and punctuation in most fields. In almost all cases we would accept what was in the record. We stopped spending time deleting extra fields such as local call numbers and subject headings that did not have tags used at Rice (e.g., 092 call numbers and non-LC subject headings). We decided that these fields could be globally deleted or ignored by our future online system. Extra "clean-up" editing, such as deleting "and co." and "etc." from the imprint and looking up and adding dates for period subdivisions in subject headings was abandoned. Contents notes for single volume works were no longer added if they did not appear on the record.

Save File Overloaded

All this streamlining, plus the addition of several more Recon Assistants, brought production up from about 450 records updated for each of the first two months of the project to over 1,300 for October. Unfortunately, I was still revising all the records that were edited. It became increasingly difficult to keep the save file clear.

An additional factor in the save file problem was new input. Upon completion of each drawer, the Recon Assistants were required to input "new" all the records in that drawer that had not been found in OCLC. Following input standards for Retrospective Conversion, they checked the online authority file, changing name headings found there to AACR2 form, and filled in all fixed and variable fields. These new input "saves" were revised first by me, then by the Principal Cataloger, before updating. As you can imagine, this process often led to bottlenecks and a full save file. I was now spending nearly all of my time at the terminal revising saves!

Help came in two forms. First, the best of the Recon Assistants was promoted to Senior Recon Assistant and began working thirty hours per week, at a higher rate of pay. She began right away to revise the work of the less experienced assistants, at first updating only DLC/DLC records and then the more straightforward member records. Finally she was put on her own, updating all the records about which she felt confident. The second solution to the save file problem was to stop doing new input as each drawer was finished. We decided to leave the non-hits, flagged with green envelopes, to be input later.

Staff Grows

Through the fall of 1981 the staff continued to grow, in spite of the anticipated turnover problems. The hours of the project were extended to cover Monday night, with the Senior Assistant acting as supervisor on Monday nights. In November, there was a major push to fill up the schedule, since we felt that the project was running smoothly at half-force. In answer to block ads in Houston's two Sunday newspapers, the applications poured in, and soon all eight terminals were scheduled for use during nearly all Recon hours. While I trained the new Recon staff in searching and tagging and familiarized them with the specifications, my Senior Assistant gave them their machine training, with the help of self-paced manuals made available by the AMIGOS Bibliographic Council.

At about this time, the Music Librarian and the Music Cataloger expressed an interest in moonlighting on Recon. Rather than waste the talents of these two new applicants on monographs, I put them to work converting the cards for scores that the Recon Assistants had already flagged. And so began the music conversion at Fondren, considerably earlier than we had expected.

New Attempt to Speed Up Project

The next major crisis came when the University Librarian informed us that the project was going much too slowly. Something drastic needed to be done to speed up progress, or the project might be cancelled altogether. At this point, I worked with the Head of the Bibliographic Processing Department, the Principal Cataloger, and the Associate Librarian to devise a list of alternatives to speed up the conversion process. Sending all or part of the project to an outside agency was again considered. Using OCLC or AMIGOS was reconsidered, and we also looked at the possibility of REMARC. Alternatives to farming out all or part of the work included everything from reasonable streamlining of the specifications to editing only main entry, title, and call number.

Once again, the recommendation made to the Librarian was to send out the bulk of the project to OCLC, with special materials to be done in-house. However, when we presented our recommendation to the librarian, he decided to continue the project in-house. Back to square one!

Specifications Again Pared Down

We began the painful process of paring the specifications one more time. What it finally boiled down to was careful editing of the access points: LCCN, main and added entries, title, call number, series tracings, and subject headings. Other fields would be edited to match the content of the card, without regard to punctuation, spacing, abbreviations, or capitalization. Fields edited only as to content included the edition statement, the imprint, pagination, and some notes. Wording in these fields did not have to match exactly, as long as the sense was the same. All of these changes added up to a lot of time saved; if fields could be left untouched, we would be spared the wait for OCLC response to changes sent online. But the most significant change turned out to be the decision to ignore the fixed fields. This was a hard decision, because it was felt that fixed field information would be helpful in searching the catalog later. However, the time spent on editing of fixed fields was prohibitive.

Production Doubles

The following month showed a 100 percent increase in Recon production (6,000 updates/month). We are now averaging 7,000 records updated per month, with a high of 9,100 records updated in one month.

An added benefit of further streamlining the specifications was that staff training time was reduced, and with it the period of revision. Recon Assistants are now able to build up to ten records per hour in a matter of a few weeks, and, depending on their background and aptitude, they can be allowed to update most records on their own in three to four months' time. While turnover has been a constant problem, a solid core of excellent staff has evolved, all of whom are updating from twelve to seventeen records per hour, mostly on their own.

Supervisor Freed for Other Duties

Allowing Recon staff members to update more records on their own has, of course, led to more free time for my Senior Assistant and me. We continue to train new staff (we have at least one new person every month), and my assistant is working on the new input at a rate of about twenty records per week. I now have time to work through the problems that are color-coded with red envelopes in the drawers, spot-check printouts of our archival tapes sent to us by AMIGOS, and learn about developments in online catalogs.

The Fondren Library Retrospective Conversion Project has been in a state of change since it began. We are constantly questioning and reconsidering policies and procedures. While I am fairly certain that no more major revisions of the specifications will be done, I am working on other ways to keep production high; promotion of friendly competition among the Recon Assistants and advanced training in machine manipulation skills for experienced Recon Assistants will both help. I have also developed an incentive pay plan whereby the hourly rate of pay increases as staff members reach and maintain certain rates of production.

SPECIFICATIONS FOR RETROSPECTIVE CONVERSION
OF MONOGRAPHS

FONDREN LIBRARY
RICE UNIVERSITY

I. *SCOPE*

These specifications cover the retrospective conversion of approximately 452,000 main entry cards contained in the catalog of the Fondren Library of Rice Univerity (RUL). However, all main entry cards produced as a result of Rice's participation in OCLC's On-Line Cataloging System are to be excluded from the conversion. The records to be converted cover all types of materials cataloged by the Library.

The project will result in machine-readable catalog records for all holdings in the card catalog. In addition, the Rice holding symbol (RCE) will appear in OCLC's On-Line Union Catalog for all of Rice's holdings.

II. *SOURCE OF CATALOGING DATA*

Conversion will be done from main entry cards only. A main entry card is defined as a full catalog entry, usually the author entry, giving all the information necessary to the complete identification of a work. This entry bears also the tracing of all the other headings under which the work in question is entered in the catalog. All main entry cards will be converted except for the ones identified below:

1. Cards originally produced at OCLC, identifiable by the OCLC control number, etc., appearing on the bottom line of a card and by the type face.

2. Information cards, including cards for series classed separately, cards for series not traced, cards referring to special bibliographies, cards referring to technical reports, collections, etc. Cards for series classed separately and cards for series not traced should be removed from the catalog when found.

3. Cards for sound recordings encountered in the Main Card Catalog. Sound recordings will be converted from cards in the Music Room Catalog at the end of the project. Sound recordings can be identified by the words "Phonodisc," or "Sound recording" after the uniform or regular title.

4. Human Relations Area File (HRAF) cards.

(For examples see Appendix A., p. 34-38.)

III. *GENERAL PROCEDURES*

The basic premise is that OCLC records will be edited to match information found on RUL main entry cards. An exception to this is that, when main entries, added entries, and/or subject headings have been changed in the data base to AACR2 form, this form should be used.

Each main entry card must match our card in all areas itemized below:

1. Bibliographic level (bib lvl)

2. Language

3. Choice of author (Form may differ — Cf. sections on Personal and Corporate Name Access Points. Occasionally choice of entry may differ — Cf. Choice of Entry.)

4. Title

5. Edition

6. Publisher

7. Copyright date or original date of publication

8. Pagination

If more than one matching record is found, a Library of Congress (LC) record should always be used if available. Otherwise, the one which most closely matches RUL's record should be used. If a matching record is found with RUL's holding symbol (RCE) already on it, the entry should be flagged with a red envelope and the problem noted on a slip of paper.

A matching record will be edited, if necessary, to include the call number and holdings information from the card. Other data elements should also be edited to reflect what appears on the card. If no matching record is found, the card will be flagged with a green envelope for input at the end of the project.

Problem Areas

Non-Roman alphabet cards, serials, scores, maps, in-analytics, and other selected analytics will not be converted until the end of the project. (See Appendix A, p.39-42, for examples of these types of materials.) Color-coded envelopes will be placed over the main cards for such items as they are encountered during the course of the conversion. (Cf. Appendix F for color-coding.)

Serials can usually be identified by the presence of a volume or date statement following the title. OCLC records for serials have an "s" in the "bib lvl" field.

Scores are identified by "M" and sometimes "MT" in the call number. "MT" can also identify a monograph, in which case the "type" will be coded "m". OCLC records for sound recordings have "i" or "j" in the type field.

Maps can be identified by the word "Map" preceding the call number. Maps are generally classified in the LC classification "G". OCLC records for maps have an "e" in the "type" field.

In-analytics can be identified by a note beginning with the word "In". This note usually comes after the title information.

Other problems will be referred directly to the retrospective conversion supervisor or will be flagged with color-coded envelopes for later handling by the retrospective conversion supervisor.

IV. *NOTES ON DATA FIELDS*

Editing and input of data should follow what is on the main entry card. Typed and handwritten corrections to all cards, including LC printed cards, should be entered as corrected.

Misspellings should be corrected. ISBD punctuation may be retained if the OCLC record has it and the card doesn't. Conversely, if the card has ISBD punctuation and the record does not, ISBD punctuation need not be added to the record.

The tracing appears on the back of some main entry cards. The notation "(over)" appears at the bottom of such cards.

Guidelines for field tagging published by OCLC should be followed. If incorrect tags are discovered in a record, they should be corrected. However, we will not attempt to send error reports on any records used in retrospective conversion.

Summary

The following fields must be edited to match EXACTLY what appears on the card:

010	1xx	600	0
011	240	610	0
049	245 ‡a, ‡b	611	0
050	4xx	630	0
086	505 for multi-vol sets	650	0
090	533	651	0
099	590	7xx	
		8xx	

Fields with the above tags that do not appear on the card must be deleted from the record, except from DLC/DLC records.

. . . .

The following fields must be edited to match the contents of the card, but punctuation, spacing, abbreviation, and capitalization need not match exactly.

250	300 ‡a	501	504
260	500	502	

(EXCEPT: all records for Rare books must match the card EXACT-LY in all fields. Rare holdings symbols: RCEH, RCEK, RCEL, RCEN, RCEP, RCEZ)

Fields with the above tags that do not appear on the card must be deleted from the record, except from DLC/DLC records.

. . . .

The following fields may be IGNORED:

Fixed fields	039	214	506
007	040	241	510
015	041	242	520
017	043	243	534
019	045	255	536
020	051	263	580
025	060	265	690
027	082	302	6xx with second indicator
034	092	350	other than zero
035	096	505 for single	
037	098	volumes	

. . . .

LCCN should be included in the converted record if printed or typed on the main entry card, with the following exceptions:

1. If a "CV" or a "V" follows an LCCN, this card number should not be entered.

2. LC printed cards for a work similar to the one being cataloged were sometimes modified with new values by either erasing and retyping, or by crossing out and typing in new data. If these changes have been made in the descriptive area of the card (i.e., title through collation line), the LCCN on the main entry card is invalid and should not be entered. Such changes are identified by noting differences in type font or type size or by noting crossed-out data.
(For examples see Appendix A, p. 43-44.)

Call Numbers

Call numbers should be entered following usual OCLC practice. If NLM classification numbers and Dewey classification numbers appear in a matching record being used, they may be left in the record. However, such call numbers appearing on a card need not be added to the OCLC record.

A summary of call number fields which will be used for the different types of material follows. (For examples see Appendix A, p. 45-48.)

1. LC Classification

    a. 050 – If RUL call number matches an LC-assigned call number, any 090 fields already in the record should be deleted. If 050 field includes more than one ≠a, but the *first* call number in the field matches the RUL call number, do not add an 090 field. If the only difference between LC and RUL call numbers is volume designation for analytics (ex.: LC – vol., RUL – no.), edit 050 to match RUL; do not add 090.

    b. 090 – If RUL call number does not match an LC-assigned call number, use RUL call number and delete any other 090 fields.

    NOTE: If our call number differs from an LC call number and must be entered in an 090 field, it is not necessary that the LC call number in the 050 field be correct. If our call number differs only slightly from a call number in the 050 field, the call number in the 050 field may simply be changed to match the call number on our card; it is not necessary to type the whole call number over in an 090 field. If the call number on the record is correct but is in an 090 field instead of an 050 field, it is not necessary to change the tag from 090 to 050. Nor is it necessary to add an indicator of "0" or "1" if no indicator has been used in an 050 field.

c. RUL numbers for analytics — Analytic call numbers can be identified by a number or volume designation as the last element of the call number. If the OCLC record has volume designations in any other language, they should be changed to the English equivalent as on RUL cards, e.g., "Bd." to "vol."

2. K Call numbers Derived from University of Chicago Law Schedule. Non-LC K call numbers (i.e. K numbers other than K, KD, KE, and KF) should be entered in an 090 field.

3. Superintendent of Documents (SuDoc) classification. 086 — If RUL has used a SuDoc number, this number should be input in the 086 field if it is not already present. RUL is profiled to have the 086 field override the other call number fields if the government document holding library symbol (RCEG) is input in the 049 field.

Holdings Data — 049

The 049 field should be input following the guidelines in the OCLC tagging manuals.

Holding Library Symbols

The holding library symbol for ǂa of the 049 field is determined by the location stamp on the card, either above or below the call number. If no specific location is present, the main holding library symbol is used. Some of the location stamps on cards to be converted (e.g., "Arch.") are no longer used and should default to the main holding library. For a complete list of holding library symbols, see Appendix B, p. 64-70.

Input Stamps

Occasionally stamps appear on cards in the margin below the call number or elsewhere on the card. These should be input in the 049 field following the holding library symbol or in a note. For a list of stamps and instructions on how and where to input, see Appendix C.

Holdings Information

Duplicate Copies

Multiple copies are indicated by a *typed* notation (e.g., ---- Copy 2) on the card. Ignore printed "copy 2" notations at the bottom of LC cards.

a. Copies in the same holding library

(1) Copies in same call number

Copy information should be input in ≠c of the 049 field. Also, a 590 note, giving holdings information in capital letters, should be input as the first note. If the added copy varies in some way from the first copy, this variation should be noted in lower-case letters in the 590 field. In addition, the holdings of an added copy of a multi-volume set should be indicated in the 590 note.

(2) Copies in different call numbers

Input on one record, using the 051 field for the call number of the second copy. We will add "≠c Copy 2. RUL" after the call number to distinguish our added copies from LC's added copies. Holdings will be indicated in the 049 field:
049 RCEA ≠c 1, 2
A 590 note is not necessary unless differences between copies or holdings of incomplete sets need to be noted.

b. Copies in different holding libraries

(1) Copies in same call number

Input the two holding library symbols in the 049 field. Indicate differences between the copies in the 590 note. If differences between copies in different holding libraries are so extensive that it is awkward to indicate all of them in one note, input copies for each holding library on a separate record. Add a "1" in the first indicator position of the 049 field

96

on the second record input to show that the second record should not bump the first record.

(2) Copies in different call numbers

Input on one record, with the holding library symbols given in the 049 field in the same order as they appear on the card. The call number of the second copy will be input in the 051 field. In ǂc of the 051 field, we will add "Copy 2. RUL", followed by the name of the appropriate holding library. For example: ǂc Copy 2. RUL WRC Axson. (The holding library name precedes or follows the call number on our cards. For the correct form of the holding library name, refer to the right-hand column of call number examples in Appendix B. If only one example is given (in the left-hand column), that is the correct form.) If differences between copies are so extensive that it is awkward to indicate all of them in one note, input copies for each holding library on a separate record. Add a "1" in the first indicator position of the 049 field on the second record input.

c. Two (or more) different editions on same card

If a DLC record can be located for the dashed-on edition(s), input each edition on a separate record. Check with supervisor to make sure OCLC record for dashed-on entry matches our record. If no DLC record is available for the dashed-on entry but a record exists for the primary work, flag the card with a red envelope and include a slip of paper identifying the problem. If no DLC record is available for either entry, flag with a green envelope.

d. Library has c.2 only

If such a penciled note appears on card, input this note in capital letters in a 590 field (as the first note). In the 049 field holdings should be: ǂc.2.

(For examples see Appendix A, p. 106-112.)

Holdings for Incomplete Monographic Sets

a. General

Holdings are indicated by notes penciled on the main entry

card. This note should be input as the first note in the 590 field in capital letters in the form in which it appears on the card. Dates of publication and variations between bibliographical volumes and physical volumes should also be included in the 590 field. In addition, holdings should be input in the 049 field in the appropriate subfields. (For examples see Appendix A, p.56 -67.)

b. RUL Holdings Differ from Holdings on DLC Copy

Sometimes the total number of volumes in a set differs on a revised DLC/DLC record from the number of volumes given on RUL's card. For example, we may have thought that a set was complete in 2 volumes and closed the set. Upon locating a revised DLC/DLC record, however, we find that there are 3 or more volumes to the set. In such a case we will not revise our card but will simply indicate our holdings on the DLC record.

If our set is still open, but the DLC/DLC record indicates that the set is complete with the number of volumes we have, we will accept the DLC holdings, without attempting to close our set.

If the DLC record has fewer volumes than we have, we will simply add our additional volumes to the DLC record. This will be done whether the DLC set was open or closed.

Personal Name Access Points (Applies to main entries, subject headings, and added entries) —1xx, 6xx, 7xx.

1. Use form of name as it appears on RUL's main entry card, unless this form of name has been converted in the data base to AACR2 form. In this case use AACR2 form. A converted entry can be recognized by a ≠w at the end of the heading, and, possibly, an 87x field at the end of the record. If some records for a main entry have been flipped to AACR2 form in OCLC, and others have not, do not change the unflipped ones to the AACR2 form. Enter heading as on card.

2. British titles should be input in ≠c of the 100, 600, and/or 700 fields regardless of their position on the RUL card.

3. It is all right to leave "Mrs." in ≠c of the 100 field. Do not add "Mrs." to a record unless the husband's first name has been used instead of the woman's first name.

4. When a maiden name is given in parenthesis on an RUL card and without parenthesis in the record in the data base, the parenthesis may be omitted. However, such parentheses need not be deleted on records.

5. Birth and death dates should be input as they appear on RUL cards. An exception to this is that a person's death date should be left on the record if it is a DLC record or, in the case of non-DLC records, if the conversion assistant can ascertain from preceding or following catalog cards that the death date is correct.

6. On older LC cards, birth and death dates for certain famous people were not given in subject headings with subdivisions. If correct dates appear on the record, they should be left; however, such dates need not be added to records.

7. When penciled parentheses have been placed around parts of personal names, the part of the name within the parenthesis should be ignored. The name should be converted as if the parenthesized part had been omitted.

8. Punctuation at the end of 1xx, 6xx, and 7xx fields may be ignored.

Corporate Name Access Points (Applies to main entries, subject headings, and added entries) — 1xx, 6xx, 7xx.

1. Use form of name as it appears on RUL's main entry card, unless this form of name has been converted in the data base to AACR2 form. In this case use AACR2 form. A converted entry can be recognized by a ≠w at the end of the heading, and, possibly, an 87x field at the end of the record.

2. Ignore capitalization of corporate names.

Choice of Entry — 1xx or 24x

If RUL's card is entered under editor and a revised DLC/DLC record has changed the entry to a title main entry, with an added entry for the editor, the revised DLC record may be accepted as is. RUL's call number must be added if the cutter number on the revised record differs from the cutter number on RUL's card. If there are other changes in the call number or in other parts of the record, the card should be flagged as a problem.

If RUL's card is entered under title and the revised DLC/DLC record is entered under an editor who was mentioned in the body of our card and given an added entry, we will accept LC's revision without changing our card. There should be a title added entry on the revised DLC record. Again, our call number must be input if the cutter number differs.

If changes in entry do not fall into these categories, cards should be flagged as a problem.

(For examples see Appendix A, p. 120-121.)

Uniform Titles – 240

1. If RUL's card matches a DLC/DLC record except for the presence of a uniform title on the DLC record, the uniform title should be retained in the record.

2. First indicator of 240 field may be ignored; second indicator must always be added; correct subfield codes must be added.

Title and Statement of Responsibility – 245

1. The entire title and subtitle (≠a and ≠b) should be input as they appear on the card, ignoring any penciled parenthesis around parts of the title or subtitle.

2. Punctuation, spacing, abbreviations, and capitalizations may be ignored.

3. If author statement appears on card but not on record, do not add if it is the same as the main entry. Conversely, if author statement appears on the record but not on the card, do not delete if it is the same as the main entry.

4. First indicator of 245 may be ignored, but second indicator in 245 field must always be filled in.

Edition Statement – 250

The 250 field must reflect the content of the edition statement, but punctuation, spacing, abbreviations and capitalization may be ignored.

Imprint – 260

1. In the publisher statement, "Inc.", "Ltd.", "and Co.", "and Sons", "and Bros." may be omitted if not on record. Do not

delete if on record.

2. "Etc." after place or publisher may be omitted but need not be deleted on monographic records.

3. Dates showing that a book is a later printing and copyright dates must be added if not on record.

4. Second place of publication may be omitted but need not be deleted.

Collation – 300

1. Preliminary leaves ("p.1."), pages or leaves given in brackets, and unpaged leaves at end of volume need not be added to pagination but if on record need not be deleted. Unbracketed Arabic pagination should match what is on the card. Exception: Pagination for rare materials should match in all respects what is on the card.

2. Illustrations and size may be ignored.

Series – 4xx

1. The form of a series statement and the series tracing should conform to what appears on the main entry card, unless the heading for personal or corporate author has been converted to AACR2 form. In this case use AACR2 form. A converted entry can be recognized by a ≠w at the end of the field, and, possibly, an 87x field at the end of the record. However, if some records for a series have been flipped to AACR2 form in OCLC, and others have not, do not change the unflipped ones to the AACR2 form. Enter headings as on card.

2. Check tracing on card to determine correct 4xx tag. On LC cards where a printed parenthesis was used around the series in the tracing, RUL has traced for the series only if the parenthesis has been removed; if the parenthesis has not been removed, the series is untraced.

3. On some main entry cards the only indication that the series may be traced in some form is the fact that the series statement is underlined. These series should be tagged 490 1, with no corresponding 8xx field. (Tracings will be added at the end of the conversion.) Tag underlined series 490 1, whether or not a

series added entry is given, as the form of the added entry is frequently incorrect.

4. "Half-title", "On cover", "Added t.-p." and editor must be omitted from series statements tagged 400, 410, 411, and 440. "Cover title" in a 4xx field should be moved to a 500 note.

5. Care should be taken to add a "≠v" before series numbering for all 4xx fields except 490.

   (For examples see Appendix A, p. 113-117.)

Notes — 5xx

1. Notes should be the same as those on RUL's main entry card. An exception to this is a revised DLC card for the same edition of a work. (A revised DLC card is identified by "//r" following the card number in the 010 field.) If the revised card matches RUL's call number, main entry, and description, notes added to the revised card may be left in the record. Check with supervisor.

2. All 500, 501, 502, and 504 notes must reflect the content of the notes on the card, but variant wording, punctuation, abbreviations, and capitalization may be ignored.

3. When the 590 note is used to show holdings, it should be the first note and be input in capital letters. Otherwise, it should be put in its appropriate place in the prescribed order of notes.

4. Notes beginning "Translation of" found at the bottom of some old cards should be put in a 500 note. Check with the supervisor on order of notes.

5. Contents notes (505) should be ignored, EXCEPT on records for multi-volume sets. On these records, contents should be input exactly as they appear on the card.

6. The 533 note should be used for micro- and macroreproductions.

Subject Headings — 6xx

1. Subject headings should be edited or input to contain the headings as they appear on the main entry card. Extra LC subject headings (600, 610, 611, 630, 650, 651 tagged with second indicator 0) that do not appear on the card should be deleted if

found on a record. (For exception, cf. 4. below.)

2. Abbreviations in subject headings found on records should be checked to be sure they are standardized abbreviations. If not, they should be spelled out. (Cf. Appendix G for a list of abbreviations.)

3. All 69x subject headings found on records should be ignored, as should 6xx subject headings with second indicator other than zero.

4. If a revised DLC card (identified by "//r" following the card number in the 010 field) matches RUL's call number, main entry, and description, it is all right if it has additional subject headings or changed subject headings. If record is not a revised or corrected LC card, change subject headings to match RUL card.

5. Any subject headings that have been lined out on the RUL card should not be entered in the converted record, unless the lined out subject heading is the same as the main entry. Check with supervisor.

Added Entries — 7xx

1. Added entries that have been lined out on the RUL card should not be entered in the converted record. If an added entry lined out on a card is the same as a subject heading on that card, the added entry should be retained.

2. Do not add inverted title added entries made up by RUL. (For example: Title = Human efficiency; Made-up title added entry = Efficiency, Human.)

3. In 7xx added entries, a second indicator of "2" should be used when the added entry is for a work contained within the work being converted. In other cases, it is not necessary to distinguish between the use of a "0" or a "1".

Dashed-on Entries (other than added copies and added editions)

If a card contains one dash entry, the dash entry will be input as a 590 note on the card for the main work. The 590 note will appear after all notes pertaining to the main entry and will begin with dashes as on the card. (If the main work has an author entry, the description of the supplement begins with 2 dashes followed by a blank and then 3 more dashes. If the main work has a title entry, the description of the supplement begins with 3 dashes.) All information pertaining to the dash entry will be given in one paragraph. The collation line, the series statement, and any notes will be separated from preceding elements by a "space dash space."

An additional 590 note will be input as the first note under the main entry. This note will give the library's holdings of both main and supplementary volumes. For example:

LIBRARY HAS MAIN VOLUME PLUS SUPPLEMENT
   [INDEX, GUIDE, etc.]
LIBRARY HAS V. 1–2 OF MAIN WORK PLUS SUPPLEMENT.
LIBRARY HAS MAIN VOLUME PLUS V. 1–3 OF SUPPLE-
   MENT.

If the main work or the supplement has incomplete holdings, holdings will also have to be input in the 049 field. The volume designations will have to be defined in ≠d of the 049 field.

Example: 049 RCEA ≠d [≠v=vol. ≠p=suppl.] ≠v 1–2 ≠p 1

If the call number for the dash entry has been typed on the card, input it as a second ≠a in the 050 or 090 field. A second ≠b will also be used in the appropriate place in the call number for the dash entry.

If there is more than one dash entry on a card or if the dash entry is in a different holding library from the main entry, flag as a problem. These items will be recataloged on separate records.

If the dash entry is for a serial, use an orange envelope to flag the whole card as a serial.

(For examples see Appendix A, p. 118-119.)

V. *MONTHLY PRODUCTION REPORTS*

Monthly reports of work accomplished will include both a summary of records converted for the month and a cumulated summary of records converted since the beginning of the project. A count of records requiring original input will also be kept.

VI. *QUALITY CONTROL*

Rice University Library in its retrospective conversion project will follow quality control methods sufficient to maintain a high degree of accuracy. These methods will include a comprehensive, intensive training program for terminal operators and supervision by a professional cataloger.

RUL has planned a program of local review of records — both updates and inputs. General spot checking of all records will also be performed.

NA
2440
.N47
M873
1971

Cooper Union for the Advancement of Science and Art,
New York. School of Art and Architecture.
Education of an architect: a point of view. An exhibition by the Cooper Union School of Art & Architecture at
the Museum of Modern Art, New York City, November
1971. ₍New York, 1971₎
323 p. illus. (part col.) 31 cm.
1. Architecture—Exhibitions. 2. Cooper Union for the Advancement of Science and Art, New York. School of Art and Architecture.
3. Architecture—Study and teaching—New York (City)   I. New
York (City). Museum of Modern Art. II. Title.
NA2440.N47M873 1971   720′.71′17471   74–184158
MARC

— —Copy 2.

049   ≠c 1, 2
590 LIBRARY HAS
C. 1, 2.

ARTS
NA
31
.F55
1966

Fleming, John, 1919–
The Penguin dictionary of architecture, ₍by₎ John Flem-
ing, Hugh Honour, Nikolaus Pevsner; drawings by David
Etherton. ₍Harmondsworth, Eng., Baltimore, Md.₎
Penguin Books ₍1966₎
247 p. illus., plans, diagrs. 20 cm. (Penguin reference books,
R13)

-- ---Copy 2-3.

1. Architecture — Dictionaries.   I. Honour, Hugh.   II. Pevsner,
Nikolaus, 1902–   III. Title.   IV. Title: Dictionary of architecture.

NA31.F55 1966a   720.3   66–70279

Library of Congress   ₍5₎

049   ≠c 1, 2, 3
590 LIBRARY HAS
C. 1, 2, 3.

Bartlett

ML
410
.B4
B2816

Beethoven—Hefte ₍aus der Musik. Berlin,
Schuster & Loeffler, 1902–27₎
18 v. illus., facsims., music, ports.
28 cm.

Imprint varies.
Made—up collection of assorted issues of
the periodical Die Musik devoted to or
containing articles about Beethoven.

1. Beethoven, Ludwig van, 1770–1827.
I. Die Musik.
— ---Copy 2 ₍of v.16₎

049 ≠c 1 ≠v 1-18
≠c 2 ≠v 16
590 LIBRARY HAS
C. 1, V. 1-18;
C. 2, V. 16.

NA
1223
.J3
F313

Faber, Tobias, 1915–
    Arne Jacobsen. ₍Translated by E. Rockwell₎ New
York, Praeger ₍1964₎
    xxiii, 175 p. illus., plans. 26 cm.
    English and German.
    —— ——Copy 2. ₍1966, c1964₎

    1. Jacobsen, Arne, 1902–

NA1223.J3F313   720.9489   64–16676

Library of Congress   ₍5₎

049   ≠c 1, 2
590 LIBRARY HAS
C. 1, 2; c. 2 has
imprint date:
1966, c1964.

AXSON
PR
3392
.W5
1795d

Cumberland, Richard, 1732–1811.
    The wheel of fortune: a comedy. Performed at the
Theatre-Royal, Drury-Lane. By Richard Cumberland
... * London, C. Dilly, 1795.
    79. ₍1₎ p. 22 cm.

    *4th ed.

-- ---Copy 2.   20 cm.
    i. Title.

                                             26–19617
Library of Congress   ₍37b1₎
                             ⌐PR1241.L6   vol. 231

049   ≠c 1, 2
590 LIBRARY HAS
C. 1, 2; c. 2 is
20 cm.

AXSON
PQ
1983
.F3
A813
1764

Favart, Charles Simon, 1710–1792.
    The Englishman in Bourdeaux. A comedy. Written in
French, by the celebrated Monsieur Favart. Acted with universal applause, at the Theatre-Royal, in Paris ... Translated
by an English lady now residing in Paris. London, G. Kearsly,
1764.
    iv, ₍2₎ 60 ₍2₎ p. 21½ᵐ.
    ₍Longe, F. Collection of plays. v. 101, no. 6₎
-- ---Copy 2.
    Imperfect: all after p. 60 wanting.
    i. Title.
-- ---Copy 3.   25—6006
    Library of Congress   PR1241.L6   vol. 101
                             ₍42b1₎

049   ≠c 1, 2, 3
590   LIBRARY
HAS C. 1, 2, 3;
c. 2 imperfect:
all after p. 60
wanting.

```
PQ      Giraudoux, Jean, 1882-
2613       Suzanne et le Pacifique ... Paris,
I74     Émile-Paul frères,1921.
S9         297p. 19cm.
           2 copies.

           I.Title.

        Copy 2 is 1930 issue.

23-363              W 536 Fr. 1-5-23.




                          c.2 = Gift. French For.
                             Office June, 1938
                             38-2979
```

049   ≠c 1, 2
590   LIBRARY
       HAS C. 1, 2;
       c. 2 is 1930
          issue.

```
N       Kandinsky, Wassily, 1866-1944.
68         Concerning the spiritual in art, and painting in particu-
.K33    lar. 1912. [A version of the Sadleir translation, with con-
1947    siderable re-translation by Francis Golffing, Michael Harri-
        son and Ferdinand Ostertag] New York, Wittenborn,
        Schultz, 1947.
           95 p. illus., port. 26 cm. (The Documents of modern art [5])
           Bibliography: p. 6.
           "Prose poems (1912-1937)": p. [79]-91.
        — ——Copy 2-3.  93 p.
           1. Aesthetics. 2. Painting.     I. Sadleir, Michael, 1888-     tr.
        II. Golffing, Francis, tr.  III. Title.  IV. Series.

           N68.K33  1947          701.17              47—12026*

        Library of Congress        [a52x1]
```

049   ≠c 1, 2, 3
590   LIBRARY
       HAS C. 1, 2, 3;
       c. 2-3 have 93 p.

```
PQ   Laclos, Pierre Ambroise François Choderlos de,
1993    1741-1803.
.L22    Poésies de Choderlos de Laclos, publiées
A 17 par Arthur Symons et Louis Thomas.  Paris,
1908 Chez Dorbon l'aîné, 1908.
           100 p.  21 cm.

        312 copies printed.  No.64.
     -- ---Copy 2.  No.25.
        I. Symons, Arthur, 1865-1945, ed.  II. Thomas,
     Louis, 1885-     jt. ed.
```

049   ≠c 1, 2
590   LIBRARY
       HAS C. 1, 2; c. 2
       is no. 25.

NA
680
.B25
1967

Banham, Reyner.
　　　Theory and design in the first machine age. 2d ed. New
York, Praeger [1970, c1960]
　　　338 p. illus., plans. 23 cm.
　　　Bibliographical footnotes.
　　　1. Architecture, Modern—20th cent.   ɪ. Title.
　　　NA680.B25 1967　　　　724.9　　　　　67-16449

　　　*"Second edition, 1967. Second printing, 1970."
-- ---Another issue. 1975, c1960. (Praeger
University series)

049　　≠c 1, 2
590　　LIBRARY
　　　HAS C. 1, 2;
　　　c. 2 is another
　　　issue with imprint
　　　date and series:
　　　1975, c1960.
　　　(Praeger Univer-
　　　sity series)

AXSON ₍Cumberland, Richard₎ 1732–1811.
PR
3392
.W4
1771

　　　The West Indian: a comedy. As it is performed at the Theatre Royal in Drury-Lane. By the author of The brothers ...
London, W. Griffin, 1771.
　　　3 p. l., 102, ₍2₎ p. 21ᶜᵐ.

　　　Imperfect? Half-title wanting?

─ ─Copy 2.
　　　Part of a collection of early drama formed by John Philip Kemble.
　　　Text inlaid with Kemble's notes on title page and verso of title
　　　page.
　　　ɪ. Title. ɪɪ. Kemble, John Philip, 1757–1823.

　　　　　　　　　　　　　　24–5987

　　　Library of Congress　　　　PR3392.W4 1771

049　　≠c 1, 2
590　　LIBRARY
　　HAS C. 1, 2; c. 2
　　is part of a collec-
　　tion of early
　　drama formed
　　by John Philip
　　Kemble; text
　　inlaid with Kem-
　　ble's notes on
　　title page and
　　verso of title
　　page.

---

a. (2) Copies in different call numbers, but in same holding library

---

NA
351
.Es6

Espouy, Hector d', 1854–
　　　Fragments d'architecture du moyen âge et de la renaissance
d'après les relevés & restaurations des anciens pensionnaires
de l'Académie de France à Rome, publiés sous la direction de
H. d'Espouy ... Paris, C. Schmid; ₍etc.,₎ c1925.
in ₍1₎
　　　2 v. ₓ 180 pl. (incl. plans) 45½ᶜᵐ.
　　　Issued in parts (in portfolios)
　　　The "Table explicative des planches" (v. 1) is by G. Daumet.
　　　Vol. ɪɪ has imprint: Paris, C. Massin et cⁱᵉ.
　　　1. Architecture, Medieval. 2. Architecture, Renaissance.. 3. Architecture—Italy.   ɪ. Daumet, Georges, 1870–1918. ɪɪ. Title.

NA　　　　　　　₍Full name: Marie Désiré Hector Jean Baptiste d'Espouy₎
111　　─ ─Copy 2. (in 2 vols..)
.E7　　─ ─Copy 3 of v1 only　　　　36–14381 Revised
　　　Library of Congress　　　NA1111.E7
　　　　　　　　　　₍r38b2₎　　　　　720.84

Input on same
record.
049　　RCEA
　　≠c 1, 2
　　≠c 3 ≠v 1
051　　NA1111
≠b .E7 ≠c₎Copy
2-3. RUL
090　　NA351
≠b .Es6
590　　LIBRARY
HAS C. 1 (2
vols. in 3), C. 2
(2 vols.), and
VOL. 1 OF C. 3.

109

Revised
APPENDIX A.   V.   Multiple copies (continued)
a. (2) Copies in different call numbers, but in same holding library (continued)

PR
1243
.I 4
v.18
Cumberland, Richard, 1732–1811.
    The wheel of fortune; a comedy, in five acts; as performed
at the Theatre Royal, Drury-Lane. By Richard Cumberland,
esq. ... With remarks by Mrs. Inchbald. London, Longman,
Hurst, Rees, Orme, and Brown ₍n. d.₎
    72 p. front. 15 cm. (Inchbald, Mrs. Elizabeth. The British theatre
... London, 1808. v. 18 ₍no. 5₎)

    I. Title.

PR
3392
.W5
Library of Congress — —Copy 2.

Input on same
record.
049   RCEA
       ǂc 1, 2
050 0 PR1243.
       ǂb .I4 v.18
051   PR3392
       ǂb .W5 ǂc Copy
       2. RUL

b. Copies in different holding libraries
(1) Call number is same

ML
410
.B4
B96
Burk, John Naglee, 1891–
    The life and works of Beethoven. ₍1st Modern Library
ed.₎ New York, Modern Library ₍1946 , c1943₎
    viii, 483 p. 19 cm. (The Modern library of the world's best
books)
    Includes music.
    "Phonograph records": p. 464–478.

Bartlett
ML
410
.B4
B96
-- ---Copy 2.

    1. Beethoven, Ludwig van, 1770–1827.

[ML.410.B4B   ]   927.8   A 48—6425*

Yale Univ. Library
for Library of Congress   ₍60d1₎

Input on same
record.
049   RCEA,
      RCEN

PR
3392
.B7 ·
1770
₍Cumberland, Richard₎ 1732–1811.
    The brothers; a comedy. As it is performed at the Theatre
Royal in Covent-Garden. London, W. Griffin, 1770.
    1 p. l.,
    ₍v, ₍3₎, 72 p. 21ᶜᵐ.
    ₍Longe, F. Collection of plays. v. 207, no. 5₎
    Engraved t. p. with vignette.

AXSON
PR
3392
.B7
1770
-- ---Copy 2.

-- ---Another issue.
    Engraved t.-p. with vignette.
    I. Title.

                              25—27580

Library of Congress   PR1241.L6 vol. 207
                           W11557 Engl. 9-19-49
                           ₍3761₎   49-7015

Input on same
record.
049   RCEA
      ǂc 1 ǂa RCEK
          ǂc 1, 2
590   LIBRARY
HAS C. 1, 2, 3;
c. 1 is in general
collection and
2 copies are in
AXSON collec-
tion; second
AXSON copy
is another issue
with engraved
t. p. with vignette.

APPENDIX A.   V. Multiple copies (continued)   Revised
b. Copies in different holding libraries (continued)
(1) Call number is the same (continued)

Input on 2 sepa-
rate records.
Extensive micro-
film note makes
it difficult to
input both cards
on one record.
Add "1" in first
indicator posi-
tion of 049 field
of second record
input.

BR
60
.G7
E6

Epiphanius, *Saint, bp. of Constantia in Cyprus.*
  Epiphanius ... hrsg. im auftrage der Kirchenväter-
commission der Königl. preussischen akademie der wissenschaften, von d. dr. Karl Holl ... Leipzig, J. C. Hinrichs, 1915–   *Library has v.1 only.*

  1 v. 24½ᶜᵐ. *(Added t.-p.:* **Die griechischen christlichen schriftsteller**
der ersten drei jahrhunderte ... (bd. 25)

Film
BR
60
.G7
E6

Epiphanius, Saint, Bp. of Constantia in Cyprus.
   Epiphanius ... hrsg. im Auftrage der
Kirchenväter-Commission der Königl. preus-
sischen Akademie der Wissenschaften, von Karl
Holl. Leipzig, J. C. Hinrichs, 1915– 33
   /v. 24 cm. (Die Griechischen christ-
lichen Schriftsteller der ersten drei
Jahrhunderte ... (Bd.37) *Library has v.3 only.*

   Microfilm (negative) Washington, D. C.,
Library of Congress, Photoduplication Service,
1969–   / reel. 35 mm.

                              (Over)
                                        20-2 5082 C

b. Copies in different holding libraries
(2) Call number is different

✻PR   **Cumberland, Richard,** 1732–1811.
1241   The Jew: a comedy. Performed at the Theatre-Royal,
.P48   Drury-Lane. By Richard Cumberland, esq. ~~The 2d ed.~~
no.3   London, C. Dilly, 1794.

           2 p. l., 75, (1) p. 20½ᶜᵐ.

AXSCN   ~~(Longe, F. Collection of plays. v. 228, no. 4)~~
PR
3392   ·— (Plays. 1753–1806. no.3)
.J4   – ---Copy 2.

           I. Title.

                                        26—10614

       Library of Congress   PR1241.L6   vol. 228
                                W2994 Engl. 12-17-28
                                (37b1)   29-137

Input on same
record.
049 RCEH,
RCEK
051 PR3392
≠b .J4 ≠c Copy 2.
RUL WRC Axson
090 PR1241
≠b .P48 no.3

```
JC      Corpus juris civilis.  Institutiones.
85         Imperatoris Iustiniani Institutionum libri quattuor, with
.L3     introductions, commentary, and excursus, by J. B. Moyle ...
C623    5th ed., Oxford, Clarendon press;  London and New York,
        H. Frowde, 1912  1923.
            vi p., 1 l., 682 p., 23cm.
            "The text ... followed is that published by Krueger in his and Momm-
        sen's edition of the Corpus juris civilis (Berlin, 1877)"—Pref.


            1. Roman law.    I. Moyle, John Baron, 1852-1930, ed.
                (Continued on next card)
                                                      13—25017
                            W2487 Anc. Hist. 10-10-27
            Library of Congress        (a37d1) 27-4623
```

Input on 2 sepa-
rate records if
DLC copy avail-
able for dashed-on
edition; otherwise,
flag with red
envelope as
problem.

```
JC      Corpus juris civilis.  Institutiones.    Impera-
85          toris Iustiniani Institutionum ...  1923.
.L3         (Card 2)
C623

JC      — —2d ed.  Oxford, Clarendon press, 1890.
85          4 p.l., 683 p.  23cm.  (At head of title:
.L3     Clarendon press series)
C621




                        W8274 Hist. 12-27-40
                            41-781
```

d. Library has copy 2 only.

```
DG      Storoni Mazzolani, Lidia.
82          The idea of the city in Roman thought: from walled city
.S8613  to spiritual commonwealth.  Translated by S. O'Donnell.
        Bloomington, Indiana University Press (1970)
            288 p.  23 cm.  6.95    Library has c. 2 only.
            Translation of L'idea di città nel mondo romano.
            Bibliography: p. 281-282.

        — —Copy 2.

            1. Rome—Civilization.  2. Cities and towns, Ancient.    I. Title.
            DG82.S8613              913.37'03              79-108947
            SBN 253-13080-5                                    MARC
            Library of Congress        70 (4)
```

049   ‡c 2
590 LIBRARY
HAS C. 2 ONLY.

a. Series is not traced — Note parenthesis around series tracing or lack of series tracing.

PF
3599
.M5
W5
1964

Wiercinski, Dorothea.
Minne; Herkunft und Anwendungsschichten eines Wortes.
Köln, Böhlau, 1964.

vi, 106 p. 24 cm. (Niederdeutsche Studien, Bd. 11)

Issued also as thesis, Münster, under title: Herkunft und Anwendungsschichten des Wortes Minne.
Bibliography: p. ₍101₎–106.

1. Minne (The world)   ɪ. Title.   (Series)

PF3599.M5W5 1964

66–95599

Library of Congress   ₍2₎

490 0   Nieder-
deutsche Studien,
≠v Bd. 11

PF
3301
.S3

Schipporeit, Luise.
Tenses and time phrases in modern German.   ₍1. Aufl.
München₎ M. Hueber ₍1971₎

203 p.   21 cm.   (Sprachen der Welt)

Bibliography: p. 199–203.

GDR***

1. German language—Tense.   I. Title.

PF330LS3   438.2'4'21   72–192042
                                           MARC

TxHR

Library of Congress   72 ₍4₎

490 0   Sprachen
der Welt

PQ
7276
.O 68

Orozco, Fernando, comp.
Cuentos y narraciones de la Ciudad de México / Fer-
nando Orozco. — ₍México₎ : Departamento del Distrito
Federal, Secretaría de Obras y Servicós, 1974.

111 p. : ill. ; 17 cm. — ₍Colección popular Ciudad de México ; 16₎

CONTENTS: Orozco, F. El cuento en México.—Couto, J. B. La
mulata de Córdoba y la historia de un peso.—Riva Palacio, V. Las
mulas de Su Excelencia.—Gutiérrez Nájera, M. La novela del tran-
vía.—Campo, A. del. El jarro.—Estrada, G. El paraíso colonial.—
López Velarde, R. Semana Mayor.—Novo, S. Lota de loco.—Avilés,
R. El hombre del cheque.
$5.00

1. Short stories, Mexican. 2. Mexico (City)—Fiction.   I. Title.
(II. Series.)

PQ7276.O68

74–235622

TxHR

Library of Congress   74 ₍2₎

490 0   Colec-
ción popular
₍Ciudad de México;
₎≠v 16

113

PP
3301
.H3

Hauser-Suida, Ulrike.
Die Vergangenheitstempora in der deutschen geschrie-
benen Sprache der Gegenwart: Untersuchungen an ausgew.
Texten/ Ulrike Hauser-Suida; Gabriel Hoppe-Beugel. —
1. Aufl. — München: Hueber; Düsseldorf: Pädagogischer
Verlag Schwann, 1972.

408 p.; 21 cm. (Heutiges Deutsch: Reihe 1, Linguistische Grundlagen; Bd. 4) DM22.00   GDB 73-A4

Bibliography: p. 387–406.

1. German language—Tense.   I. Hoppe-Beugel, Gabriele, joint
author.   II. Title.   III. Series.

TxHR

PF3301.H3   73–317612

Library of Congress   73 [2]

440 0   Heutiges
Deutsch: ≠n
Reihe 1, ≠p
Linguistische
Grundlagen;
≠v Bd. 4

PQ
1477
.G45
1969

Guernes *de Pont-Sainte-Maxence, 12th cent.*
La vie de saint Thomas le martyr, archevêque de Canterbury [par] Garnier de Pont Sainte Maxence. Publiée et
précédée d'une introd. par C. Hippeau. Genève, Slatkine
Reprints, 1969.

liv, 227 p. 23 cm. (Collection des poètes français du Moyen Age,
2)   Sw***

Reprint of the Paris 1859 ed.
Includes bibliographical references.

1. Thomas à Becket, Saint, Abp. of Canterbury, 1118?-1170—
Poetry.   I. Hippeau, Célestin, 1803–1883, ed.   II. Title.   Series

TxER   PQ1477.G45 1969   73–480538

Library of Congress   70 [2]

440 0   Collec-
tion des poètes
français du Moyen
Age, ≠v 2

PF
3599
.L5
S9
1975

Sucharowski, Wolfgang, 1945-
"Liberal" im gegenwärtigen Sprachgebrauch : linguist., psy-
cholinguist. u. semant. Studien zum Jahr 1971 / Wolfgang Sucharowski. — München : Fink, 1975.

409 p. ; 21 cm. — (Münchner Universitäts-Schriften : Philosophische Fakul-
tät) (Münchener germanistische Beiträge ; Bd. 19)   GFR76-A
A revision of the author's thesis, Munich, 1973.
Bibliography: p. 400–408.
ISBN 3-7705-1169-7 : DM78.00

1. German language—Semantics. 2. Liberal (The German word) 3. German philology—Political aspects.   I. Title.   II. Series: Münchener germanistische Beiträge ; Bd. 19.   III. Series: Münchener Universitäts-Schriften.
Reihe der Philosophischen Fakultät.
PF3599.L5S9 1975   76-459147
                                                      MARC

TxHR

Library of Congress   76

490 1   Münch-
ner Universitäts-
Schriften: Philo-
sophische Fakul-
tät
490 1   Münch-
ner germani-
stische Beiträge;
≠v Bd. 19
840 0   Münche-
ner germani-
stische Beiträge; ≠v
Bd. 19.
840 0   Münche-
ner Universitäts-
Schriften. Reihe
der Philosophi-
schen Fakultät.

Underlining of series heading indicates that a series added entry has been made.

```
Z        -Cole, George Watson, 1850–
1008        An index to bibliographical papers published by the Biblio-
.B4      graphical society and the Library association, London, 1877–
Reference 1932, by George Watson Cole ...   Chicago, Ill., Pub. for the
         Bibliographical society of America at the University of Chi-
         cago press ₁1933₁
              ix, 262 p.  22ᶜᵐ.  ₁Bibliographical society of America.  Special pub-
           lication₁
              Author and subject index.
              Indexes also the Library, a quarterly review of bibliography.
              "List of publications indexed": p. vii–ix.
              Reference books consulted cited in "Addenda".
              1. Bibliography—Bibl.  2. Bibliographical society, London—Bibl.  3.
Z          Library association—Bibl.  4. Library science—Bibl.  5. Indexes.   I.
1008       The Library; a quarterly      review of bibliography.   (Indexes)
.B4        II. Title.                     W4566 Gen'l.11-14-33
              Library of Congress         Z1008.B585      33–33065
           ————Copy 2.                                34–41
           Copyright   A 67127            ₁5₁                    016.01
```

490 1   [Biblio-
graphical Society
of America.
Special publica-
tion]

No 8XX field
is added.

```
LB       Abelson, Paul, 1878–
5           ... The seven liberal arts, a study in mediæval culture.  By
.C8      Paul Abelson ...  New York, Teachers' college, Columbia
no.11    university, 1939.

              x, 150 p.  23½ cm.  (Columbia university.  Teachers' college.
           Contributions to education, no. 11)

              "Critical bibliography": p. 137–150.



              1. Education   Medieval.   I. Title.
                                                      7—13492
              Library of Congress       LA96.A25
                                          W12763
                                         ₁51i½₁
```

490 1   Colum-
bia University.
Teachers' College.
Contributions
to education,
≠v no. 11

No 8XX field
is added.

```
PQ       Abraham, Claude Kurt, 1931–
1772        Pierre Corneille, by Claude Abraham.  New York, Twayne
.A54     Publishers ₁1972₁
              169 p.  21 cm.  (Twayne's world authors series, (TWAS) 214.
           (France)
              Bibliography: p. 163–166.



              1. Corneille, Pierre, 1606–1684.   Series
              PQ1772.A54          842'.4              76–186715
                                                         MARC
              Library of Congress         72 ₁4₁
```

When inputting
series in 4XX
field, omit part
of series that is
enclosed in paren-
thesis.

Entry for series
is: 440 ɓ0
Twayne's world
authors series,
≠v 214

E
540
.I3 A2
v.2

Abel, Annie Heloise, 1873–
The American Indian as participant in the civil war, by Annie Heloise Abel ... Cleveland, The Arthur H. Clark company, 1919.

403 p. incl. front. (facsim.) port., double map, 2 fold. facsim. 24½ᶜᵐ. (*Her* The slaveholding Indians, vol. II) $5.00

"Selected bibliography": p. ₍353₎–367.

1. Indians of North America—Hist.—Civil war. 2. Indian Territory—Hist.—Civil war. 3. U. S.—Hist.—Civil war—Indian troops.   I. Title.

Library of Congress   E540.I 3A2

————— Copy 2.   19—5303

Copyright   A 512837   (2812)

Entry for series
is: 400 11 Her
≠t Slaveholding
Indians; ≠v v. 2

HM
132
.P63

Ponzio, Augusto.
La relazione interpersonale. Bari, Adriatica, 1967.

103 p. 22 cm. (Pubblicazioni della Facoltà di lettere e filosofia della Università degli studi di Bari, 4) 1200   It 68–July

At head of title: Università degli studi di Bari, Facoltà di lettere e filosofia.
Includes bibliographical references.

1. Interpersonal relations.   I. Title.   Series: Bari Università. Facoltà di lettere e filosofia. Pubblicazioni, 4

TxHR   HM132.P63

Library of Congress   69 ₍1₎   73–377980

Form of series
in collation line
is different from
series tracing.
Series must be
input in both
4XX and 8XX
fields.

---

c. Omissions from series statements

PT
1703
.A3
Z6

Abraham *a Sancta Clara,* 1644?–1709.
Etwas für alle. Von Abraham a Santa Clara. Hrsg. und mit einer einleitung versehen von Richard Zoozmann. ₍Dresden, H. Angermann, 1905₎

xxxv, 488 p. incl. 13 pl., port. 21½ᶜᵐ. (*Added t.-p.:* Angermann's Bibliothek für bibliophilen ... 3. bd.)

Illustrated series half-title.
Extracts from the original. with facsimiles of the engravings and of the t.-p.: "Etwas für alle, das ist: eine kurtze beschreibung allerley stands- ambts- und gewerbs-personnen, mit beygeruckter sittlichen lehre und biblischen concepten, durch welche der fromme mit gebührendem lob

(Continued on next card)

5–26509 rev.
₍r33b2₎

"Added t. p."
should be omitted
when inputting
series.

JA
81
.S3

Sabine, George Holland, 1880–
    A history of political theory, by George H. Sabine ...   New
York, H. Holt and company [*1937]
        xvi, 797 p. 22ᶜᵐ. (*Half-title:* American political science series; general editor, E. S. Corwin)
    "Selected bibliography" at end of most of the chapters.

1. Political science—Hist.   ɪ. Title.
                                                              37–12544
    Library of Congress   JA81.S3
    ———— Copy 2. ————   W6562 Phil.6-12-37
                                        37–4558
    Copyright A 107217   [10]   320.9

"Half-title"
and "general
editor, E. S.
Corwin" should
be omitted when
inputting series.

PQ
7276
.M3

Martínez, José Luis, *comp.*
    Literatura indígena moderna: A. Médiz Bolio, E. Abreu
Gómez, A. Henestrosa ...   Introducción y selección de José
Luis Martínez. México, Ediciones Mensaje, 1942.
        3 p. l., 9–165 p., 1 l. 19ᶜᵐ. (*On cover:* Selecciones hispano americanas)
    "Notas" (bibliographical) : p. 24–25.
    CONTENTS.—Médiz Bolio, Antonio. La tierra del faisán y del venado.—
Abreu Gómez, Ermilo. Canek.—Henestrosa, Andrés. Los hombres que
dispersó la danza.

    1. Mayas—Fiction.   ɪ. Médiz Bolio, Antonio, 1884–   ɪɪ. Abreu
Gómez, Ermilo, 1894–   ɪɪɪ. Henestrosa, Andrés. ɪᴠ. Title.
                                        W27716   A 43–1892
    Harvard univ. Library
      for Library of Congress   PQ7276.M3
                                          [4]†   860.9

"On cover" should
be omitted when
inputting series.

```
AI      Sutton, Roberta (Briggs)
3            Speech index; an index to 259 collections of world famous
.S85     orations and speeches for various occasions. 4th ed., rev.
1966     and enl. New York, Scarecrow Press, 1966.
REF.        vii, 947 p.  21 cm.

            "Incorporates all the materials in the three previous Speech In-
         dexes: 1935, 1935–55, and 1956–1961, and augments it [sic] with ...
         new publications ... through 1965."

         -- ---Supplement.  1966-70--      .  Metuchen,
         N. J., Scarecrow Press.
            2 v.  23 cm.  Library has 1966-70--
                                          1971-75

                        (Continued on next card)
                  [145-2]
                                              [Over]
```

Dash entry is for a serial — Flag whole card as a serial (with orange envelope)

```
HG     Donaldson, Elvin Frank, 1903–
173         Personal finance [by] Elvin F. Donaldson and John K.
.D6      Pfahl. 3d ed. New York, Ronald Press Co. [1961]
1961        717 p. illus. 24 cm.

         Includes bibliography.

         ——— ———Instructor's manual.  New York, Ronald Press
         Co. [1961]
            96 p. 23 cm.

                              HG173.D6  1961  Manual

            1. Finance, Personal.   I. Pfahl, John K., joint author.

         HG173.D6. 1961        332.024          61—7071 ‡

         Library of Congress        [64r62t3]
```

590 LIBRARY HAS MAIN VOLUME PLUS MANUAL. 504 Includes bibliography. 590 — —Instructor's manual. New York, Ronald Press Co. [1961] -- 96 p. 23 cm.

```
E     North Carolina.  General assembly
573.3 Roster of North Carolina troops in the war
.N87 between the states.  Raleigh, Ash & Gatling, state
      printers, 1882.
         4 v.  23 cm.

      --- --- Index [of names] ... filmed from card
FILM index in the North Carolina Department of Ar-
E     chives and History.  Raleigh, N. C., 1958.
573.3 15 reels.
.N87
Index    Microfilm copy (16 mm, positive)
      "Compiled by the     W. P. A. Historical Re-
      cords Survey."
```

Dash entry is in a different holding library. Flag as a problem (with red envelope).

```
ARTS
N          Akademie der Künste, Berlin.
5070          Die Kataloge der Berliner Akademie-Ausstellungen 1786–
.B4          1850, bearb. von Helmut Börsch-Supan.  Berlin, B. Hess-
A7          ling, 1971.
ARTS          2 v.   20 x 27 cm.   (Quellen und Schriften zur bildenden Kunst, 4)
N                                                              GDB•••
5070          —————— Registerband.  Berlin, B. Hessling, 1971.
.B4          165 p.   20 x 27 cm.
A7                                          N5070.B4A7   Suppl.
Suppl.

              1. Art--Exhibitions.     I. Börsch-Supan, Helmut, ed.   II. Title.
              N5070.B4A7                                          76–599662
              ISBN 3-7720-0101-2
  TxCP        Library of Congress            71 ,2,
```

050 0   N5070
.B4 ≠b A7
≠a N5070.B4
≠b A7 Suppl.
590 LIBRARY
HAS MAIN WORK
PLUS SUPPLE-
MENT.
590 – –Register-
band. Berlin,
B. Hessling,
1971. – 165 p.
20 x 27 cm.

```
D          Biegański, Stanisław, ed.
763          Działania 2. Korpusu we Włoszech.  [Opracowali: Stani-
.I 8          sław Biegański et al.]   Z przedm. Władysława Andersa.
B48          Londyn, Komisja Historyczna 2. Korpusu, 1963–
              1 v.   25 cm.    Library has v. I only.
              On p. [i] v. 1–   : Sekcja Historyczna 2. Korpusu.
D          —————— Szkice.  Londyn, Sekcja Historyczna 2. Korpusu,
763          1956–         Library has v I only.
.I 8           1 v.   illus., maps (part fold.), plans (part fold.)  24 cm.
B48                                          D763.I 8B48
Suppl.          1. World War, 1939–1945—Campaigns—Italy.  2. Poland.  Polskie
              Siły Zbrojne.  2. Korpus.  3. World War, 1939–1945—Regimental his-
              tories—Poland—2. Korpus.   I. Title.
              D763.I 8B48                                          65–66322
  TxHR        Library of Congress            [1]
```

049 RCEA
≠d (≠v = vol.
≠p = suppl. vol.)
≠v 1 ≠p 1
050 0 D763.I8
≠b B48
≠a D763.I8
≠b B48 Suppl.
590 LIBRARY
HAS VOL. 1 OF
MAIN WORK
AND VOL. 1 OF
SUPPLEMENT.
500 On p. [ii]
v. 1- : Sekcja
Historyczna
2. Korpusu.
590 – –Szkice.
London, Sekcja
Historyczna 2.
Korpusu, 1956- –
v. illus., maps
(part fold.),
plans (part fold.)
24 cm.

```
PQ        Cotelo, Rubén, comp.
8517.5        Narradores uruguayos; antología. [Caracas]
.C68      Monte Avila [1969]
               289 p.  18 cm.  (Colección Continente)


          Includes bio-bibliographical sketches of
          the authors.


          1. Short stories, Uruguayan.  I. Title.
IxHR
                         NUC70-1767
```

RUL card —
Entered under
compiler, with
title added entry.

OCLC Record

1	010	78-11466
2	040	DLC ǂc DLC
3	050 0	PQ8517.5 ǂb .N35
4	082	863/.01
5	090	ǂb
6	049	RCEA
7	245 00	Narradores uruguayos : ǂb antologia / ǂc Rubén Cotelo [compilador]
8	260 0	Caracas : ǂb Monte Avila, ǂc [1969]
9	300	289 p. ; ǂc 18 cm.
10	650 0	Short stories, Uruguayan.
11	700 10	Cotelo, Rubén, ǂd 1930–

OCLC record entered under title, with added entry for compiler.
Subject heading is same; call number is same, except for cutter
number.

Use OCLC record as is; change cutter number in 050 to match what
is on card. Add our series and note.

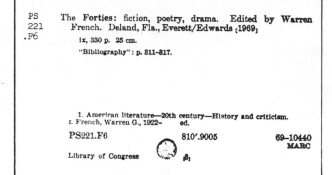

RUL card —
Entered under
title, with editor
added entry.

OCLC Record

1	010	69-10440//r70
2	040	DLC ≠c DLC
3	050 0	PS221 ≠b .F67
4	082	810/.9005
5	090	≠b
6	049	RCEA
7	100 10	French, Warren G., ≠d 1922--
8	245 14	The Forties: fiction, poetry, drama. ≠c Edited by Warren French.
9	260 0	Deland, Fla., ≠b Everett/Edwards ≠c [1969]
10	300	ix, 330 p. ≠c 25 cm.
11	504	Bibliography: p. 311–317.
12	650 0	American literature ≠y 20th century ≠x History and criticism.

OCLC record entered under editor, with added entry for title.
Subject heading is same; call number is same, except for cutter
number.

Use OCLC record as is; change cutter number in 050 to match what
is on our card.

CONVERSION USING OCR

Gary M. Pitkin

This paper is based on two conversion experiences. The first is the actual conversion of the Sangamon State University Library's main shelf-list to machine-readable form through the optical-character-recognition method. The second is the analysis, as a consultant, of the conversion needs of Southern Illinois University at Edwardsville. The analysis included assessments of conversion alternatives and a recommendation with appropriate methodology.

The Sangamon State University Conversion

In early 1979, the Illinois Board of Higher Education was awarded a Higher Education Cooperative Act (HECA) grant to be used for the conversion of shelf-lists to machine-readable form during the 1979-80 fiscal year. Converted records were to be used for participation in the Library Resource Sharing Network which was based on the University of Illinois' Library Computer System (LCS). Many academic institutions in Illinois applied for a portion of these funds. Fourteen received awards, including Sangamon State University.

The Plan

Several months prior to this notification, in December of 1978, I had submitted a report, which was the culmination of a year of research, including an OCLC conversion statistical sampling of the Library's main shelf-list. The report recommended "that we convert the shelf-list to machine-readable form through a commercial vendor utilitzing the Optical-Character-Recognition (OCR) method and that we request the necessary bids as soon as possible." The document stipulated staffing needs as "two to three current civil service positions, one current professional position, and seven CETA positions". This recommendation was for the main, or Library of Congress classification, shelf-list only.

Also proposed was a recommendation to utilize a keypunch processor. We would keypunch to magnetic type directly from shelf-list cards for conversion of the Library's two other shelf-lists — the government documents shelf-list and the periodicals shelf-list.

Both recommendations were accepted in anticipation that the Sangamon State University Library would receive a HECA grant for fiscal year 1979-80. On April 20, 1979, the Illinois Board of Higher Education notified the Library that Sangamon State University had been recommended as a HECA recipient. The Grant Agreement was signed by the University's president on July 1, 1979.

The Reality

Later that month we were notified that staffing for the conversion project would not be at the requested level. We were not granted the three civil service positions. We were granted the one professional position, and the seven CETA positions were reduced to four. The eleven positions, which were considered absolutely mandatory to the success of the project, were thus cut to five positions. Also, the HECA grant was for one year only. We were expected to convert 250,000 LC classed bibliographic records in twelve months with five staff members — of which four had absolutely no library training.

It was a traumatic twelve months to say the least. But our vendor, Blackwell North America, produced a machine-readable shelf-list of excellent quality twelve months from the time we shipped them the first batch of OCR sheets. The technical specifications, all MARC-based, were met. The specification requiring that the vendor produce shelf-list cards for editing purposes two weeks after receipt of each Friday shipment of sheets was never met.

Besides a high quality end product, the project produced, through constant examination and revision, a set of procedural documents and performance assessment charts that could be adopted, with moderate revisions, by any library for retrospective conversion through OCR.

The Southern Illinois University Conversion Proposal

In January of 1980, Southern Illinois University at Edwardsville was designated by the Illinois Board of Higher Education as a fiscal year 1980-81 recipient of HECA funds to become a participant in the Library Resource Sharing Network. I was hired as a consultant to recommend the scope of conversion and the method or methods to be used. The "scope of conversion" meant either short record to support circulation control only, or full record to support an on-line catalog. As the University of Illinois had developed specifications for what it called FBR, or Full Bibliographic Record, and as LCS member libraries were told that this would eventually become associated with LCS, the Edwardsville administration favored full record conversion.

A recommendation on the method or methods to be used was to be based on a time frame of twelve months. Each alternative was to identify both contractual and personnel costs. The recommendation presented to Southern Illinois University was a combination of OCR and OCLC and was based on 1) cost effectiveness, and 2) the OCR methodology developed at Sangamon State University.

The cost analysis that follows is based on contractual costs provided by vendors and personnel costs provided by the University, both effective during the first half of 1980, and is taken directly from the consulting report. Cost effectiveness is presented under the headings of: 1) Methods and Costs; 2) Non-MARC-based vendors; 3) OCLC; 4) MARC-based vendors; 5) and the recommended combination of BNA/OCLC.

Shelf-list Conversion: Methods and Costs

The first step involved with implementing any automated bibliographic system is the conversion of manual shelf-lists to the machine-readable format compatible with the new system. In the case of the LCS/FBR combination, the necessary machine-readable format is MARC.

There are three methods for converting shelf-lists to MARC available to SIU-E. These are 1) non-MARC-based vendors; 2) OCLC; and 3) MARC-based vendors. If the Southern Illinois University at Edwardsville system is to be automated efficiently beyond circulation control, all bibliographic elements of the shelf-list record must be converted to machine-readable form. The shelf-list record includes approximately 368,500 records in the main shelf-list, which is made up of bibliography, stacks, reference, East St. Louis, children's collection, and high school collection shelf-lists. Approximately 7,700 records in the periodicals control file, 840 records in the theses shelf-list, and 15,000 records in the recordings shelf-list are also included.

Non-MARC-Based Vendor

In utilizing a non-MARC-based vendor, either for short or full record conversion, the method would involve shipping the shelf-list to the vendor for conversion. The shelf-lists would be sent to the vendor on a predetermined schedule as conversion to LCS/FBR is to be completed within a twelve-month period. The bibliographic elements, including holdings, for each shelf-list entry would be copied by the vendor and transferred to tape. The cards would be returned to the library with print-out copies of the produced tape. Several clerical positions, with training in descriptive cataloging, would be designated to edit the print-outs to insure tape accuracy. Errors would be identified on the print-outs, which would be returned to the vendor for correction. The edit reports, with a correction report produced for each edit report, would be returned to the library for further editing. Each edit report would represent a shelf-list drawer, and the editor would "sign-off" on the appropriate correction report when all errors for the respective drawer had been corrected.

The number of editors needed depends on the employment of short record or full record conversion. As stipulated in the following cost figures, it is estimated that, for conversion of approximately 392,040 records and based on experiences at Sangamon State University and elsewhere, fourteen editors would be needed for full record conversion and ten for short record conversion.

Non-MARC-Based Vendor: Costs

(The rates as of early 1980 are those of Electronic Keyboarding, Inc. of St. Louis, the vendor used by the University of Illinois for short record conversion and by the Library of Congress for creation of MARC tapes)

Short Record Conversion

Main Shelf-list
    368,500 records @ $ .15 $ 55,275

Periodicals Control File
    7,700 records @ $ .15 $ 1,155

Theses Shelf-list
    840 records @ $ .15 $ 126

Recordings Shelf-list
    15,000 records @ $ .15 $ 2,250

Ten Library-Clerk II Editors
    @ $6,360 annually $ 63,600

TOTAL FUNDS NEEDED: $122,406

Main Shelf-list
   368,500 records @ $ .78 $287,430

Periodicals Control File
   7,700 records @ $ .78 $ 6,006

Theses Shelf-list
   840 records @ $ .78 $ 655

Recordings Shelf-list
   15,000 records @ $ .78 $ 11,700

Fourteen Library-Clerk II Editors
   @ $6,360 annually   <u>$ 89,040</u>

TOTAL FUNDS NEEDED: $394,831

OCLC

The second method is to utilize OCLC. Application for retrospective conversion authorization would have to be made, and the OCLC profile would have to be changed to include all internal locations as holding libraries (to be entered as input stamps).

Procedures would involve matching the shelf-list entry with the OCLC entry, inputting the holding library, actual holdings, and local call number. No other bibliographic information would be input because of the HECA-imposed twelve-month conversion time limit. This would produce a "dirty" data base, and the records would have to be edited via LCS maintenance terminals after conversion had been completed. This editing would include descriptive cataloging decisions and would, consequently, require substantial professional time. Note that, as this would not be done during the original conversion process, the editing cost is not included in the cost figures for OCLC.

Shelf-list entries not found in the OCLC data base would be referred to the head of the cataloging department for original cataloging. Records would be entered into the "save" file for verification prior to tape production. The three existing OCLC terminals would be used for daily cataloging only. Six additional terminals for conversion would be leased and would be staffed at seventy hours a week each; a total of twelve LTA I's (double-shift) would input records into the "save" file, and four professional catalogers would process the saved records and enter original records.

Lease six terminals for twelve months:

Terminal Rental and Maintenance @ $155 per month per terminal	$ 11,160
Terminal Installation one @ $87.50; five @ $17.50	$ 175
Twelve LTA I's @ $8,280 annually	$ 99,360
Four Professional Catalogers @ $20,000 annually	$ 80,000

TOTAL FUNDS NEEDED: $190,695

Note 1:   This does not include the substantial cost in professional cataloging time needed to edit the "dirty" records created by not editing the fixed and variable fields during the conversion process.

Note 2:   Considerable savings would be realized if LTA I's could be given the responsibility of inputting records directly to the OCLC data base.

MARC-Based Vendors: Blackwell North America and Brodart

The third method of conversion is to utilize a MARC-based vendor with optical-character-recognition (OCR). Based on research into data base quality and quantity, conversion procedures, and reactions of clients, two vendors, Blackwell North America (BNA) and BRODART are identified as able to convert the SIU-E main, periodicals, and recordings shelf-lists. This statement is based on discussions with BNA, BRODART, Autographics, and Baker & Taylor, evaluation of descriptive documents provided by these vendors, and extensive discussions with libraries using each vendor. The following comparison is based on information provided by BNA and BRODART in 1979. The difference between employing either vendor can be defined in terms of the time required to complete input, editing, and original cataloging input. This discussion is based on a full-time staff of ten.

According to the HECA grant proposal, conversion is to be completed within a twelve-month period. Using the optical-character-recognition (OCR) method, with IBM Selectric typewriters (it is assumed that the Library can get these typewriters through the University at no cost) and OCR "A" p/P1 typing elements, this time frame could be met through simultaneous input and editing. Simply, this means that the OCR sheets are typed with minimal bibliographic information, proofread, and mailed to the vendor on a weekly basis. Two weeks later, the entries are returned to the library for editing of those found in the data base and for original cataloging input of those not found.

With simultaneous OCR input and output entry editing, it is estimated that this part of the conversion process would take ten months. Original cataloging input, i.e., typing the full bibliographic record on to the OCR sheet for records not in the vendor's data base, would be done during this same ten-month period. This procedure would continue for another two months.

This time frame can be met by BNA, as it is BNA's policy to produce weekly runs against their data base for all customers. Records that are found are returned in the form of shelf-list cards and, when edited, replace the former cards in the shelf-list. BRODART does not have a weekly run policy for its customers. Instead, it runs the entire shelf-list against the data base after all the input documents have been received. As stated above, the input is estimated to take ten months and the editing and original cataloging input twelve months. Also, BRODART provides records of all items in print-out form. Library staff would have to transfer that information to shelf-list cards in-house. To summarize, BNA can meet the projected twelve-month time frame; BRODART would take twenty-four months. In addition, BRODART's data base is not as comprehensive as BNA's.

BRODART's data base is composed of MARC: BOOKS only. Consequently, BRODART estimates that only sixty percent of the shelf-list would be located in its data base. With 391,200 shelf-list records (main, periodicals, and recordings), the staff would have to provide original cataloging input for 156,490 records. The sixty percent figure is not based on any statistical data, since BRODART does not have a system for shelf-list analysis.

BNA, on the other hand, does conduct shelf-list analysis for potential customers. This analysis was not conducted for the Southern Illinois University at Edwardsville Library, but analyses of libraries of similar size have yielded estimates that eighty percent of their shelf-list records could be located in the BNA data base. This means that the staff would have to provide original cataloging input for 78,240 records — exactly half of the number projected for BRODART. The eighty percent figure is possible because the BNA data base includes MARC: BOOKS, MARC: SERIALS, MARC: SCORES and PHONODISCS, MARC: AUDIO-VISUAL, Canadian MARC, and British MARC. Approximately ten percent of the records found in the data base would need corrections or field updates. At Sangamon State University, BNA's shelf-list analysis projected a hit rate of 80 percent and an error rate of 8 percent. Both projections proved to be accurate.

Because the amount of original cataloging input necessary for BRODART is exactly double that of BNA and because BRODART does not allow simultaneous input, editing, and original cataloging input, it is estimated that original cataloging input for BRODART would require nine months more than the twenty-four months projected for BNA. Included in original cataloging input are typing the OCR sheets, editing the returned print-outs, and producing the shelf-list cards.

Staffing, based on the Sangamon State University experience, would require ten clerk-typist II positions for OCR typing, microfiche title index scanning, and output editing. Two LTA I positions would be needed to code the non-hits for OCR. Staff would also be required to do preliminary sorting of the shelf-list, including stamping "bin" numbers. These terms will be fully described shortly.

MARC Based Vendor: Costs

Optical-Character-Recognition through BNA

Main Shelf-list

MARC Hits (80%) @ $ .18	$ 53,064
Hit Corrections (10%) @ $ .20	$ 5,896
Non-Hits (20%) @ $ .50	$ 36,850

Periodicals Control File

MARC Hits (80%) @ $ .18	$ 1,110
Hit Corrections (10%) @ $ .20	$ 125
Non-Hits (20%) @ $ .50	$ 770

Recordings Shelf-list

MARC Hits (80%) @ $ .18	$ 2,160
Hit Corrections (10%) @ $ .20	$ 540
Non-Hits (20%) @ $ .50	$ 1,500

BNA Microfiche Title Index

First copy $720; second copy $400; third copy $400	$ 1,520

OCR "A" p/P1 Typing Elements

Five @ $16.20	$ 81

Lion C-75 Number-stamps

Ten @ $41.95	$ 420

Ten Clerk-Typist II's

@ $6,360 annually	$ 63,600

Two LTA I's

@ $8,280 annually	$ 16,560

TOTAL FUNDS NEEDED:	$184,196

Note: The theses shelf-list is not included here as none of those titles would be in the BNA data base. Conversion of the 840 theses would be done through OCLC and would be worked into the current daily cataloging routine.

Conversion — BNA/OCLC

An alternative to these three basic approaches is a combination of the MARC-based vendor, in this case Blackwell North America, and OCLC. There are several advantages to this arrangement. First of all, the eighty percent of the main, periodicals, and recordings shelf-lists processed through the BNA data base will be full, clean bibliographic records. No clean-up will be necessary, as would be the case with a fast twelve-month conversion through OCLC.

Another very important advantage is that OCLC will provide greater control over the BNA non-hits, which, experience has shown, invariably are bibliographic cataloging problems. The cost analysis provided below plans for a professional librarian to check, through the "save" file, the records entered by the four LTA I's. With this size staff involved with the OCLC part of the conversion process, there will be enough time to do full record editing of the BNA non-hits and full record entry of the theses shelf-list. This project would have two terminals, each staffed at seventy hours per week.

A third advantage is the time saved in processing the BNA non-hits through OCLC. The procedure would call for entering the item into the "save" file from information provided on the shelf-list card with, in many cases, some bibliographic interpretation, and, later, revising the "save" file. Processing the non-hits through BNA would entail bibliographic interpretation, transferring the information to a code sheet containing OCR tags, or writing the OCR tags on the shelf-list card itself, typing that information onto the OCR sheet, and, later, editing the shelf-list card provided by BNA.

Based on these advantages, the necessity of full bibliographic conversion, and the cost analysis provided below, it was recommended that a combination of 1) optical-character-recognition, through Blackwell North America, and 2) OCLC be used for conversion of the four Southern Illinois University at Edwardsville shelf-lists.

A staffing recommendation of ten for the BNA process is based on the Sangamon State University experience and will provide the flexibility of having OCR typing, BNA title index searching, and output editing done simultaneously and will allow the employee the flexibility of performing all tasks on a rotating basis. The best approach is to assign each staff member a call number range for typing and title index searching. Staff would also be required to do preliminary sorting of the shelf-list.

Three copies of the BNA title index should be used, two staff per index, so that a maximum of six staff can be searching non-matches simultaneously. This means, of course, that the conversion project will have to usurp six microfiche readers from the library's collection. The library will also have to obtain five IBM Selectric typewriters from the University. These typewriters must have 10-pitch type available (which is not the case with all IBM Selectric typewriters).

BNA and OCLC: Costs

Blackwell North America

Main Shelf-list
    MARC Hits (80%) @ $ .18 $ 53,064
        Hit Corrections (10%) @ $ .20 $ 5,896

Periodicals Control File

    MARC Hits (80%) @ $ .18 $ 1,110
        Hit Corrections (10%) @ $ .20 $ 125

Recordings Shelf-list

MARC Hits (80%) @ $ .18	$ 2,160
Hit Corrections (10%) @ $ .20	$ 540

Microfiche Title Index

First copy $720; second copy $400; third copy $400	$ 1,520

OCR "A" p/P1 Typing Elements

Five @ $16.20	$ 81

Lion C-75 Number-stamps

Ten @ $41.95	$ 420

OCLC (BNA Non-Hits: 78,240; Theses Shelf-List: 840)

Two Terminals

Rental and Maintenance @ $155/mo./terminal	$ 1,860
Installation @ $87.50 and @ $17.50	$ 105

Staffing

Blackwell North America Process

Ten Clerk-typist II's @ $6,630 annually	$ 63,600

OCLC Process

Four LTA I's @ $8,280 annually	$ 33,120
One Professional Cataloger @ $20,000	$ 20,000

TOTAL FUNDS NEEDED: $183,601

Outline of Conversion Process

The following outline provides a breakdown of each step in the conversion process and is inclusive for the main, periodicals, and recordings shelf-lists. It deals with bibliographic conversion only and does not include copy/volume conversion. The theses shelf-list will be done through OCLC.

A. Preparatory Sorting (Attachment A)

1. Step one — separate OCLC card sets into a separate section at the back of each drawer.

2. Step two — assign "bin" numbers to remaining card sets. The "bin" number, assigned sequentially, identifies the entry on the OCR code sheet and on the BNA shelf-list card.

    a) Purchase ten Lion C-75 number-stamps. These contain six digits with the first being an alpha character.

    b) Divide the main shelf-list into eight areas and assign each area an alpha character. Also assign an alpha character to the Periodicals Control File and an alpha character to the recordings shelf-list.

    c) Each staff member hired for the BNA process will be responsible for numbering a section of the shelf-list.

3. Step three — identify and pull MARC exact matches from the first section of each drawer. These card sets are filed at the front of each drawer.

4. When the sorting has been completed, each shelf-list drawer will be in three sections: 1) exact matches, 2) non-exact matches, and 3) OCLC. It should be understood that everything added to the collection, barring government documents, should now be cataloged through OCLC for automatic transfer to the LCS (Library Computer System) data base. All OCLC cards received during the conversion process are to be filed in the OCLC section of the respective drawer.

B. BNA Title Index (Attachment B)

1. The non-exact matches, section two of each drawer, as identified in A.3. above, are searched by title in the BNA microfiche title index. When a record is found, the differences are circled on the card in pencil, and the BNA title number is written at the top of the card.

2. Those records that are not located in the title index are filed in call number order, behind the non-exact match section.

These are the BNA non-hits, and these card sets become the third section of each drawer; the OCLC section becomes the fourth section.

3. When the non-matches have been examined against the BNA title index, count the sections of the drawer and record the counts on the workform provided as *Attachment C*. This will provide a statistical analysis of the project and will provide an official title count for the collection.

C. Typing Exact Matches *(Attachment E)*. *(Attachment D* is the "OCR Numeric Input Typing General Procedures" manual as prepared by Blackwell North America)

1. The first section of each drawer, the exact matches, are OCR-typed using only the location code, Library of Congress card number, and bin number.

2. This "input" typing is edited and corrected, and edited sheets are shipped to the BNA scanner every week. Typing accuracy is monitored through *Attachment F*. BNA accuracy is monitored through *Attachment G*.

3. Two shelf-list card sets, each representing a typed entry and the corresponding tape record, are received, and the "output" is edited against the original shelf-list card set. Those sets that match the shelf-list entry are interfiled with the OCLC sets in section four of the drawer. The BNA duplicate is discarded along with the old shelf-list card set.

4. Errors identified during output editing are circled in red on both copies of the BNA shelf-list set. One is returned to BNA for correction of the master tape, and the other is filed in section four.

5. Card sets remaining in section one should be examined against the BNA title index. Those found in the index should be treated as non-exact matches. Those not found in the index should be treated as non-hits.

D. Typing Non-Exact Matches *(Attachment H)*

1. The second section of each drawer, the non-exact matches, are OCR-typed using location code, bin number, all circled items, and BNA title number. Holdings are not typed.

2. Numbers 2, 3, and 4 are done as described under C.

E. Conversion of Card Sets Not Found in the BNA Title Index —
   BNA Non-Hits

   1. As the identification of non-hits is completed for each
      drawer, the person in charge of collection development for
      the call number range involved should be notified through
      Attachment J. The procedures identified in *Attachment K*
      should be followed in weeding the non-hits. *Attachment L*
      should be used in keeping track of the weeding process.

   2. Card sets representing non-hits to be kept in the collection
      should be converted to machine-readable form through
      OCLC.

F. Conversion of Copy/Volume Data (Manual will be supplied
   by LCS)

   LCS hardware was installed in October, 1980. As BNA tapes
   are added to the LCS data base, copy/volume conversion should
   be scheduled on LCS maintenance terminals.

ATTACHMENT A

SHELF-LIST SORTING

(Card implies card set including holdings card and card 2, card 3, etc.)
Step One

Each drawer is separated into three sections divided by pink cards placed in clear plastic covers. The three sections are:

1) at the rear of the drawer are filed, in call number order, all OCLC cards. These cards are identified by "IAS_" at the bottom of the card:

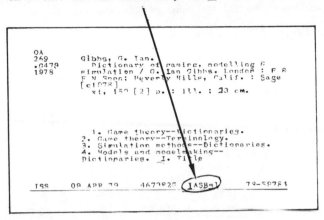

Interfile green slips marked "new card set ordered through OCLC" with OCLC cards.

2) all Abel cards are filed in the middle of the drawer in call number order; these are cards with CUSG or ZCUSG or RCUSG:

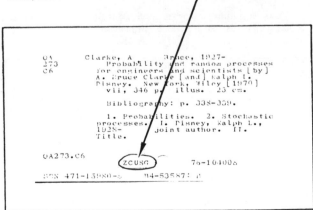

3) at the beginning of the drawer are filed, in call number order, all other cards.

Step Two

All cards in the first section of each drawer are stamped with a six-digit roll-stamp as close to the bottom of the card as possible. The first card in the first drawer will be 000001. Numbering continues consecutively throughout the first section of the shelf-list; for example, the last card in section one of drawer one is 000999; the first card in section one of drawer two will be 001000.

Step Three

Section one of each shelf-list drawer is examined card by card. Pull, for each drawer, the cards that match all of the following criteria:

1) Library of Congress Card Number in the lower right-hand corner:

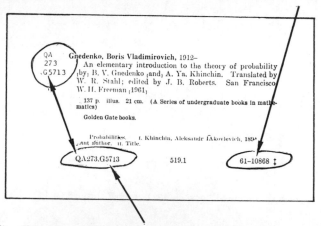

2) call number in the upper left-hand corner matches one of the call numbers listed at the bottom of the card:

3) card lists page numbers, or the equivalent for audio-visual materials; do *not* pull cards that have a "v" in place of page numbers:

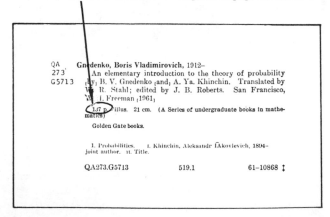

Do *not* pull cards that have the following characteristics:

1) "x" at end of call number
2) dashed-on entries:

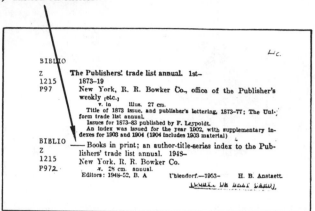

3) typed in or penciled in changes or additions (this does not include words like Alanar or BRODART):

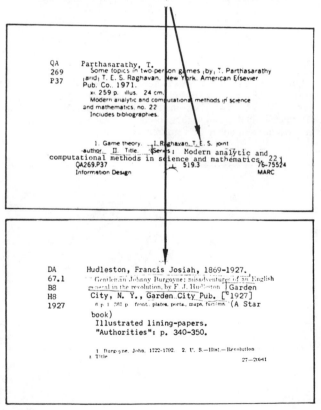

4) more than one volume or copy, or followed by holdings card:

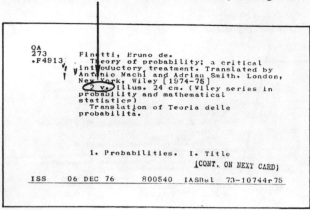

```
QA
273         Finetti, Bruno de.
.F4913          Theory of probability; a critical
            introductory treatment. Translated by
            Antonio Machi and Adrian Smith. London,
            New York, Wiley [1974-75]
               2 v. illus. 24 cm. (Wiley series in
            probability and mathematical
            statistics)
               Translation of Teoria delle
            probabilita.




               1. Probabilities.  I. Title
                                 (CONT. ON NEXT CARD)
   ISS     06 DEC 76      800540   IASBsl  73-10744r75
```

The cards that are pulled for each drawer are filed at the beginning of that drawer in call number order. This becomes section one and is the LCCN Exact Matches. Those not pulled are section two and are Non-Exact Matches.

NOTE: *All cards that indicate "PHONODISC" are to be given to the Project Director.*

Step Three

Additional Instructions:
1) While sorting shelf-list cards in accordance with the attached instructions, check cards for the indicator "IASB" or "CUSG", "RCUSG", or "ZCUSG." "IASB" means that the card is an OCLC card and should be filed in call number order in the last section of that drawer. An example of an OCLC card is:

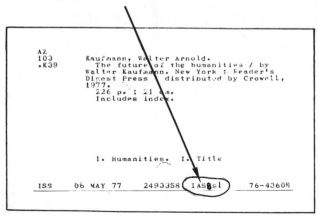

```
AZ
103         Kaufmann, Walter Arnold.
.K39            The future of the humanities / by
            Walter Kaufmann. New York : Reader's
            Digest Press : distributed by Crowell,
            1977.
               226 p. ; 21 cm.
               Includes index.




               1. Humanities.  I. Title
   ISS     06 MAY 77     2493358   IASBsl   76-43608
```

140

"CUSG," "RCUSG," or "ZCUSG" means that the card is an Abel card and should be filed in call number order in the middle section of that drawer. An example of an Abel card is:

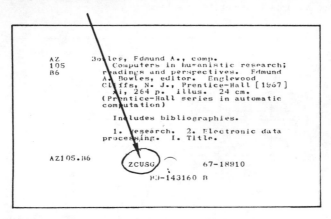

2) If an OCLC or Abel card is found that is stamped with a five-digit number or has a five-digit number written in red at the bottom of the card, white-out that number with Liquid Paper and file that card in the proper section. An example of a numbered card is:

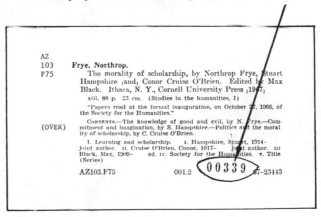

3) If a card is found that says "Card 2," "Card 3," "Card 4," etc., or is a holdings card, and is either stamped or has a number written on it at the bottom, or has no card 1, pull the set for the project director. An example of a holdings card is:

REMEMBER: Throughout the manual, "Card" refers to card set, which is all cards with the same call number.

142

BNA TITLE INDEX PROCEDURES

The BNA Title Index is in microfiche and is arranged alphabetically by title. Section II, the non-exact matches, of each drawer is to be compared to the Title Index.

Procedure:
I. Identify title of card set (disregard *a, an,* or *the*)
   A. Title main entry

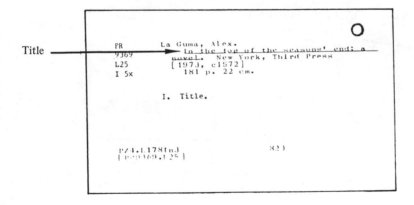

Title ⟶

B. Author main entry

Title ⟶

II. Locate the microfiche to be placed in the reader. The letters included on each microfiche are given at the top of each column.

143

III. After the entry has been located in the Title Index, compare the
areas identified below with the card set.
A. BNA entry

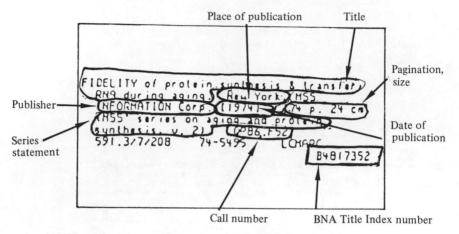

NOTE: If there is an author main entry, it will follow the title.
If there is an edition statement, it will appear between the author
and title.

B. Card set

IV. In pencil, circle on the first card of the card set all areas that do not
agree with the Title Index entry or are not included in the Title
Index entry. Write the BNA Title Index\number, located in the
lower right hand corner of the Title Index entry, on the first card
of the card set in the upper right hand corner.

144

An example of a completed card set is:

```
                                          B48/7352

QP  Fidelity of protein synthesis & transfer RNA during aging.
86    (Papers by Fay Dingley, B. J. Harrison, Robin Holliday,
F52    et al. / New York, MSS Information Corp. [1974]
          174 p.  illus.  24 cm.  (MSS' series on aging and protein synthe-
       sis, v. 2).
          Includes bibliographical references.
          1. Aging—Addresses, essays, lectures.  2. Protein biosynthesis
       Addresses, essays, lectures.  3. Ribonucleic acid—Addresses, essays,
       lectures.   I. Dingley, Fay.  II. Series


      SL
                                          F.10127
```

V. Card sets that are not found in the Title Index are put aside, in call number order, until all of Section II of the drawer has been compared to the Title Index. A pink card is placed behind those Section II card sets that were found in the Title Index. The card sets not found in the Title Index are placed behind the pink card and become Section III of the shelf-list drawer. The Abel card sets make up Section IV, and the OCLC card sets are in Section V.

ATTACHMENT C

CALL NUMBERS OF DRAWER	CARD SETS EXACT MATCHES	CARD SETS NON-EXACT MATCHES	CARD SETS NON-HITS	CARD SETS OCLC	CARD SETS TOTAL	INITIALS OF COUNTER

146

(prepared by Blackwell North America)

OCR NUMERIC INPUT TYPING GENERAL PROCEDURES

A. Typewriter

1. Use only a Selectric typewriter specifically certified by IBM for OCR. An IBM local office will certify machines in the field for a standard charge.

2. Use only the proper typing element: IBM OCR "A" p/P1 { IBM part 170 } .

3. Use 10 pitch type. NEVER USE 12 PITCH TYPE.

4. Do not use the half space key.

5. Do not vary the vertical line spacing. Always use the vertical spacing indicated on the OCR paper.

6. Do not reuse typewriter ribbons.

7. Use only standard carbon single-use ribbons. Other ribbons can cause errors as ink is not evenly distributed on the impression.

B. Paper

1. Use only the special preprinted paper form supplied. Do not fold, spindle, staple, punch, or mutilate.

2. Do not expose to excessive moisture or extremes of temperature.

3. Do not use paper which has been mutilated, crinkled, stained, etc. Paper must be dirt-free.

4. Ship paper flat in waterproof boxes or in boxes wrapped in water-proof wrapping.

5. Do not type into the red margin.

6. Do not submit pages with smudged type.

7. Do not use paper which is torn in any way. All four corners must be clean and square.

8. Do not write on, stamp, or mark in any way the back of the paper.

9. All marks on the paper must be made with a typewriter. Do not try to fill in characters with a pencil or pen.

10. Align paper exactly. Paper must be level.

147

C. Character Set:

ABCDEFGHIJKLMNOPQRSTUVWXYZ

abcdefghijklmnopqrstuvwxyz

1234567890-=∎;',./

Ɏ♪⌐¢%|&*{}→∎:",.?

1. Never attempt to create a character set by combining two other characters.

2. The "hook" ♪ is used to input the quadrille {#}.

D. Errors

1. Correct errors by overstriking with the obliterate character {∎}. One strike is made over each character error. DO NOT OVERSTRIKE WITH ANY OTHER CHARACTER.

2. Do not use liquid correction fluid, erasures, or ink eradicator.

3. No record started on one page should be continued on the next page.

4. In order to delete a line in which multiple errors make it expedient to re-type the entire line, use the "—" through the line.

EXAMPLES:

ɎMBERS   *BNA ∎C1234567*LOL $a638.84 A312a

~~Ɏ   *LOL $J♪⌐¢%|&~~

E. Continuation

If a field (OCR tag and its data) has been completed on a line, simply begin the next field on the next line.

If a single field is too long for a line, use a hyphen as in normal typing procedures. If you wish to preserve the hyphen at the end of a line, use two hyphens.

EXAMPLES:

ɎMBERS *BNA C1234567*LOL $kMuseum collection, War Memorial Mothers of the Last Great Battle

Ɏ   *BNA B3458279*LOL $kSpecial collection of the city-- county accounting offices

OCR TYPING PROCEDURES FOR EXACT MATCHES

I. The page heading
   A. On line 1, beginning at the left margin, a three segment number is typed.
     1. The first segment is always ⊢1211 followed by a |.
     2. The second segment is the typist's identification number. These are assigned as follows:

       01 - Ruth Cook
       02 - Francine Walker
       03 - Virginia Latonis
       04 - Ronnie Wieber
       05 - Patricia Neuman
       06 - Dorothy Wilson
       07 - Florence Green

     This is followed by a |.
     3. The third segment is the page number which must be three characters.
     4. An example of a page heading is:

     ⊢1211|01|023

     This would be the twenty-third page typed by Ruth.

II. The record request
   A. On line 2, beginning at the left margin, type the record request symbol, ⊬, and the location code.
     1. Location codes are as follows:

       CUSG   (no location indicator is above the call number on the card set)
       CUSGR (REFERENCE is above the call number on the card set)
       CUSGI (INDEX is above the call number on the card set)
       CUSGB (BIBLIO is above the call number on the card set)
       CUSGD (DOC INDEX is above the call number on the card set)
       CUSGO (OVERSIZE is above the call number on the card set)
       CUSGS (SPEC COLL is above the call number on the card set)
       CUSGF (FILM is above the call number on the card set)
       CUSGG (GAME is above the call number on the card set)
       CUSGK (KIT is above the call number on the card set)
       CUSGL (RECORD is above the call number on the card set)
       CUSGV (VIDEOTAPE is above the call number on the card set)

   B. Return the carriage to the ⊬ and space 10 positions. Data fields *always* begin at column 10.
     1. At column 10, type an asterisk (*) followed, with no space, by LCN, one space, and the Library of Congress Card Number from the lower right hand corner of the card set.
     2. The last number of the Library of Congress Card Number is followed by, with no space, another asterisk (*) and LOL.
     3. LOL is followed by a space and $p and, with no space, the bin number, which is either stamped or written in red on the first card of the card set.

C. Examples are given below and are repeated on the attached OCR sheet.

YCUSGO   *LCN 72-179277*LOL $p26147

YCUSG   *LCN 74-22181*LOL $p25978

Y   *LCN 66-70003*LOL $pD11543

D. On line 3, the next record is input the same as for line 2. The only exception is that the location code is not repeated if it is the same as the previous line.

E. If a card set is not assigned a bin number, the Library of Congress Card Number is the only field input for that card set.

III. Delete line
A. If an entry cannot be corrected as described in the general procedures, strike through it with a single line:

~~Y   PNQ DAA CISG~~

Γ˙˙. When a page has been completed, clip the card sets to the page and give both to Ruth.

ⱶ1211|01|023

YCUSGO *LCN 72-179277*LOL $P26147

YCUSG *LCN 74-22181*LOL $p25978

Y   *LCN 66-70003*LOL $pD11543

Typist _____

Date OCR Sheets Edited	Number of Sheets	Number of Entries	Number of Typing Errors	Number of Typing Errors Per Record	Comments: Type of Error, Consistency of Error	Editor's Initial

Date OCR Sheets Shipped To BNA	Number of Sheets Shipped	Date Edit Cards Received	% of Errors	Date Errors Returned to BNA	Date Corrected Cards Received	% Needing Additional Corrections.

ATTACHMENT H

OCR TYPING PROCEDURES FOR NON-EXACT MATCHES

I. The page heading
   A. On line 1, beginning at the left margin, a three segment number is typed.
      1. The first segment is always ⌐1211 followed by a |.
      2. The second segment is the typist's identification number. These are assigned as follows:

        02 - Francine Walker
        03 - Virginia Latonis
        04 - Ronnie Wieber
        05 - Patricia Neuman
        06 - Dorothy Wilson
        07 - Barbara Mackay

      This is followed by a |.
      3. The third segment is the page number, which must be three characters.
      4. An example of a page heading is:

      ⌐1211|02|023

      This would be the twenty-third page typed by Francine.

II. The record request and location code
   A. On line 2, beginning at the left margin, type the record request symbol, Ч, and the location code.
      1. Location codes are as follows:

      CUSG   (no location indicator is above the call number on the card set)
      CUSGR (REFERENCE is above the call number on the card set)
      CUSGI (INDEX is above the call number on the card set)
      CUSGB (BIBLIO is above the call number on the card set)
      CUSGD (DOC INDEX is above the call number on the card set)
      CUSGO (OVERSIZE is above the call number on the card set)
      CUSGS (SPEC COLL is above the call number on the card set)
      CUSGF (FILM is above the call number on the card set)
      CUSGG (GAME is above the call number on the card set)
      CUSGK (KIT is above the call number on the card set)
      CUSGL (RECORD is above the call number on the card set)
      CUSGV (VIDEOTAPE is above the call number on the card set)

III. Return the carriage to the Ч and space 10 position. Data fields *always* begin at column 10 with an asterisk {*} typed in that column, followed by the first data fields.
   A. The data fields involved with typing the non-exact matches are as follows and are to be typed in the order shown:

DATA FIELD	TYPING SYMBOL
Library of Congress Card Number	LCN
BNA Access Number	BNA
Library of Congress Call Number	LOL
Edition	EDN
Imprint	IMP
Collation	COL
General Note	NOG

154

B. Not all data fields will apply to all shelf-list card sets. Those that are not appropriate are to be skipped.

C. Typing procedures are the same as for typing the exact matches.
1. At column 10, type an asterisk {*} followed, with no space, by the typing symbol of the first appropriate field.
2. The symbol is followed by a space and the appropriate information, which is followed by, with no space, another asterisk {*} and the typing symbol for the next appropriate field.
3. Subfields are typed by following the typing symbol with a space, $, and the appropriate subfield indicator.
4. There are no spaces between subfields in the same data field.

IV. Data fields to be typed for each shelf-list card set are identified by being circled in pencil. An exception is the Library of Congress Card number, which is located in the lower right hand corner of the first card of the card set. Another exception is the BNA Access Number, which is written in pencil in the upper right hand corner of the first card of the card set. Examples of the data fields follow:

A. Library of Congress Card Number

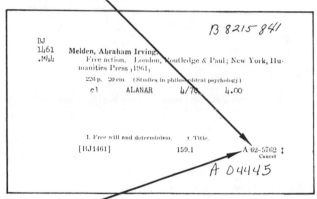

YCUSG   *LCN A62-5762*BNA B8215841*LOL $pA04445

B. BNA Access Number

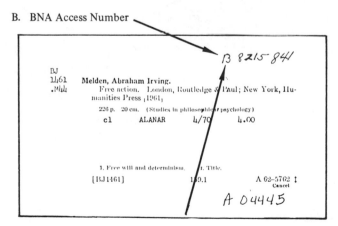

YCUSG   *LCN A62-5762*BNA B8215841*LOL $pA04445

C. Library of Congress Call Number

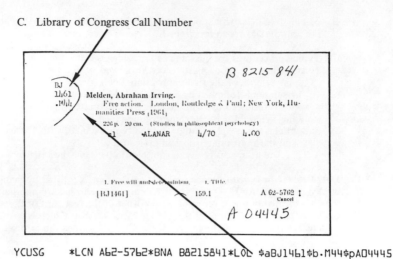

YCUSG   *LCN A62-5762*BNA B8215841*LOL $aBJ1461$b.M44$pA04445

The subfields for the Library of Congress call number data field are:
1. $a local classification number {BJ 1461}
2. $b cutter number {.M44}
3. $c volume or year
4. $p BIN number

The BIN number is to be part of every entry, as was true with the exact matches.

D. Edition

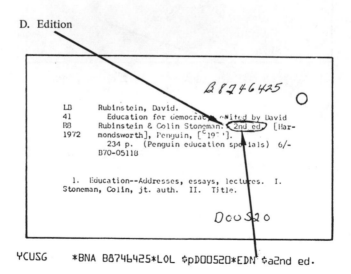

YCUSG   *BNA B8746425*LOL $pD00520*EDN $a2nd ed.

E. Imprint

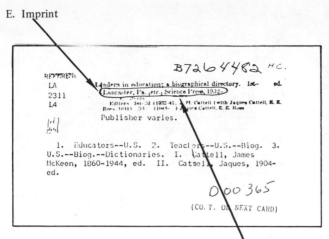

YCUSGR   *BNA B7264482*LOL $pD00365*IMP $aLancaster,Pa
.$bScience Press$c1932-

The subfields for the imprint data field are:
1. $a place of publication
2. $b publisher
3. $c date of publication

F. Collation

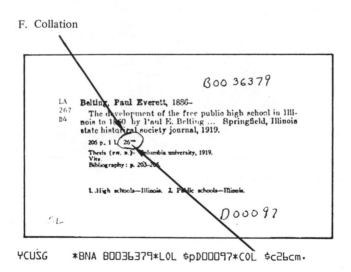

YCUSG   *BNA B0036379*LOL $pD00097*COL $c26cm.

The subfields for the collation data field are:
1. $a pagination
2. $b illustrative matter
3. $c size

G. General Note

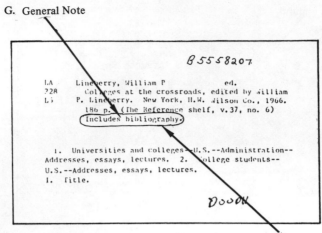

YCUSG   *BNA B5558207*LOL $pD00011*NOG $aIncludes bibliography.

V. Author statements and series statements, even if circled in pencil, are not
included in the typing process.

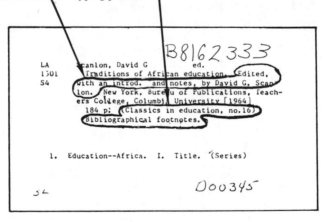

YCUSG   *BNA B8162333*LOL $pD00345

TO:

FROM: Shelf-list Conversion Project

DATE:

RE: Weeding BNA Non-hits

    The shelf-list drawers(s) listed below are ready for weeding those entries not located in the Blackwell North America (BNA) data base. The call numbers involved are under your direction for collection development.

Call Number Range	Number of Non-hits
_____	_____
_____	_____
_____	_____
_____	_____
_____	_____
_____	_____
_____	_____
_____	_____
_____	_____
_____	_____

    The non-hit section is the third section in each shelf-list drawer. As weeding will be done in the stacks, please place the shelf-list card in the item to be withdrawn, and give those items to the conversion supervisor. Cards representing items to be kept should be refiled in the appropriate section of the drawer. Please weed as quickly as possible, as the HECA grant requires that bibliographic conversion be completed within a twelve-month period. We cannot convert the non-hits until the weeding process has been completed.

ATTACHMENT K

PROCEDURE FOR WEEDING NON-HITS

I. Upon receipt of letter notification that one or more drawers are ready for weeding, go to the shelf-list and remove the cards representing non-hits. These will be in the third section of the drawer.

   A. Remove cards from only one drawer at a time.

   B. Be sure to place a drop slip in the section. This should be a 3" X 5" slip, available at the shelf-list. Write the call number range across the top and write your name and date near the bottom. If possible, arrange to have the cards, per drawer, for only one working day.

II. Take the shelf-list cards to the shelf and examine each shelved item.

   A. If an item is to be withdrawn, place the shelf-list card in the book.

   B. Keep cards representing items to be kept in a separate stack.

   C. If an item is not on the shelf, check pre-sort areas.

   D. If an item is not located, place the respective shelf-list card in the stack representing items to be kept.

III. After all of the non-hits for the particular shelf-list drawer, have gone through the weeding process, return cards to technical services.

   A. Cards representing items to be kept should be placed, in call number order, back in the third section of the appropriate drawer.

   B. Drop slips should be made for cards that have been placed in books to be withdrawn. Write the call number in the upper left hand corner. Write "to be withdrawn" across the middle of the slip. Write your name and date at the bottom of the slip. File the slips in call number order in the non-hit section of the drawer.

   C. Place the shelf-list card back in the item to be withdrawn and give all items to the conversion supervisor.

Shelf-list drawer call numbers	Librarian Responsible	Non-hits identified	Weeding done	Shelf-list drawer call numbers	Librarian Responsible	Non-hits identified	Weeding done	Shelf-list drawer call numbers	Librarian Responsible	Non-hits identified	Weeding done

"COM CAT"
IS COMING!

COM CATALOG – THE OCR ROUTE

Lois E. Shumaker

Rather than deal in general advice on the various steps in the conversion process, such as writing specs, talking to vendors and other librarians, training staff and reviewing their work, I'm going to be very specific and zero in on how Sacramento Public Library managed to get through its conversion and come up with a COM catalog.

It is, quite frankly, a "how we did it good" approach. I'll try to point out some of the most glaring problems that faced us, and the solutions we chose to overcome them. No doubt some general principles for coping will emerge as I describe the process.

OCR Process

Before I begin, let me give a brief description of the OCR batch process. It consists of typing machine-readable information from a source document (the shelflist or catalog cards, or a combination), using an OCR (optical character recognition) typewriter element on a Selectric typewriter on special optical scanning paper. The information typed (generally, Library of Congress Card Numbers, LCCNs, or a combination of author-title-publisher-date) is called a search argument. This search argument is used to search a machine-readable database for titles which match your own. When matches are found, they are duplicated into your own database, and this eliminates the need to type all the information for your own titles. When matches are not found, however, you must type all the information, or all that is missing.

Why SPL Chose OCR

Michael Gorman, in a speech he gave on closing the catalog, described the card catalog as the single most embarrassing encumbrance to be found in the library; instead of a continuum of records interfiled over the years, it actually shows layers and layers of geological

strata. The strata represent both the various decisions made locally as well as the rule changes imposed by those who set cataloging standards.

Because SPL is an old library and has been through many organizational changes, the geological layers and atrocities are quite evident in the shelflist. They are excellent examples of the types of decisions which are constantly called for in the conversion process.

At SPL we had several reasons for going with the batch conversion process over other alternatives. The spectre of Proposition 13 was upon us, and we were pressed for time in terms of labor. We were preparing card printing masters for some 18,000 titles per year; preparing branch shelflists for Central, 26 branches, and Technical Services; and filing about 500,000 cards per year. We were also pressed for time in terms of money, as costs of card stock, printing, and catalog furniture were rising rapidly. We had revenue-sharing money set aside for half of the project, but we had to budget for the remainder. This money was for a one-time expense, with no prospect for ongoing special funds.

As we rapidly weighed the pros and cons of such a project, the advantages of conversion in general became apparent: 1) branch catalogs had never had subject cross reference cards made for them by Technical Services, and this would be remedied by a COM catalog; 2) branches had no union catalog — 1 FTE was scheduled in Technical Services at all times to answer the phone and give locations of books to branch staff; 3) we had no authority files; 4) we could stop handling all those catalog cards and devote more staff time to public service; 5) we could get a bibliographical database established that would stand us in good stead for whatever other changes the future would bring.

How We Did It

We started planning in 1975/76, appealed for grant money, which we failed to get, and finally, in 1977, had half of the necessary money. We decided to take the rest from our operating budget.

We made a quantum leap of faith; we simply decided to get started and plowed right in. We decided to close the card catalog, planned to quit making any cards for public catalogs one year in advance of the first anticipated full COM edition, and even quit making shelflist cards. Some branches mounted great weeding projects, and, needless to say, were heartily encouraged in this endeavor by Technical Services.

In arriving at budget estimates for the project, we had a great deal of help from vendors and from other librarians who had been through similar experiences. We asked countless questions of anyone who even sounded knowledgeable about COM catalogs. We found that some of the best and most recent information on projects such as this came from vendors, and they were the most willing to help. They spent a great deal of time patiently explaining their services to us, and thereby, in a sense, training us to evaluate their own services.

Keeping the Staff Informed

The FIRST STEP was to set up a staff COM Committee, comprised of staff from small branches and from large branches, some line and staff supervisors, and some administrative staff. The purpose of this committee was to help write specifications for the catalog, to invite its input to the project, and to encourage it to tell Technical Services of branch concerns for the catalog.

The welcome by-products of this committee were that the staff learned the need for and agreed to decisions which were quite difficult to make and not easy to live with once made. It also helped the staff know and explain the product to patrons. The latter was especially important at that time, because the catalog came to fruition just as Proposition 13 passed.

Throughout the planning process and early stages of implementation, I sent many memos to all staff outlining the progress and hang-ups in the project. Probably this committee, combined with the memos, was the single most important step in the training of staff and patrons. *Keeping the staff informed at all levels is the chief suggestion I would make to guarantee that the project will ultimately be acceptable to the public service staff and through them to the patrons.* Even with all the memos, meetings, and training, however, there were times when branches simply couldn't swallow one more inconvenience or catalog problem, and the calls and complaints would come in.

Specifications and Vendors

The SECOND STEP was to write "specs" and send out "RFPs." At that stage I had never even seen specs or heard the mystical letters "RFP." I was told that it was merely a matter of cutting and pasting.

So I started to accumulate material to cut and paste; I called vendors and other librarians and asked for sample specifications and RFPs. I began reading and gradually learned both some spec jargon and some desirable COM features. The cutting and pasting then began, and, finally, I came up with a preliminary draft.

Again, I called upon the vendors. We showed our draft to several vendors and got valuable advice. Also, we showed the draft to our

168

...ct:

_...ject: TEC Update

TEC is holding up well under the conversion project, a...
typing continues at a very steady pace. When you are at Franklin/...
hesitate to ask for an explanation of the procedures if
interested.

...d several inquir' ...out the recent use of blank
...g to minimiz **The decision to join** ...time spent in physical
we are r across the country which jobber paste in the
...ic j' the following: is on them, and
jackets is on

1. The growing cooperation among libraries, fc
systems, and planning for a national library
...r having bibliographical informat...
for~at. This will, in turn, le
national union catalogs which
More people will have
...are housed at greater dist
...ighter, fewer libraries
s but will still have a...

To: All Staff

From: Lois Shumaker, TEC

Subject: COM Catalog

Installation of the COM Catalogs is scheduled for mid-January. I have t...
anticipate questions you might have concerning it, and have given what ar'/ing.
I have. Don't hesitate to call if you have further questions, while remer...
that all the answers aren't in yet. I'll keep a list of your questions and...
distribute answers to everyone.

631, adult fiction

Lois Shumake...mber, and October rovides most of ou...
...nust, and Septembe card catalog i-
...1000 othercomputer
...late

1. WHAT IS ON THE FIRST FILM?

From the shelflist: Adult nonfiction thr... **Subject:**
through author O, juvenile fiction throug All is COM in TEC
Titles for which you have never had card:
adult review tables (titles which have b
juvenile review tables (titles which hav With the installation of COM in February, many question:
titles cataloged before July but for wh I did not anticipate in my Jan. 2 memo. Here are some o
another 4000 titles cataloged both befc of TEC's responses.
tables and which went to CEN only. Th

1. HOW DO WE TELL TEC ABOUT MISTAKES ON COM?

If the mistake pertains to a specific title, please n
2. WHAT ABOUT TITLES NOT YET ON COM? include the COM Accession no., and send to TEC. We will f.
along with all the 1170s you have been sending since July,
You should handle inquiries abo' tackle the project of keying in these corrections. Send th
Use your card catalog for older titl to tell us of mistakes in locations and copy nos., as well a
some 1977-78 imprints not on COM, a' errors, misspellings, duplicate entries for the same title,
will prevail. However, call TEC if If the error is one of filing, subject headings, or som
track it down. pertaining to a specific title, please call or send a note.
holding these messages is growing daily!

3. ARE THE BRANCH LOCATIONS AVAIL 2. WHAT ABOUT TITLES ON COM WHICH BRANCHES HAVE NOT RECEIVED?

Yes. For each title, the b' This happens because we catalog the book and send the inf
ARC 3 COO 4,5 RAN 6. This infor the computer just as the review table period is ending. Wher
multiple copies, if we have to try more than 1 book jobber r
order is cancelled, it means COM holds information on multi-
4. HOW ARE ENTRIES FILED? which we have not received. We are taking steps to elim
'tarting with the February table. However, the solution
The catalog is a dictionary 'ads to another: if we don't put the record into the
'ntries (main, title, subject 'oks have arrived, they show up on COM
'e. Titles which begin wit 'ore they could be on the shelves for
order. HERE ARE TITLES WHICH BEGIN WITH NUMERALS?
Titles which begin with numerals are *'
Titles which begin with a sm...
The distinction see...
age, but yo...l...

169

May 10, 1978

Sacramento City Council
c/o City Clerk, Room 203
City Hall, 915 I Street
Sacramento, California 95814

Dear Sir:

We are pleased to respond to your request for Proposal concerning
production of an automated catalog for Sacramento Public Library.
I believe that our demonstrated experience, proven technical competence
and financial strength make us uniquely well-qualified to provide SPL
with a superior level of service and we would enjoy the opportunity
to work closely with the Library to make its automated catalog an unqualified success.

May 5, 1978

City of Sacramento, California
Purchasing Division
City Clerk, Room 203, City Hall
Sacramento, CA 95814

Reference: Bid Number 067
COM CATALOG, EQUIPMENT AND SERVICES

Dear Sirs:

We are please to submit our quotation for the equipment section of the
above request for bids.

Purchasing Division
City of Sacramento
915 I Street
Sacramento, California 95814   tion Design manufact.
                                      publi
Gentlemen: nal which is currently

        Attached is our response to Bid No. 067 for COM Catalog,   he United States and
Equipment and Services for the Sacramento Public Library. Auto-
Graphics fully meets all the requirements as outlined in your re-
quest for bid.

        Undoubtedly, one of the concerns of the Sacramento Public
Library when selecting a vendor for their COM catalog project is
the capability of the vendor to handle large projects and t
all of the technical specifications. We believe
demonstrated its ability to do both. The S
network Catalog, containing approv:
exploded to Author, Title
demonstrate this

We are pleased to respond to your request for bid number 067, COM Catalogs for
the Sacramento Public Library.

Our proposal contains what we term "fully automatic heading edit and subject
authority control". This feature ensures a quality SPL database with little
or no editing effort on the part of the library staff. Without this feature,
each of the 220,000 records will have to be reviewed one-by-one by the staff
to be certain that the form and choice of entry is consistent in terms of syntax,
spelling, and authority and that the subject headings conform to the latest edition
of Library of Congress Subject Headings, 8th Edition. Each of the 18,000 new
records added per year will also require reviewing.

Since the LCSH/8 is constantly being revised and updated by LC, without the
benefit of heading edit and subject authority control, it would be necessary
for the staff to review 220,000+ records every time a new catalog is produced.
In the course of the first year alone, then, the staff would be required to
review 220,000+ titles six times. Stated differently, the staff would be requir
d to review 1,320,000+ records per year. This task includes the transmittal
thousands of edit instructions and output edit sheets and requires extensive
ling, and control. Bidders without automatic authority control simp'
into this untenable position while offering low prices. I
de computer service bureau type services and leave t'

                                              almost impossible process.
                                                   of price and qua
                                                   ed as the

purchasing agent, to the library administration, and to any other librarians I could con into reading and criticizing it. Another general guideline I could offer here is to *stay on good terms with all your colleagues, and don't hesitate to call upon them for help when you need it.*

We learned that specifications should not: 1) eliminate any vendor who can offer the basic product; 2) back the library into a corner by making the definitions of its needs too tight; 3) allow either the vendor or the library too much room for later changes because definitions were too vague.

One of our weaknesses in writing the specifications was failure to be aware of the need for evaluating the bids. Specifications should be written so it is easy to judge responses and so it is easy to explain the decisions. This is especially true if you have the freedom to decide on a vendor on a basis other than merely lowest price estimate. One should be able to explain the final choice to the losing vendors. I feel strongly that a vendor's failure to win a contract is not a reason for cutting off communications with him/her. You never know what will happen in the future, and staying on good terms with *all* vendors is the safest course.

Planning the Workflow

The THIRD STEP was planning the workflow. We started, of course, with the premise that all input would be done by OCR. We divided the input into two parallel processes: 1) backfile conversion and 2) ongoing input. We decided to use our own staff, as they were accustomed to our shelflist and teaching its interpretation would be unnecessary. We had a little additional help in the form of volunteers and CETA staff, but they were closely watched by our own typists. We made our own staff available to this project by freeing those formerly involved in catalog card production. We ceased all card production before input was started, and for several months branches had no catalog cards for new books. This is where that staff COM committee came in handy for selling difficult and unpopular decisions. For the backfile conversion portion of the project, we spent nine months typing. We had 11 typewriters, and approximately 17 people who could type.

We first determined that the shelflist would serve as our source document, as the COM was to be a union catalog showing copy numbers as well as branch holdings. With the help of the vendor, we decided what to type as search arguments: LCCN, if present, and author-title-publisher-date, if not. We also typed the call numbers, branch codes, and copy numbers for each title. We estimated our shelflist to hold about 220,000 titles.

171

Next, we picked out as many variations in our shelflist as possible, to identify all potential problems and decide what to do about them. For example:

a) city and county cards showed duplicate copy numbers — we typed as is. (SPL consists of two administratively merged but legally separate libraries: city and county, each consisting of several branches.)

b) new and old branch names — we changed all to the newer 3-letter codes.

c) information was on both fronts and backs of cards — typists were reminded to check the versos.

d) the same title sometimes turned up in 2 different class numbers (the city/county thing again) — we typed them as we came upon them.

e) many titles were older than 1968 (no MARC tapes were available) — we automatically typed author-title-publisher-date.

f) questionable cataloging practices loomed from the past (as when many editions of the same title were simply added to the present holdings on the existing shelflist card) — we typed them as they appeared.

g) many post-1968 titles had LCCNs, but many were without — we used author-title-publisher-date.

h) if only a county branch held a title, there was probably no Cutter number. To guarantee proper machine filing of the shelflist, we provided it.

i) biographies had various classification symbols: L (for life), B with Cutter, B with name of biographee — we changed all to the last version. This, of course, meant branches had either to be aware of this apparent discrepancy or change all of their books with the old class symbols.

j) due to space problems, Central's copy of a title might have been put in a storage area known as the Inactive Collection — we invented the new branch name INA.

When conversion typing started, this handout was prepared to help branches explain the fact that new books were not represented by cards in the catalog.

A "PAWS" IN SERVICE

In early 1979, all libraries in Sacramento City and County will change from the use of the card catalog to a new computerized catalog, henceforth known as "COM CAT." The new catalog will list all the titles owned by the Sacramento Public Library and in which branches they are located. Library patrons will have the advantage, with the new system, of immediate access to the location of the title in which they are interested.

Preparation for the changeover to the new catalog will result in the following short-term changes in service to the patron:

1. Catalog cards for books with 1977 or 1978 publication dates will no longer be available in the card catalog.

2. Library staff will be unable to accommodate library patron requests to determine which branch, other than their own, holds a particular title or to accept patron requests to borrow books published in 1977 or 1978 from other branches.

Plans for this changeover were developed in 1976. The temporary curtailment of these services is NOT related to the passage of Proposition 13. Full catalog service will again become available to you in early 1979.

The library staff asks for your patience and understanding during this period as we prepare for the new catalog which will be more helpful than ever.

"COM CAT" FACTS

Over 100 libraries and library systems across the country are converting to computerized catalogs based on the growing cooperation among libraries in planning for a national library information network. As a result, library patrons will have increased access to a far greater number of materials and fewer libraries will need to duplicate their holdings due to the access they will obtain to the holdings of neighboring libraries and library systems.

Funding for the Sacramento Public Library computerized catalog consists of combined Federal Revenue Sharing funds and savings realized in the library department in fiscal year 1977-78. Special arrangements have been made to hold the funds for use in 1979. The ongoing costs of the computerized catalog are comparable to those previously budgeted annually for the cards, card cabinets and manpower for the operation of the traditional card catalog.

The computerized catalog will offer taxpayers increased service and efficiency WITHOUT increased dollar spending.

IT PAYS TO USE YOUR PUBLIC LIBRARY!

SACRAMENTO PUBLIC LIBRARY

Shelflist cards

/ Potential| problems, examples a-e

q641.5 Beck, Simone.
 B393   Mastering the art of French cooking, by
       Simone Beck, Louisette Bertholle and Julia
       Child. New York, Knopf, 1961-
          v. illus. 26 cm.

       1-ff, v. 1 10.00   6-ch
       2-rio x72   7-carm
       3-carm   8-arc
re: 4-rc   9-fq
q641.5 5-sg   1-carm v. 2 12.50
 C536   1. Cookery, French. I. Bertholle, Louisette.
author: II. Child, Julia. III. Title. **(Over)**
Child

q641.5 Beck, Simone.
 B393   Mastering the art of French cooking, by
       Simone Beck, Louisette Bertholle and Julia
       Child. New York, Knopf, 1961-
          v. illus. 26 cm.

       1-main v. 1 10.00 6-ml v. 1 10.00 k72
       2-op   7-mlk
       3-mck   1-main v. 2 12.50 76
re: 4-ekm   2-ekm
q641.5 5-tb Tka   3-mg
 C536   1. Cookery, French. I. Bertholle, Louisette.
author: II. Child, Julia. III. Title. (Over)
Child

Shelflist card

Potential problems, example f

CARD 2

```
*
  IA   Brontë, Charlotte, 1816-1855
         Jane Eyre; illustrations by Helen
       Sewell.   Oxford Univ. Press [1938]


  c.19 May 64 Random 2.19FO          c.30 Aug 66 Gift
  c.20   (1950, Modern Lib.)cp+as       (1962,Macm,,
  c.21 Anc                               il.by A.For-
  c.22 ARD *                             berg)  Rio
  c.23 Go
  c.24 Nov 64 F.F. 1.55 Frt           31-isl(Dodd-3.95)
  c.25 (1963, New American            32-earm (Macmillan
  c.26FP            Library)                     4.94)
  c.27SH                              33-fol    "    "
  c.28FL                 )            34-ard×7=3.95
  c.29                                35-or  ×76
```

```
                  CEN
  58- 85 (Signet 1.55)                74-ns  (Signet 1.68
  59- mc    "     "          (  )     IA 75-mlk (Dodd,Mead4.50
  60- mg    "     "                    76-mlk
  61- h (World, c1946   2.50)          77-mlk
  62-CEN (Heritage Press 2.50)75       78-mlk
  63-CEN(Dodd, Mead ; 3.95)75          79-mlk
  64-ekm    "     "     "              80-mlk
  65-    (q Watts 7.95 LT)             81-mlk (World, 2.88)
  66- CEN (Harcourt, Brace 3.95)75     82-mlk
  67- CEN    "        "                83-op
  68-ns (Macmillan 4.94) L10/69
  69-tb (Dodd, Mead 3.95) ssc
  70-dp (Signet) 1.68
  71-ekm    "     "
  72-mck    "
  73-mck    "
```

Crispi, Francesco
Crispi, Francesco   172054
Memoirs ... translated by Mary Prichard-
Agnetti, from the documents collected and
edited by Thomas Palamenghi-Crispi. 1912.
3.v. (Library has v.1-2)

33 '35 '38 *56 6 MAIN
'35 8 *56 6 2MAIN

172056
B
Crocker, Aimee (Princess Galitzine)
And I'd do it again.   New York, Coward
McCann, 1936.
291p. front.,plates,ports. 22cm. 3.00

*106959 AND Ch r m .

172058   shelf list a-t
CROCKETT, DAVID, 1786-1836.

B   Crockett, David, 1786-1836.
Crockett A narrative of the life of David Crockett
1973   of the State of Tennessee. A facsim. ed. with
        annotations and an introd. by James A. Shack-
        ford and Stanley J. Folmsbee. Knoxville,
        University of Tennessee Press [1973, c1834]
        xx, 211 p. illus. 20 x 22 cm. (Tennes-
        seana editions)
        Original ed. published by E. L. Carey and
        A. Hart, Philadelphia.

                            (Continued on next card)
                            MAR 19 1976
                            (over)

176

k) city branches once used accession numbers on books instead of copy numbers. If the only copy was at Central, we changed the number to 1; if there were additional copies, we used the accession numbers. This practice has subsequently caused confusion among those librarians who have been with us long enough to remember when the accession number was indeed used instead of a copy number and not, as now, used as a record identification in the database.

The Retrospective Inputting Begins

Finally, we started the actual conversion input typing. Again, there were several steps.

FIRST, there was the assigning of a number to each title. This number was a Source Document Number (SDNO), which served as the identification number of the source document throughout the input process until the computer successfully added the record to the database and assigned it a new number, called the Accession Number (ACCN). We used a Bates stamper for this. Finding that these machines cost $90 each, we bought 2, only to find that we needed several people to stamp shelflist cards in order to stay ahead of the typists. Someone remembered the old accession number practice and scouted city branches for some of the old stamping machines. Five were found, but they had only 5 digits rather than the required 8. Since we pre-assigned blocks of 8-digit numbers to shelflist drawers, and the drawers held only 1,000 or so cards, it was easy to supply the first 3 digits mentally as the cards were typed. It was another thing for the typists to remember, however. We wrote detailed instructions for this number stamping task and set to it, adding Cutter numbers to "County only" titles and updating the biography classifications. We also tried to make any other corrections to the cards that would make the typing easier.

Having found that we needed to pre-assign blocks of SDNOs to shelflist drawers in order to accommodate several stampers at once, we also found it to be useful so that typing need not be done in shelflist order. This became a concern as we began to realize that the first edition of the COM catalog would be incomplete, since we would have input only adult nonfiction titles. We quickly redrew some plans and shifted typing to some fiction and juvenile drawers so that a portion of everything would show up on the first catalog. As we finished stamping cards in each drawer, we put a sticker on the outside showing the inclusive numbers.

11-7-78 Machineno.5 Dobbins

SDNO, **Backfile Conversion**

ℐℐ30285043

ⱯO10 76-029915 Ⱨ930 fic Ⱨ940 cen1hag2kin3mcc4mck5nsa6car7arc8ard9elk10fai
Ɏ11nhi12ran14rio15sou16syl17 > call numbers

ℐℐ30285044

ⱯO10 72-305715 Ⱨ930 S611·018 L581 1972 Ⱨ940 cen1cou2 > branches and copy numbers

ℐℐ30285045 reg numbers

ⱯO10 77-007340 Ⱨ930 574·8732 P853 1977 Ⱨ940 cen1

ℐℐ30285046 > LC card numbers

ⱯO10 76-008378 Ⱨ930 q625·19 L668 1974 Ⱨ940 cen1

ℐℐ30285047

ⱯO10 77-008008 Ⱨ930 q738 C411 1977 Ⱨ940 art1ran2

ℐℐ30285048

ⱯO10 77-376446 Ⱨ930 q738·3 B879 1977 Ⱨ940 art1

ℐℐ30285049

ⱯO10 76-046053 Ⱨ930 618·92 N565 1977 Ⱨ940 cen1kin2car3arc4ard5elk6fai7fol8
Ɏnhi9ran10rio11sou12syl13

ℐℐ30285050 ← correction - record crossed off

Ⱨ100 Martin, David Ⱨ245 The cremony of innocence Ⱨ260 Secker & Warburg
Ⱨ262 1977 Ⱨ930 fic Ⱨ940 cen1

ℐℐ30285051 author-title-publisher-date

Ⱨ100 Sagan, Françoise Ⱨ245 A certain smile Ⱨ250 1st ed· Ⱨ260 J· Murray
Ⱨ262 1956 Ⱨ930 fic Ⱨ940 cen1

ℐℐ30285052

ⱯO10 76-007742 Ⱨ930 618·86 D687 1977 Ⱨ940 cen1,2

ℐℐ30285053

ⱯO10 77-072282 Ⱨ930 q259 4 C43536 1977 Ⱨ940 art1

The SECOND STEP in the typing process was actually typing. We got a procedures manual from the vendor and copied parts of it for each typist, paraphrasing, amending, and giving examples when we could. The typists started out, learning the necessary fields with their tag numbers. We proofread each scan sheet, correcting it if necessary, and mailed the sheets to the vendor on a weekly basis. As the typing of each shelflist drawer was completed, we put a new sticker on the front indicating that it was closed and that no further changes to the shelflist cards could be made. This caused some consternation, as the shelflist card has always been considered the sacrosanct record of library holdings. Its obsolescence was a bit of a shock.

During the course of the typing process, various situations necessitated new decisions. The very fact that the shelflist had always been considered the master record of the collection meant that new procedures had to be devised for recording holdings changes. When the last copy of a title was lost after the card was stamped, but before it was typed, we crossed through the number and the card but left it filed in place to preserve the numbering sequence. To record holdings changes which occurred after a card was typed, we designed a new form and started a new file to hold these forms, thereby collecting changes to be made in the catalog long before the catalog even appeared. All such changes, of course, would be input via OCR typing. It soon became evident that a COM catalog which showed holdings would always be out of date.

Administratively, one of the hardest steps in this whole process was mailing a week's scan sheets to the vendor. It was as if they were sent into a black hole, and the time lag between mailing and seeing any results was cause for much frustration. The vendor returned all scan sheets after they were scanned, and, for some mysterious reason, I kept them all. This turned out to be fortunate, because several times I had to return batches of scan sheets for re-scanning, as gaps in the catalog were discovered.

The Inputting of Current Items

Now to the other portion of the project — the ongoing input of new acquisitions. For the most part, this was a simpler process, with fewer on-the-spot decisions necessary.

Again, we typed search arguments (almost always the LCCNs) on scan sheets and sent them to the vendor, identified by SDNOs. This time the search arguments were for searching for new title records on MARC tapes held by the vendor, and the SDNOs were devised according to date. We could keep track of all search arguments sent and cross them off our lists as the MARC records were located and print-

Search arguments for ongoing input of new acquisitions

~~9-28-79 Machine No. 1~~ Kato

~~****~~51   *MARC search*

79390001 POLEACTIVWFAB9   *arguments*

79390002 78-004416

79390003 77-027592

79390004 78-018908   ← *LC card number*

79390005 MONTBEDTI***H8

79390006 POLEBOOK*EOTB9

79390007 78-025600   ← *Author-title algorithm*

79390008 78-059155

79390009 77-088638

79390010 78-031100

79390011 78-069869

79390012 78-005031

79390013 78-009685

79390014 77-024135

79390015 78-007879

79390016 78-005289

79390017 78-005920

79390018 78-004574

79390019 78-009053

79390020 78-009842

79390021 78-007251

79390022 78-008710

79390023 79-050114

79390024 78-010156

79390025 78-010135

180

Printout of new titles found on MARC tape

```
MARC HIT
SACRAMENTO PUBLIC LIBRAPROOF LIST   DATE 80110                          PAGE 0120
ACCNO   00010375**
SDNO.1  78280709
010.1   76-016723
020.1   0671224395 :
082.1   332.6/78
100.1   Sargent, David R.
245.1   Stock market profits and higher income for you /
247.1   by David R. Sargent.
250.1   Rev. and updated ed.
259.1   New York :
260.1   Simon and Schuster,
262.1   c1976.
300.1   285 p. : Sb graphs ;
301.1   25 cm.
500.1   Includes index.
650.1   Investments.
```

181

Edit sheet used as catalog work sheet

```
ACCNC  00012485**
SDNC.I  76310002
01C.1  77-011542
02C.1  C0o0107278 :
C82.1  813/.5/4
10C.1  Chayefsky, Paddy,
131.1  1923-
245.1  The -experiment : Altered states
246.1  a novel /
247.1  by Paddy Chavevsky.
25C.1  1st U.S. ed.
259.1  New York :
26C.1  Harper & Row,
262.1  c1978.
30C.1  p. cm.
```

n?30 fic   Additions + changes
                               to MARC

n?40 cen 1,2 coo 3 Kin 4 car 5 arc 6 fai 7

      ran 8 cou 9 cyl 10 rev 11,12,13,14

      8.45

+R   E245 = Altered states :

+R   E250 = 1st ed.

+R   E300 = 184 p. ;

+A   E301 = 22 cm.

8-22-78 RR.

182

OCR typing showing local changes/additions to MARC record now in the library's database

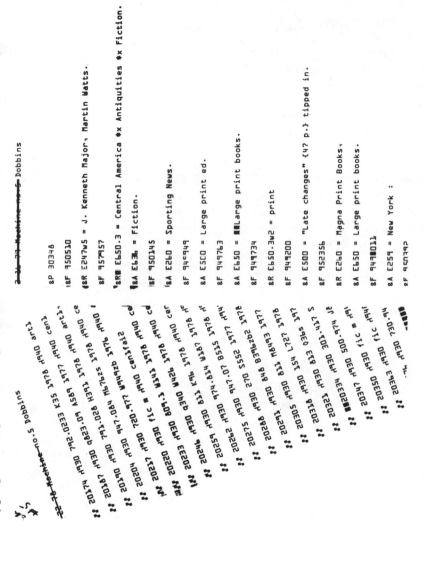

183

outs were mailed back to us.

We used these printouts, or edit sheets, as catalog work sheets, indicated any changes and/or additions on them, and sent them to the typists for more OCR typing. Again, the scan sheets were mailed to the vendor, and again, the frustrations of batch processing were painful.

The Project Director

During the course of the entire project, we felt that the successful completion of the backfile conversions and the smooth ongoing input operation was due in large part to our project supervisor. He is our chief cataloger, has good rapport with the staff, is patient and tolerant at training and supervising, and comprehends how data is handled by a computer. He is also able to solve the day-to-day problems independently.

I made all contacts with the vendor, so the two of us knew all steps in the process, and we could discuss any larger problems as they arose. It turned out to be a very good division of labor. Another guideline can be stated here: *have a project director who not only understands the data processing principles involved, but also the people problems involved.*

Editing at the End of the Project

The THIRD AND ONGOING STEP in the conversion to COM process is the cleanup of problems — which become apparent immediately upon receipt of the first COM output. Some typical examples:

1) incomplete records due to incomplete input, no matches, or poor matches on the vendor's database. Any missing fields must be OCR-typed and sent to the vendor.

2) missing records. The vendor provided lists of SDNOs missing in sequence, and they had to be matched with the shelflist cards. Unfortunately for us, many were missing in the fiction area — between George Orwell and Jean Plaidy — not a popular problem with the public service staff. This is when I was happy not to have thrown out the returned scan sheets, as I could identify those missing SDNOs and return the scan sheets for re-processing.

3) Wrong hits because of duplicate assignments of LCCNs. This evidently happened some years ago when the same block of

LC card numbers was given both to various American publishers and to some Indian publishers. For us, the matching process using these LCCNs resulted in the appearance in our COM catalog of several titles dealing with agricultural problems in Calcutta, with juvenile call numbers, mainly in the JE, or picture book, area.

4) unwanted data from another database. Our vendor used another library's database for searching some of our titles, and the matches held information input by the other library but not necessarily wanted by us.

A word of caution could serve as another general guideline here: the origin of data to be adopted for your catalog should be thoroughly checked out for its acceptability to you for your specific use. One library's catalog needs can be quite different from another library's needs.

The FOURTH AND ONGOING step in the project is the constant assessing of the catalog and the constant correcting of errors and upgrading of standards. A comparison of our second COM edition with our sixth, 2 years later, shows not only cleanup of the data, but also format changes designed to save film space and be more legible on the screen. We have also added subject cross references and name cross references.

In conclusion, I would say that we have found our COM catalog to be basically satisfactory. We have many of the same kinds of problems as we had with cards — standards, authority lists, class numbers suggested by LC and despaired of by public service staff. But a new, more versatile catalog has emerged. It is machine-readable, useful for other products, easier to change, easier to duplicate, and complete on a roll of film. We are now more ready for a circulation system, an online catalog, and for any cooperative efforts to share catalog databases among libraries.

Technical Services is now more or less back to normal. Given the same choices, the same timing, and the same financial picture, we probably would do it again.

"COM CAT" IS HERE!

HELPFUL HINTS

FOR SURVIVING YOUR

COM CATALOG

1. Talk to as many vendors and COM-using libraries as possible. Get as many examples of output as possible, from specifications right through to COM film itself. Learn about vendors' normal procedures and output before deciding what changes in the library's procedures to make or to resist. Collect as much information as possible so that decisions and changes can be carefully considered, but be prepared for the need to rethink and change again, perhaps many times. Be flexible.

2. Involve as many staff as possible in the planning process, and keep everyone informed of progress throughout the project. Emphasize to public service staff the advantages the COM will offer over cards, but prepare them for the inadequacies of the first few COM editions.

3. Assign a project supervisor. Keep this person involved in all decisions so staff questions can be answered promptly. Keep him/her available to staff throughout the implementation of the COM Catalog.

4. Don't promise anything to staff or patrons for a specific date. No matter how liberally you plan a timeline, there will be unforeseen holdups. Holdups may originate anywhere at any stage of the project — with the vendor, with government or library bureaucracy, with your own staff. Be flexible.

5. Don't emphasize to patrons the computer connection with the COM catalog. The public will tend to identify it with many other computerized services which make them feel depersonalized. Public service staff should feel free to explain to patrons that COM is merely microfilm, and that it simply repeats exactly the same information which they formerly found on cards.

6. Plan the stationing of COM readers so they are in view of public service staff, and emphasize the necessity for simple routine maintenance on the readers.

7. Stay as upbeat as possible with all staff. When despair sets in, try to confine it to a few supervisory staff who can help you get over the hump. Avoid contact with pathological perfectionists. Be flexible.

AUTOMATION IN MISSISSIPPI PUBLIC LIBRARIES

David M. Woodburn
and
Gerald Buchanan

Introduction

Mississippi has not been an innovator in automation of public libraries. The absence of innovation in automation does not connote absence of interest but does acknowledge the pressing needs and political realities that dictated other priorities.

In the 1950s, we ensured that public library service was available to people in every one of our 82 counties. In the 1960s, we supplemented local book collections by providing long-term loans from the state agency, by establishing a telephone/telegraph interlibrary loan network, and by beginning centralized cataloging and processing for public libraries lacking professionally trained staff.

Our innovative efforts in the 1970s were concentrated on constructing or renovating library buildings and on assuring professional staff for the public libraries of the state. Using more than $20 million in state revenue sharing and local funds, we have since built, expanded, or renovated public library buildings in 86 cities and towns.

Our entirely state-funded personnel grants program puts more than $1.5 million annually into salaries for public librarians across Mississippi. In operation since 1972, this program has given us the professional expertise essential to building a resource-sharing network across our state.

Early Automation Projects

In automation we chose to benefit from the developmental efforts of other states rather than to experiment with our own fugitive dollars.

We were, however, not entirely idle. In the decade of the 1970s, we:

1. Published the first and second editions of *Mississippiana: A Union Catalog*, prepared under a state-funded grant by

Mississippi State University and produced by Science Press.

2. Produced the first and second editions of the *Mississippi Union List of Periodicals*, both funded by LSCA grants, the first to the Gulfport-Harrison County Library and the second to the Mississippi Research and Development Center. Both editions used the facilities of the state Central Data Processing Center.

3. Began a continuing monthly keyword-in-context index to state publications, with annual and five-year cumulations.

4. Adapted the Baker and Taylor Automated Buying System (BATAB) to our needs as a centralized processing center serving public, state agency, and state institution libraries. BATAB has served us well since 1975.

5. Studied carefully the merits of both SOLINET/OCLC and the Washington Library Network as vehicles to meet the needs of a Mississippi resource-sharing network.

SOLINET/OCLC Membership

In this same decade, the three largest state universities became SOLINET/OCLC members. In 1979, the Mississippi Library Commission took its first giant step in automation by also going online with SOLINET/OCLC. We chose this route because of:

1. Existing membership by Mississippi universities.

2. Expected membership by other Mississippi academic, special, and large public libraries.

3. Access to a rapidly growing regional and national data base for both cataloging and interlibrary loan — the latter being considered essential to Mississippi libraries of every type and size.

At the time of the decision to join SOLINET/OCLC, we also recognized that a minuscule number of Mississippi public libraries could ever afford the annual costs of SOLINET/OCLC membership for themselves.

Our one unchanging goal in Mississippi has been to make the total library resources of our state easily and freely available to the total population of the state. With this goal in mind, we began exploring ways in which patrons in even the smallest of libraries could benefit from library automation at the state level.

Retrospective Conversion

This exploration led to the second significant automation decision: to convert the adult non-fiction holdings of the Library Commission itself to machine-readable form. To do so, within the constraints of staff time and the remaining budget year, we chose to use short entry optical character recognition input as the method and Auto-Graphics, Inc. as the vendor. In 3 months our staff and Auto-Graphics prepared OCR input for 110,250 records. Auto-Graphics matched these against MARC Tapes, gave us 53% hits and 47% short entries (author and title only), and produced a divided computer-output microfiche catalog, which we distributed to all except school libraries.

The decision to use this type of conversion had long-range implications. It was much faster and also less expensive than OCLC conversion. The major long-range implication, however, was that SOLINET/OCLC would not accept tape input from this conversion, even for the MARC hits. The result was that, for the first time, the Mississippi library community had real access to the MLC collection through our long-standing interlibrary loan network, but that the data was split into retrospective holdings via Auto-Graphics and current acquisitions via SOLINET/OCLC.

Partial Union Catalog

The next year, 1980, we used the SOLINET/OCLC archival tapes from the centralized processing center libraries to update the original Auto-Graphics conversion. We also merged the SOLINET/OCLC archival tape from the Jackson Metropolitan Library System. We thus produced the first partial union catalog, which:

1. Was on computer-output microfiche.

2. Was distributed free to nearly 300 public, academic, and special libraries.

3. Cost $66 per copy.

4. Was divided into author, title, and subject sections.

5. Contained full bibliographic information at each entry.

6. Listed holdings only at the main entry.

191

Updating has been easy — as long as we update via SOLINET/OCLC archival tapes. ORC update proved to create more problems than it solved. We did experience some difficulty in replacing short entries (no-hits) from the original conversion.

The catalog had three major faults: (1) it was issued annually and already several months out of date when issued; (2) no substantive procedure for correcting entries from other contributing libraries was in place (deletion of entries and holdings was difficult); and (3) holdings were shown at only one location, thus creating additional searching for the user.

The 1981 edition was essentially the same as the 1980 edition, except that partial holdings of the First Regional Library were added via a conversion already under way for them by the General Research Corporation. The First Regional Library is, with over 100,000 titles, the second largest public library in total holdings. Auto-Graphics also did a partial retrospective conversion of the Jackson Metropolitan Library System shelf list.

The 1982 edition of the union catalog added a conversion by Auto-Graphics of the Columbus-Lowndes County Library System, which has more than 30,000 titles. We also made the catalog easier to use. We displayed holdings at every author, title, and subject entry, but not at joint author and similar added entries. We also grouped libraries by type and geographic location to facilitate borrowing from the nearest library.

As we evaluated the 1982 catalog and planned for the 1983 edition, we considered these factors:

1. The catalog is drawn from a variety of conversion sources.

2. Other than the Library Commission itself, the catalog includes one large public library in the center of the state, one fairly large public library in the northwestern corner, and one medium-sized public library in the northeast quarter of the state. All other entries and holdings are from small public libraries which purchase fewer than 2,000 titles per year — and the rate of duplication is high in these small libraries. No academic libraries are included.

3. The catalog is still published only once a year and is out-of-date at the time of issue.

4. The Jackson Metropolitan Library System has borne the brunt of heavy interlibrary loan traffic, lending far more than it borrows.

5. State budget cuts of about $100,000 forced cessation of centralized processing, thus making unavailable holdings data from the more than 20 small public libraries.

6. Our automation efforts are irrevocably linked with interlibrary loan networking. Automation is a way to make more library resources available to greater numbers of people and has been specifically intended to include non-SOLINET/OCLC libraries.

Our problem for 1983, then, was to find a way to extend the data base both in number of titles and geographic coverage and to improve the interlibrary loan network.

Online Network for Retrospective Conversion

Our solution was to create a tiered, or layered, network based both on SOLINET/OCLC and on the union catalog data base created through Auto-Graphics. To do this, we chose to use AGILE II, the online system created by Auto-Graphics.

Our choice was based on these factors:

1. We were pleased with the results and working relationship since 1979 with the Auto-Graphics staff, particularly our sales representative, Peter Adler, who has helped to solve many a problem.

2. AGILE is the only online system that easily handles input from a variety of sources, both OCLC and non-OCLC.

3. Two site visits to the AGILE installation at the Birmingham (Alabama) Public Library and talks there with George Stewart and Norfleet Day enabled us to evaluate the system in action.

In contrast to OCLC, AGILE maintains separate data bases for the MARC Tapes and for each of its customers. All customers, however, have access to all data bases. The terminal operator sets up a search path which determines which, how many, and in what order the data bases are to be searched. These are searched sequentially until the desired title is found. It is quite simple to add an entry from the MARC Tapes or from another library's data base to your own data base.

Charges are also different from OCLC. Instead of first time use, display holdings, or other use charges on OCLC, AGILE charges are based on the number of titles stored. The current annual charge is 5 cents per title. SOLINET's LAMBDA is around 20 cents per title.

AGILE also has electronic mail capability, an interlibrary loan module, and keyword title searching. It will soon have the capability of printing cards locally.

Our next step was to select sites for AGILE installations for continued retrospective conversion. The critical factors were size of collection and geographic location. Host libraries selected were the Gulfport-Harrison County Library, the Tombigbee Regional Library, and the Washington County Library System. The Jackson-George Regional Library and the Judge George W. Amstrong Library were clustered with Gulfport-Harrison County. The Columbus-Lowndes County Library, the Bolivar County Library, and the Sunflower County Library were clustered with Tombigbee Regional. With the other libraries that were already contributing to the data base, we now have at least one primary public library in virtually every area of the state. (See map.)

Offline Libraries

Every other public library in the state contributes to the union catalog through its current acquisitions from Baker & Taylor. For 15 cents per title, Baker & Taylor provides a MARC record for each library. These records are merged annually by Auto-Graphics into the union catalog data base. Deletions, corrections, and other clean-up work are being handled online at the Library Commission itself. The 1983 union catalog is expected to have about 350,000 titles.

Network Access

The network we have developed is both layered and somewhat decentralized. (See chart.) It emphasizes use of local, sectional, and state sources before use of regional and national sources.

The general public has access through microfiche catalogs in most branch libraries and in all public library headquarters units. College students and faculty have access through microfiche catalogs in all academic libraries. Employees in agencies which have special libraries have access through microfiche catalogs in their libraries. School libraries have access through local public libraries.

Requests for titles owned by the Library Commission come directly to us by regularly scheduled telephone calls or by mail, since we are geared to handle a large volume of daily interlibrary loan. Requests for titles not owned by the Library Commission go directly to the nearest owning library.

Requests for titles not listed in the microfiche union catalog come to the Library Commission, are searched on AGILE and SOLINET/OCLC, and, if a state location is identified, are forwarded to that library for direct loan to the requesting library. If only out-of-state locations are identified, the locations are sent to the requesting library, which then uses printed interlibrary loan forms to request the book. If budget permits, we hope to begin third-party out-of-state interlibrary loans through SOLINET/OCLC to shorten time and lessen paperwork.

AGILE Costs and Problems

Costs of the AGILE online project currently underway include;

Personnel — 11 FTE	$ 59,301
Terminal charges (6 terminals, 3 sites)	95,480
Supplies, equipment, etc.	22,228
Total:	$177,009

At the present rate of conversion, each record will cost about 74 cents.

We have experienced the same problems that we did with SOLINET/OCLC: excessive downtime and slow response time. Downtime during the first few months was near 25 percent, and, unlike OCLC, increased our per title cost alarmingly. According to Auto-Graphics, the problem was in the quality of telephone lines to Mississippi. Auto-Graphics installed new line-monitoring equipment, and the problem has been partially resolved. The cause of slow response time was that Auto-Graphics was running batch projects on the computer during AGILE operating hours. Our sales representative was able to resolve this problem with the company president. Dealing with a private vendor has enabled us to solve problems much more quickly than with SOLINET/OCLC.

Further Networking

Because the online conversion project ended on September 30, we now have additional critical decisions to make about the future of the Mississippi network. We have a data base of 1/3 million titles with the potential for online interlibrary loan, cataloging, and electronic mail. We also have the option of more frequent updates from SOLINET/OCLC and Baker & Taylor tapes.

Our desire is to continue online service. To do this, we are asking public libraries to assume part of the costs. For the next fiscal year we are offering grants of one-half the cost (up to $10,000 each) to the three current host libraries. We will also fund demonstration projects for dial-up terminals in five other libraries. We would then have 8 of the 43 administrative units online next year.

Conclusion

Our feeling is one of pride in what we have been able to accomplish in Mississippi. It is, also, one of satisfaction, both with the system and with the vendor. Perhaps, more than anything else, it is a feeling of optimism that the automation configuration we have selected will, in reality, provide faster and better library services to our people.

Entries from Mississippi Union Catalog

Examples

Full Entry

Author

FRANKEL, LAWRENCE J.
    Be alive as long as you live: the older person's complete guide to
exercise for joyful living / by Lawrence Frankel and Betty Byrd Richard.
1st ed. New York: Lippincott & Crowell, c1980. 239 p.: ill.
ISBN:0690018924 [80-010384] (00059601)
    Includes index.
    Bibliography: p. 227-236.
    1. Aged--Health and hygiene. 2. Exercise for the aged.
I. Richard, Betty Byrd, joint author. II. Title
        MLC: MLC-613.71024 F829 1980
        SY: BOL-613.71024 F829 1980   FI-613.71 Fra
        TW: OKT-613.71024 F829 1980
        EW: JX-613.71 F829b   MAD-613.71024 F829 1980
                    NES-613.71024 F829 1980
        JS: HAN-613.71024 F829 1980
        RW: PA-613.71024 F829 1980

Author main entries are generally in
boldface type.

Note differences in call numbers of
holding libraries.

Title

Be alive as long as you live.
    Frankel, Lawrence J.
        Be alive as long as you live: the older person's
    complete guide to exercise for joyful living by Lawrence
    Frankel and Betty Byrd Richard. 1st ed. New York:
    Lippincott & Crowell, c1980. [80-010384]
        MLC: MLC-613.71024 F829 1980
        SY: BOL-613.71024 F829 1980   FI-613.71 Fra
        TW: OKT-613.71024 F829 1980
        EW: JX-613.71 F829b   MAD-613.71024 F829 1980
                    NES-613.71024 F829 1980
        JS: HAN-613.71024 F829 1980
        RW: PA-613.71024 F829 1980

No tracings are given at the title
entry.

Holding codes appear at author, title
and subject entries.

Subject

AGED--HEALTH AND HYGIENE.
    Frankel, Lawrence J.
        Be alive as long as you live: the older person's
    complete guide to exercise for joyful living by Lawrence
    Frankel and Betty Byrd Richard. 1st ed. New York:
    Lippincott & Crowell, c1980. [80-010384]
        1. Exercise for the aged.
        MLC: MLC-613.71024 F829 1980
        SY: BOL-613.71024 F829 1980   FI-613.71 Fra
        TW: OKT-613.71024 F829 1980
        EW: JX-613.71 F829b   MAD-613.71024 F829 1980
                    NES-613.71024 F829 1980
        JS: HAN-613.71024 F829 1980
        RW: PA-613.71024 F829 1980

Added Entry

Richard, Betty Byrd, joint author.
    Frankel, Lawrence J.
        Be alive as long as you live: the older person's
    complete guide to exercise for joyful living by Lawrence
    Frankel and Betty Byrd Richard. 1st ed. New York:
    Lippincott & Crowell, c1980. [80-010384]

No holdings codes are listed for
added entries.

197

Short Entry

Author

DAY, GERALD WILLIAM LANGSTON
New worlds beyond the atom (00136615)
I. Title.
MLC: MLC-501 D

With short entries, there are no tracings or imprint information.

Title

New worlds beyond the atom.
Day, Gerald William Langston
New worlds beyond the atom
MLC: MLC-501 D

Mississippi's Automated Union Catalog

July 1983

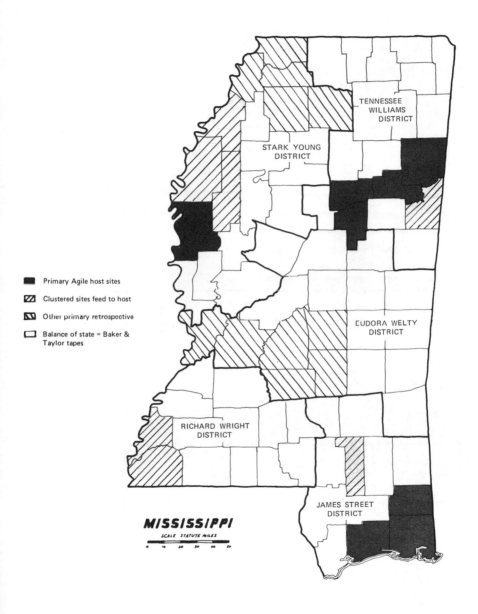

Primary Agile host sites

Clustered sites feed to host

Other primary retrospective

Balance of state = Baker & Taylor tapes

TENNESSEE WILLIAMS DISTRICT

STARK YOUNG DISTRICT

EUDORA WELTY DISTRICT

RICHARD WRIGHT DISTRICT

JAMES STREET DISTRICT

MISSISSIPPI

SCALE STATUTE MILES

0   10   20   30   40   50

Mississippi's Layered Interlibrary Loan Network

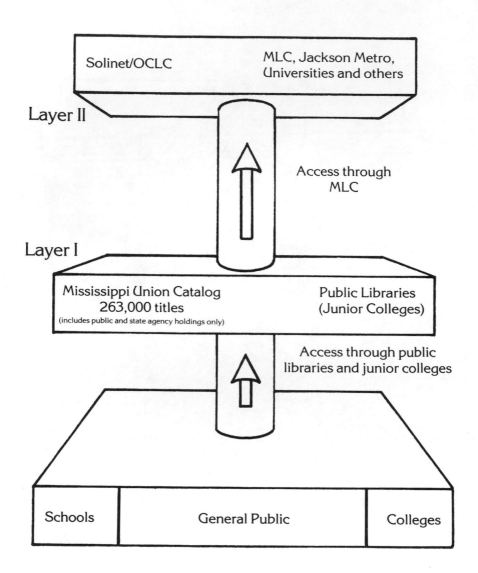

CORAL CONVERSION AND RESOURCE ENHANCEMENT PROJECT

Ruby E. Miller

The Council of Research and Academic Libraries (CORAL), a consortium of twenty-eight libraries in the San Antonio area, received a grant to convert an estimated 40,000 records from the special collections of seven of its member libraries. The grant was entitled "Monographic Resource Assessment and Union List Enhancement Project" and was funded by the Texas State Library with LSCA Funds.[1] In addition to converting the 40,000 bibliographic records, the grant also included the funds to add the Stanford University Graduate Library tapes, the Books for College Libraries tapes, and the Choice Outstanding Academic Books of the Year from 1972 to 1981 to the CORAL Union List of Monographs on Microfiche.

The basic purpose of the grant was twofold: to increase the holdings of the CORAL Union List of Monographs on Microfiche; and to utilize the Union List as a collection management tool by adding the Stanford University Undergraduate tapes and the special bibliographies.

The Union List project was especially suited to the purposes of LSCA funds because CORAL is a multitype library consortium of academic, public, and special libraries located in and around the San Antonio area. In its fifteen years of existence, CORAL has sponsored a variety of cooperative projects aimed at resource sharing and mutual aid among its members, including an inter-lending and delivery system between all the libraries in the group; cooperative acquisitions programs; and union lists of monographs, motion pictures, government documents, and serials. The heart of CORAL is the concept of resource sharing. The most basic requirement for resource sharing is bibliographic control, and producing union lists is one method of sharing library resources.

The CORAL Union List of Monographs on Microfiche has been

---

[1] Published with funds granted under the Library Services and Construction Act, Title I (P.L. 84-597, as amended by P.L. 95-123).

in existence since 1975. It began with the holdings of eight of the CORAL libraries and some 800,000 records. The most recent CORAL Union List, published in 1982, includes twenty libraries and a little over 1.6 million titles. With this edition, the CORAL Union List not only expanded its holdings, but it also added a facility to do collection management. Thus, the grant was seen by the consortium as an additional building block toward bibliographic control of materials in the San Antonio area.

Choosing a Vendor

The grant proposal was written by a committee of technical services librarians from several of the CORAL libraries. This same committee served as an advisory committee to the project director during the grant year. The first decision to be made by the grant committee was the choice of a vendor for the conversion of the bibliographic records.

The vendors considered by the committee included MARCIVE/ EKI, Blackwell North America (BNA), and Amigos. The Amigos option was eliminated because only one of the seven libraries to be converted was an OCLC member, and there was no clear method for utilizing OCLC services for nonmembers at that particular time. After reviewing the remaining two vendors, Blackwell North America was chosen, because their pricing was slightly lower and they could provide a full MARC record. The MARCIVE/EKI original input system, at that time, did not include all the fixed fields. In reality, however, both vendors were used, because MARCIVE did all the conversion work of the Choice records from the MARC database. MARCIVE also prepared the Books for College Libraries tapes and the Stanford University Undergraduate Library tapes for inclusion in the Union List of Monographs. In addition, MARCIVE did all the merging of the tapes of the CORAL libraries and produced the COM tapes for the Union List on microfiche.

Establishing Library Profiles

Once Blackwell North America was chosen to do the conversion, the next step was to establish a profile for each library. The seven libraries to be included in the conversion were: Incarnate Word College, Our Lady of the Lake University of San Antonio, Oblate College of the Southwest, Texas Lutheran College, Southwest Foundation for Research and Education, Southwest Research Institute, and the School of Aerospace Medicine, Brooks Air Force Base. The holdings to be converted for these seven libraries were carefully selected from those areas of their shelflist that represented the most unique collections in each library. For example, the titles from the subject area related to Catholic religion were converted for the Oblate College of the Southwest. The profile for each library was prepared by the project director, in consultation with each of the libraries.

Since CORAL was not interested in actual catalog cards, the profiles were relatively simple. The basic choices were the type of call number to be used, location stamps, if any, and what database to search on the large BNA database. While Blackwell was building the profiles for each of the seven libraries, the collection of access numbers and/or actual copies of shelflist cards was begun. The typing of the access numbers could not begin until the profiles were established on the BNA computers. It required more time than was anticipated for the establishment of the profiles, and, thus, none of the typing could begin until midway through the contract year.

Procedure Used for Conversion

The grant provided for a clerical staff person to search for access numbers, type scanning sheets, etc., for the conversion. Instead of hiring one full-time person, several part-time workers were hired. These workers included some students and some library staff members who worked off-hours on the project. The advantage of these workers was that most of them had library experience and therefore required little training. Their disadvantage was that we had to spend time coordinating the work, as well as the workers.

The basic procedure for each library was to gather access numbers — Library of Congress card numbers or ISBN numbers — for those titles to be converted, type them on scanning sheets with an IBM OCR, type A font, and submit the sheets to a scanning bureau in California. The bureau in California would then send a tape to BNA. Blackwell would read the tape from the scanning bureau, search its database, and copy the appropriate bibliographic record onto the individual computer file for each of the seven libraries. As a part of copying the record, BNA also produced a dummy shelflist on flimsy paper and returned it to the project director. Once the flimsies were received, they were matched against the shelflist, and those records not found were pulled. The "not founds" were then searched on the Blackwell title fiche. Those with access numbers were typed on scanning sheets, and those without access numbers were sent for original input. The bibliographic titles that had access numbers were processed easily and relatively quickly. Those that had no access numbers were more time-consuming.

Problems Encountered

The whole process sounds rather simple. However, there were problems along the way. The major problem consisted of the poor quality of the bibliographic record found in some shelflists. Another problem was in the delay while waiting for the profiles to be established. The time required to match, refile the shelflist in title order, and search for access numbers was longer than had been anticipated because of the high number of "no hits" in the case of two libraries.

The manual provided by BNA for the typing of the scanning sheets was inaccurate and necessitated some retyping of these sheets. An added problem was that the OCR, type A font ball could only be used on an IBM Selectric II with 10 pitch. There were some libraries that did not have a typewriter, and the typing had to be done in another location. One benefit from the project was that BNA revised its manual, and the instructions are now much clearer.

The problem that was the hardest to deal with was the lack of complete bibliographic data in the various shelflists. The shelflists of two libraries simply could not be used because they were incomplete. One library had a mixture of complete and incomplete records, and four had shelflists that were, for the most part, complete.

The libraries with the most incomplete records represented the largest bulk of the total number of titles to be converted. Thus, the first word of advice for any conversion project is to evaluate the quality of the shelflist and to make plans for using alternative sources of information. It was difficult to find an alternative in this case because of the time imposed by the grant. Another piece of advice is to try not to have strict deadlines during a conversion project.

How Shelflists in Each Library Were Handled

The two libraries with the incomplete shelflists were handled rather differently. In one library, it was found to be easier to take the numbers from the books on the shelf, type the scanning sheets, and then deal with the "not founds" when matching the flimsies from BNA. Surprisingly, there were relatively few incorrect records retrieved because of bad LC numbers in books. These titles were marked in the shelflist, and the library plans to correct them when the conversion is complete. In the other library, however, the shelflist had to be photocopied, refiled in title order, and searched manually. The advantage here was that the "not founds" were identified early. However, in order to submit the titles for original keying, another copy of the card had to be provided. Because of the time constraints on the grant, more access numbers were sought from other areas of the shelflist, in order to avoid submitting so many for original keying.

The partially good shelflist of the one library was totally photo-copied. Items with access numbers were typed, and items without numbers were separated. Those without numbers were then refiled in title order and searched manually on the BNA title fiche. Of the titles searched on the BNA fiche, the "not founds" were then sorted by the quality of the shelflist, and only those with complete biblio-graphic data were sent for original keying. Naturally, some of the incomplete ones slipped in, because some of the workers did not real-ly understand what a full record should contain. However, BNA returned those titles and did not try to keyboard them.

Two of the libraries had very good shelflists, and these were photocopied in their entirety. Items with access numbers were typed, and those without access numbers were separated and sent for origi-nal keying. There was no attempt to search these titles on the BNA fiche. These two libraries had access numbers on most of their shelf-lists and had a very high hit rate when searched on the BNA data-base. The matching and sorting process for these two libraries was much simpler than for the others.

The two smallest libraries did almost all the work in-house. Each library provided lists of access numbers, matched its own shelflist, and sent photocopies of the "no hits." The only work done by the project was the typing of the scanning sheets.

Rush at End of Project

As can be seen, each of the libraries required a unique proce-dure, and each had its own problems. The difference in the quality of the shelflist, was, perhaps, the major problem. But the amount of time necessary to photocopy, type, sort, search, and match was somewhat underestimated and caused a virtual flurry at the end of the grant period. In addition, most of the original keyboarding could not be identified until late in the grant year, and this placed a lot of pressure on the vendor, BNA. There was a lot of concern that the deadline could not be met, but, fortunately, the last library made it under the wire. Once all the conversion was complete, BNA had to prepare the tapes and ship them to MARCIVE to be included in the CORAL Union List. During the preparation of the tapes, BNA was able to delete the duplicate entries caused by a typing mixup.

In retrospect, a better understanding of the quality of the shelf-list in each library earlier in the grant writing process would have been beneficial in planning the staffing for the grant. The original keyboarding was left too late in the grant year and caused a lot of panic on both the project director's part and the vendor's part.

Cost of Project

The total cost of the project was $54,367. The computer services used for the conversion cost $33,920, for an average cost of $.74 per title. Staffing costs added another $.22 per title, for a total cost of $.96 per title. There were actually 45,653 records converted, with 9,476 titles requiring original input. This represented 21 percent of the titles converted. However, the breakdown per library ranged from 14 percent to a little over 50 percent. The age of the collections should be evaluated when planning a retrospective conversion project, in order to project the overall costs.

Conclusion

In conclusion, the amount of service provided by the grant will be measured by the increased access to resources within the greater San Antonio area. CORAL has developed a cooperative borrowing system that now includes all the CORAL libraries, as well as an efficient delivery service that enables patrons to borrow easily. The Union List provides the basic bibliographic tool for finding materials within the CORAL libraries. Moreover, the addition of the collection management aspect will provide a means for a library to build an order file of basic titles that are missing from its collections. A special printout of the Choice titles was prepared, and many of the CORAL libraries have used the list to check their holdings.

Each of the seven libraries has received its tapes and can continue to complete its own conversion. In addition, these records have been added to the Union List and to the computer tapes of the combined holdings of CORAL. This tape can now be utilized in other automated systems within the San Antonio area. The grant provided a variety of problems and challenges that were sometimes frustrating but often rewarding in their solutions.[2]

---

[2]The activity which is the subject of this report was supported in whole, or in part, by the U.S. Department of Education. However, the opinions expressed herein do not necessarily reflect the position or policy of the U.S. Department of Education, and no official endorsement by the U.S. Department of Education should be inferred.

RETROSPECTIVE CONVERSION AT
THE NATIONAL AGRICULTURAL LIBRARY

Patricia L. John

In the current environment of online public catalogs and integrated library systems, many libraries are trying to determine how, when, and how much it will cost them to get out from under their often unwieldy, unmanageable, and sometimes outmoded public card catalog. The solution for most libraries today — those able to justify the cost — is the online bibliographic catalog, usually obtained in conjunction with an online circulation system.

Once the vision of an online catalog begins to materialize, various problems present themselves. The usual and most glaring one is that of having a relatively small percentage of public catalog records in a machine-readable format. The National Agricultural Library, or NAL, is no exception.

In 1979, when the National Agricultural Library leased an online circulation system to double also as an online catalog, it had approximately 185,000 machine-readable catalog records; this represented slightly over 28 percent of the approximate total of 650,000 records, which dated back to 1862. The records were physically housed in two public catalogs. The original 1862–1965 dictionary catalog consisted of about 450,000 records. The divided catalog, started in 1966 when NAL opted for the Library of Congress classification scheme in lieu of the classification scheme developed for NAL in 1889, consisted of approximately 200,000 records.

1966–1969 Monograph Records to be Converted by EKI

To provide the easiest access for both the catalog and circulation system users, monograph records in the divided card catalog and the entire file of 39,000 machine-readable serial records located in both card catalogs had to be loaded as an online catalog file. This file arrangement would require a maximum of two lookups. The only problem, however, was that the machine-readable monograph records went back only to 1970. The immediate need was to key the 1966–1969 monograph records so that the online file would correspond to the divided catalog. Therefore, when the Request for Proposals, or RFP, soliciting for an online circulation system was announced in August 1979, it included an additional requirement that all catalog records had to be keyboarded and entered directly into the online system.

NAL awarded the contract for the online system and record conversion to DataPhase Systems in December 1979. The firm which DataPhase selected to perform the subcontract keyboarding project was Electronic Keyboarding Incorporated, referred to as EKI, a St. Louis-based firm specializing in data entry and conversion. Although EKI had not previously handled a project which required identifying and assigning MARC tags and indicators to catalog records, NAL staff felt that the firm would be able to handle the project because of its strong performance on the Library of Congress name authority record conversion project.

Fortunately, NAL has all of its catalog records going back to 1862 in printed book catalogs. The *National Agricultural Library Catalog*, published since 1966 and corresponding to the second public catalog, is currently published monthly. Although there is an eight-volume cumulative version for the years 1966–1970, it could not be used as the keying source document because of the need to avoid duplicating all of the 1970 records already in a machine-readable format. Instead, NAL located and shipped to EKI for the record conversion project two archival sixteen-volume sets of the bound monthly and quarterly catalog issues covering the specific years to be keyed, 1966–1969.

NAL Tagging Guidelines

MARC tagging guidelines, prepared by NAL, accompanied the shipment of the archival book catalogs, which were sent within one week of the first meeting with the DataPhase consultants. The seven-page input requirements document provided to EKI contained a list of the specific 1,476 pages of the quarterly cumulations from which EKI was to key the monographs. They also contained instructions identifying serial records not to be keyed, so that EKI would avoid creating duplicate records. The guidelines included examples of the default values to be used in the fixed and variable fields for both the I-level, or full level, monograph records and the K-level, or minimal level, translation and analytic records. They further specified the mandatory data, spacing, and coding requirements for the variable fields. Finally, there were examples of actual records from the book catalog keyed in the MARC record format, with examples of all the fixed fields, variable fields, spacing, and coding.

In addition, the guidelines contained two specific coding change requests. The first request was that EKI input the proper filing indicator in the title field to provide better retrieval. Complicating this request was the fact that nearly fifty percent of the records for EKI keying were in a variety of foreign languages. Therefore, NAL compiled a table of the leading articles in the major foreign languages which EKI could expect to encounter. The second request was that EKI convert the two-digit obsolete AGRICOLA subject category code in the 1966--1969 records to the corresponding six-digit numerical code, which NAL was using at the time of the conversion project. To support the change request, NAL compiled and included a conversion table of the fifteen AGRICOLA codes for EKI to use.

Two weeks after DataPhase had received the book catalogs and guidelines for EKI, DataPhase asked that NAL provide additional guidelines to aid EKI in identifying the various fields in the foreign language records and to aid them is assigning the proper MARC tags and indicators. NAL provided an additional twelve-page guideline document containing examples of records from the book catalog, utilizing the proper MARC tags and indicators for all expected variable field possibilities. NAL arranged the variable field examples in numerical order, providing actual book catalog examples under each MARC tag and field heading. NAL highlighted with a pointer the segment in the record examples corresponding to the MARC variable field tag. Although more than 65 percent of the record examples provided were in a variety of foreign languages as requested, NAL also provided several English-language record examples of corporate and conference main entries and series fields.

EKI's Coordination of Programming Requirements

With the MARC tagging guidelines, the foreign-language tagging guidelines, and the two sets of the *National Agricultural Library Catalog*, EKI proceeded with the conversion project. In setting up the project initially, an EKI library analyst coordinated with the DataPhase consultant and key cataloging staff at NAL. This coordinated effort enabled the EKI analyst to interpret properly the book catalog records and to define system parameters for achieving the desired tape output for DataPhase specifications.

EKI coordinated the programming requirements for three levels of need — for NAL, for DataPhase, and for EKI itself. Among NAL's programming needs was a conversion table of the revised AGRICOLA subject category codes. The EKI keyers were able to key the two-digit code in the catalog record, and a program converted it to the appropriate six-digit code. DataPhase required the design of an output program to format the data according to system specifications. EKI's own input and quality control procedures required a third level of programming. EKI included edit programs to detect logical errors in the MARC record, such as incorrect indicators and missing fields or subfield codes. EKI provided programs to generate recurring data elements, thus eliminating duplicate keyboarding and reducing human error. One example is the two-digit mnemonic tags which EKI used in the keying process, converting them to the proper three-digit MARC tag after the records were processed through EKI's internal system.

After programming the levels of need for all three parties involved, an EKI library analyst prepared encoding and keyboarding instructions for the data preparation staff. The nineteen pages of instructions which NAL provided generated an EKI input document of over 135 pages, corresponding to the EKI programmed specifications and NAL's data input requirements.

Keying of Records and Quality Control

EKI trained sixteen data preparation staff to perform the keying and quality control checks. It trained staff members in more than one aspect of the job, so that some keyers also did proofreading and some proofreaders also did keying. Because EKI is a cottage industry, its staff keyed much of the project in their homes, while full time in-house staff were responsible for workflow coordination. A library analyst directing the project coordinated the project workflow and supervised the staff.

Once the project began, EKI staff coded the catalog records with the two-digit EKI record tags. After finishing the markup, they keyed the records. EKI keyers rigidly adhered to the document control of the catalog and workflow procedures, which insured that they would key all of the appropriate records.

EKI then converted the data by using OCR (optical character recognition) typing and scanning. Next, the subcontractor generated a printout for the proofreaders to review against the source document after the data was in the computer. EKI keyers rekeyed corrected input errors, identified on the record printout by the proofreaders, and ran the input against the EKI edit programs to check for logical errors.

In the initial stages of the project, EKI performed a quality review check, examining every tenth record of each work batch for accuracy, reproofing every record in any batch with an excessive number of errors. If EKI found few or no errors, the EKI proofreaders spot-checked the remaining 90 percent of the records. If the review process identified patterns of recurring errors, EKI prepared supplemental instructions to assist the keyers in eliminating the problem.

Once the keying and quality review process was running smooth-ly, EKI replaced the quality review check with a final quality assur-ance check performed at the end of the processing cycle. EKI also reviewed ten percent of all records in the quality assurance check and assured a minimal quality level of 99.975 percent accuracy rate for all proofed materials, or one keystroke error per 4,000. In addition, before acceptance, NAL requested edit proof printouts of approxi-mately ten percent of the records keyed by EKI over the two-month period for quality control and for identification of any pro-gramming errors in the MARC tag conversion.

After two months of keying, EKI delivered 30,113 MARC records to DataPhase for input to the online file. The records aver-aged 400 characters in length at a unit price of $1.65. The EKI in-ternal programming, defining of MARC specifications, training, cod-ing, and keying covered a four-month time frame, February to May 1980. Since the project ended, EKI has refined many of its pro-cedures. It now uses more library professionals for the actual coding and uses electronic typewriters for creating micro-cassettes. In addi-tion, it now transfers data electronically into the computer rather than using the OCR-type scan procedure.

Conclusion

Although this first introduction in monitoring a contract for keying bibliographic data was, in actuality, a subcontract, the result was a rewarding learning experience for both EKI, which had never performed a MARC record coding and conversion project, and for NAL staff, who had never prepared specifications and monitored a contract. This might not have been the case. Involvement in a sub-contract project can be a disadvantage, if the contractor insists on playing the game strictly by the book. The contractor can insist that every issue or question which arises go directly through his office. He will relay the problem to the subcontractor, and vice versa, on the grounds that the contractor is responsible for the final product being delivered to the customer.

A working relationship that allows direct but informal com-munication between the customer and the subcontractor avoids un-necessary delays, frustration, and lack of communication. To estab-lish such a relationship, DataPhase readily agreed to have NAL and EKI handle the project questions directly. This arrangement bene-fited all three parties and aided the project from inception to com-pletion.

VENDOR-BASED RETROSPECTIVE CONVERSION AT GEORGE WASHINGTON UNIVERSITY

Andrew Lisowski

In 1981, George Washington University's Gelman Library began a retrospective conversion project to support its DataPhase ALIS-II automated library system. Gelman, the main library of George Washington University, contains collections numbering 986,000 volumes. Its DataPhase system is designed to support a variety of library functions, including circulation control, reserves, acquisitions, and a public access catalog.

Circulation control was the first function scheduled for implementation. The initial database for the system was derived from 120,000 OCLC archive tape records produced between 1975 and 1981. This left about 370,000 pre-OCLC titles in the shelflist without bibliographic records in the system. DataPhase uses a full MARC format for its bibliographic records. Individual copies are identified in the system by OCR label numbers linked to the corresponding MARC bibliographic record.

Goals of Conversion

Two problems were confronted in readying the database for the initial circulation activity: (1) the need to create individual item records in the system for materials already represented by the OCLC records, and (2) the short-term goal of converting and then linking bibliographic records for pre-1975 circulating titles. The project's long term goal was to provide online access to all materials in the collection when the public access catalog became available, but all titles would not be needed to initiate circulation functions. It was recognized, however, that, because of the research orientation of Gelman's collections, a significant portion of the pre-1975 collection was in active circulation, requiring that bibliographic records be available when circulation was implemented.

To address both the short and long term goals, a committee was formed to develop a retrospective conversion program and select appropriate methodologies. Members of the committee decided that retrospective conversion should be done on the basis of actual or anticipated circulation, rather than in strict shelflist order. This was because: (1) the system would be used first for circulation; (2) it would permit a significant part of the circulating collection to be in the system at the time of implementation, thus reducing the chance of having lines of frustrated patrons forming at the circulation desk; and (3) given the projected implementation schedule, time simply was not available for an "A through Z" conversion.

Material to be Converted in Two Stages

A two-phase approach was planned. First, all materials in the most frequently used areas of the collection would be labeled with OCR labels, and a duplicate label would be affixed to the corresponding shelflist card. By reviewing circulation statistics, the "H" (Business-Social Sciences) and "L" (Education) classifications were selected as the most frequently used areas and became the primary focus for retrospective conversion.

Next, all materials returning from circulation would be labeled. It was assumed that, if an item circulated once, it was likely to circulate again. Because this identification took place in the Circulation Department, the shelflist card would not receive the duplicate label; rather, it would be placed on a card to be matched later with the shelflist card. This formed the secondary conversion file. In both phases, materials already produced on OCLC could be linked directly on DataPhase terminals, while pre-OCLC titles would require retrospective conversion.

To avoid a second linking project after conversion and duplication of effort, it was determined that the OCR numbers for the conversion items should be entered into the conversion record. The DataPhase system allows one to input the OCR number in a MARC 949 field. DataPhase software then reads the number and automatically creates a linked item record at the same time that the bibliographic record is added to the database. Automatic linking was a very attractive feature of the DataPhase system. It would allow the library to direct maximum resources towards retrospective conversion rather than diverting resources into linking.

Decision to Use Vendors in Project

Early in the planning stages, the library decided to have vendors assist with the project. Vendors would be able to convert the large amount of material from the labeling projects in a shorter time period than could in-house staff, and, since conversion speed was important, the use of vendors seemed an appropriate course for meeting the implementation schedule.

Once this decision was made, several options were considered. The library could contract with a vendor to use OCLC at Gelman Library, or at the vendor's site, to match library records against the vendor's database or to have the records keyed from scratch. Each method had advantages and disadvantages related to speed, cost, and the nature of the bibliographic records produced.

Vendors were contacted, and six proposals were received. Selection criteria included proposed speed of conversion, use of a full MARC record, ability to include a 949 field, accuracy, projected hit rate, compatibility of the tape product with the DataPhase system, and, of course, cost. The library decided to use two different vendors for the two phases of the project — Electronic Keyboarding (EKI) of St. Louis for the first phase and ProLibra Associates of Maplewood, New Jersey, for the second.

Why Each Vendor Was Selected

EKI was selected for its ability to handle rapidly a large number of titles. They proposed to key a full MARC record onto tape for the approximately 40,000 "H" and "L" titles requiring conversion, at a cost of $1.75 per record. Full proofreading was to be included. The unit conversion cost was high, but these materials were in high demand and needed to be entered into the system as swiftly as possible. EKI also had previously worked with other DataPhase libraries and had a reputation for accuracy as well as speed. The keying project was to take six months. Disadvantages to original keying, in addition to cost, included the lack of access points in AACR2 form and the absence of holdings symbols in OCLC for these titles. However, each item requiring conversion would have a record; there would be no non-hits.

ProLibra was selected to convert materials in the second phase of the project because they offered a complete package at a very reasonable cost and on a timely schedule. They proposed sorting label cards and matching them with the shelflist, pulling the shelflist cards, converting approximately 20,000 titles on OCLC, and refiling the cards at a cost of $.80 per title, not including OCLC retrospective conversion charges.

The OCLC work was to be done at ProLibra's own sites during non-prime time hours. This avoided problems in scheduling Gelman terminals or with supervising ProLibra workers after hours. Their use of OCLC assured a high hit rate, access points in AACR2 form, and the appearance of holdings for converted items in the system. Another advantage ProLibra offered was a staff experienced with other OCLC conversion projects. Although conversion time was not as critical for the second phase of the project, it was still an important consideration.

Other vendors had proposed sending staff to Gelman Library to use the OCLC terminals, matching Gelman's records with their databases, or installing their own terminals at Gelman. In each case, however, either the unit cost was higher than ProLibra's, the projected conversion time was not short enough, or the database hit rate was questionable. Also considered was the OCLC conversion service itself, but it was not chosen since it was backlogged for several months. After selecting EKI and ProLibra, the staff checked with other libraries who had used these vendors and were given positive assessments of their work.

Preparing Materials for EKI Conversion

To label the materials that the staff anticipated would circulate and to create the EKI conversion file, a Special Projects Week was held in May, 1981. The library closed for an entire week while staff from all departments participated, providing an opportunity for all to have a role in the DataPhase implementation. Participants worked in the stacks in teams of two and labeled all books in the "H" and "L" classifications and their corresponding shelflist cards. Additional cards were used to accommodate multiple labels for multi-volume sets.

Instead of sending the labeled shelflist cards to EKI, EKI suggested that the library have the cards microfilmed and send them the film. EKI planned to produce hard copy from the file though a copyflo process and then key bibliographic records from the photocopies. Filming of the cards was accomplished during July and August of 1981 by a local microfilm service. EKI staff members had met earlier with the Gelman staff to discuss specifications for the bibliographic record format, including tagging and keying conventions, field editing requirements, and the format for the 949 field. EKI received the first microfilm in August and began keying.

A test tape was prepared in October and was reviewed by Data-Phase. DataPhase gave assurance that the tape would load into Gelman's system, although 949 fields were not present on the test records and the automatic linking function could not be checked. Gelman was the first DataPhase library to use the 949 field for linking, and EKI needed additional time to add this field to its keying programs.

Loading of Tape into DataPhase

The first production tape arrived in January, 1982. Two problems occurred when the tape was loaded into ALIS. First, it would not load properly and several times caused the system to cease operating. The tape was sent to DataPhase for examination, and a report was made to EKI. DataPhase and EKI concluded that the loading the problem was caused by fields containing an excessive number of characters, and EKI promised to remedy this.

The second problem appeared when records that had been successfully loaded into the system were reviewed. A large number of them contained keying errors. This was a serious problem for access points, because errors would affect the retrievability of the records in the system. EKI agreed to correct these records and to check subsequent tapes. By February the problems had been resolved, and Gelman was receiving and loading tapes on schedule. The final tape was received in April, 1982, in time to be loaded into ALIS-II before circulation began in May.

Preparing Materials for ProLibra Conversion

Labeling of materials for the ProLibra project began in June, 1981, and continued through December. As an item returned from circulation, the Circulation Department staff placed an OCR label in the book and a duplicate on a yellow transaction card, on which was also recorded the call number. Cataloging Department staff then collected these cards and matched them with the shelflist. When a transaction card was matched with an OCLC card in the shelflist, the item was linked on a DataPhase terminal. Some OCLC retrospective conversion was done in-house on OCLC during this period, but the emphasis was on linking. From June through December, 1981, cataloging staff linked more than 20,000 titles on Data-Phase and converted 3,600. Simultaneously, a file of 20,000 cards requiring conversion and 18,000 requiring linking was readied for ProLibra.

Gelman and ProLibra staff also met to plan the project's parameters. For retrospective conversion, ProLibra would follow the library's OCLC record selection and editing guidelines and add the 949 field. In mid-December, 1981, about 30 ProLibra workers recruited from the Washington area came to Gelman Library to sort the 36,000 yellow cards and pull and sort their shelflist cards. The ProLibra supervisory staff instructed workers in their tasks, requiring about eight hours one Saturday. During that time, the shelflist cards to be converted or linked were pulled and sorted into OCLC and non-OCLC groups, and temporary slips were placed in the shelflist. Margaret Bennett, the president of ProLibra, personally transported the non-OCLC cards to New Jersey to begin conversion. The OCLC cards remained at Gelman for other ProLibra staff to link on DataPhase.

ProLibra Conversion and Linkage of Records

Working from late December, 1981, through March, 1982, at various New Jersey OCLC sites, the ProLibra conversion staff completed the 20,000 titles. Conversion supervisors contacted Gelman frequently, and several modifications to procedures were made to expedite the process. About 3,500 titles were not found on OCLC or turned out to be problems that the ProLibra staff could not handle. Each problem was noted individually on the card, and, later, Gelman's own staff worked with these.

The converted shelflist cards were returned to Gelman via air express to assure prompt and safe delivery. When all the cards were back at Gelman, the ProLibra staff returned to refile them. Bibliographic records for items converted by ProLibra were received as part of the weekly OCLC subscription tape, loaded into DataPhase with no problems, and successfully linked automatically.

While the retrospective conversion process was underway, four ProLibra staff members used DataPhase terminals at Gelman Library to link the 18,000 cards with OCLC records already in the system. ProLibra completed its part of the project in April, 1982. Gelman Library was very pleased with ProLibra's efficient organization and the accuracy of the conversion operators.

Short Term Goal Met

With the completion of the EKI and ProLibra projects, the short term goal of converting high-use materials prior to system implementation was met. When the DataPhase circulation functions were initiated in May, 1982, 190,000 records were in the database. Currently, only ten percent of all circulating items have no records in the system. Therefore, the staff believes that basing conversion priority on anticipated use of materials was a most successful strategy. Despite some problems with accuracy and delivery schedules, the experience with vendor retrospective conversion was also a success. An in-house conversion of the 60,000 high-use items could not have been completed in the same amount of time.

Retrospective conversion, with the goal of complete conversion of the shelflist continues to be a priority at Gelman Library. Following the EKI and ProLibra projects, emphasis was placed on in-house OCLC conversion of items that had circulated on DataPhase but did not yet have records and on the ongoing conversion of high-use materials. Now, plans are being made for a large-scale project over the next three years to finish the remaining 275,000 titles.

A vendor will be used for this, and again, priority will be determined by anticipated use.

Gelman Library believes that use of a vendor is the most efficient way to complete a large conversion project within a reasonable time; it avoids in-house staffing, scheduling, and training problems. Future selection of vendors will be based on Gelman's previous experience in comparing costs and services and in evaluating performance.

MITINET/RETRO: RETROSPECTIVE CONVERSION
ON AN APPLE*

Hank Epstein

The MITINET/retro (pronounced "mighty-net") system was developed to support retrospective conversion for small and medium-sized school, public, academic, and special libraries that do not have access to bibliographic networks. To use the system, libraries require access to an Apple II Plus or Apple IIe microcomputer, with 48K of storage, DOS 3.3, and one floppy disk drive, the MITINET/retro software ($85), and a custom-edition COM microfiche catalog of 1,100,000+ LC MARC titles ($90) or an existing COM union catalog.

If any library with an Apple micro wishes to convert its complete catalog to machine-readable form in the MARC format and to obtain any COM catalog or tape products, MITINET/retro will provide the required interface between the library and the COM vendor. The MITINET/retro system allows the library to supply data in machine-readable form, for use by the COM vendor.

The library needs to have the local holdings data added to an LC MARC record or an existing union catalog record. When the library uses the LC MARC fiche, the vendor copies the full LC MARC bibliographic record and adds the local library data. When the library uses the union catalog fiche, the vendor adds the library's data to an existing union catalog bibliographic record.

This is accomplished with a minimum of library effort and vastly improved accuracy compared to any other current method of retrospective conversion. When retrospective conversion has been completed, the library can purchase COM products and MARC tapes from the vendor.

---

*An earlier version of this chapter appeared in *Information Technology and Libraries*, June 1983.

In Wisconsin, the system was tested in school, public, and special libraries. The libraries' costs included student and staff labor to search the fiche catalog and enter the brief data on the Apple, at an average input speed of thirty-six titles per hour (seven to twenty cents per title for labor costs).

Introduction to MITINET/retro

The MITINET/retro system is a retrospective conversion tool permitting libraries with a microfiche reader and an Apple microcomputer to convert their bibliographic and holdings files to computer-readable tapes in the MARC format. These computer tapes can then be used:

by a COM vendor to generate a local or union catalog on microfilm or microfiche;

by the library to generate a bibliographic title file, an item inventory file, and custom item (book) labels for an online circulation system;

by the library to generate bibliographic and holdings files for an online union catalog or other type of automated system.

The Basic Process:
From Fiche to Floppys to Files

The object of retrospective conversion is to obtain a computer-readable file of bibliographic and holdings data for a library. Fortunately, it is not necessary to enter by hand either the complete bibliographic information or the complete holdings information. A special edition of an LC MARC fiche COM catalog, the fiche reader, the MITINET/retro software, and the Apple micro provide the necessary ingredients to reduce the cost, time, and labor of retrospective conversion.

The Fiche Catalog

The LC MARC-MITINET/retro special edition fiche COM catalog contains approximately 1.1 million unique titles of English-language books and AV materials, cataloged by the Library of Congress and distributed as part of the LC MARC distribution service. The bibliographic records were initially converted to machine-readable form by

LC and distributed in the form of computer tapes. A COM catalog vendor (Brodart, in this case) converted the data on the tape to a microfiche master and reproduced copies of the fiche, which are supplied to each library.

The fiche contains English-language books cataloged by LC since 1968 and includes a small number of pre-1968 titles. The AV materials contain titles cataloged since 1972 for films, filmstrips, videotapes, slides, and kits. LC is scheduled to begin an LC MARC subscription for sound recordings, including phonodiscs, cassettes, and cartridges, sometime during 1983. This material is therefore not included on the current LC MARC fiche.

The bibliographic records on the fiche are presented in title order. Each title record contains the full bibliographic record (including authors, titles, subjects, publication data, notes), with an average of 600–750 characters of bibliographic data. Included in the fiche record is the LC Card Number (LCCN) and an appended check digit (modulus 11). The LCCN with the added check digit is used as a unique record identification number. (See figure 1.)

Matching Titles

For each title in a library's collection, the library searches the LC MARC fiche and records the LCCN and check digit on the catalog card.

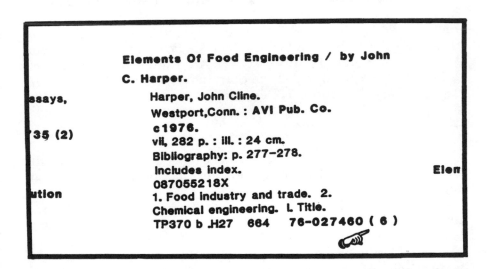

Fig. 1. Sample LC MARC Record from LC MARC Fiche. (Note the Check Digit [6], Following the LCCN.)

```
MITINET (WI)      13:RECORD NO & HOLDINGS
STATUS: UNUSED DISK SPACE = 87 RECORDS
REC NO: (75-432561)(8) NEW,CHA,DEL:(NEW)

CALL NO: (690.23 R42          )

ENTER COPY AND LOCATION DATA BELOW:
LOCN.     NO.   LOCN.    NO.   LOCN.     NO.

ART      (  )   MAIN    (2 )   WRIGHT   (  )
BANT     (  )   MONROE  (1 )
DENS     (1 )   NORTON  (  )
EMPIRE   (  )   PORTER  (  )
FREEMON  (1 )   REFEREN (  )
HAVID    (1 )   ROSSMOR (1 )
LORIM    (  )   STEVENS (  )

 + = ADD MORE COPY & LOCATION DATA FIRST
 R =  REVISE  INPUT DATA ON THIS SCREEN
 A =  ADD  RECORD TO WISC DATA BASE
 D =  DELETE  THIS DATA (IGNORE INPUT)
 O = GO TO  OPTION  SCREEN

      OPTION CODE: (A)
```

Fig. 2. Holdings Screen Filled in by User. (User Input Data Are Shown in Bold; All Other Data Are Presented by the System. Certain Data ["NEW" Above] Are Automatically Displayed by the System to Aid the User; the User Can Change the Data If Another Option Is Desired.)

MITINET/retro and Floppys

Using the Apple, the library enters the LCCN and check digit, the library's local call number, and copy and location information. (See figure 2.)

The LCCN, with a supplementary check digit entered by the library and immediately validated by the MITINET/retro software, is used by the library to identify which of the 1.1 million records on the LC MARC fiche is called for by the library. In most cases, the system will prevent the library from entering an incorrect LCCN for the desired title. This feature of MITINET/retro also reduces the amount of library keying required for unique title matching by more than 75 percent (six to ten characters versus thirty to forty-eight characters for an LCCN plus author and title data; for comparison, see figures 2 and 3.)

The MITINET/retro system automatically displays the names of all of the library's branches on the Apple screens after the library has identified the branch names the first time the system is used. From then on, the library is only required to enter the number of copies held by each branch, by filling in a form on the screen. (See figure 2.) The system then adds the number of copies held to the branch name and records this copy/location data, the library's call number, and the LCCN on the floppy disk. This feature of MITI-NET/retro reduces the amount of library keying required to define local holdings (copy/location data) by approximately 80--90 percent (one or two characters per branch versus ten or twelve characters if the branch names, and MARC codes, had to be entered).

When complete, the floppy disks with the library's data are sent by mail to a regional, school district, or statewide database

```
MITINET (WI)          15:MARC SEARCH INPUT
STATUS: UNUSED DISK SPACE = 86 RECORDS
LCCN/ISBN: (LCCN)(77-024468) BK,AV (BK)

AUTHOR'S NAME/CORPORATE NAME/CONFERENCE
AU/CN/CF/MT: (AU) ( LEWY, ANTHONY R.
                                            )

FOUR OR MORE TITLE WORDS. OMIT:A,AN,THE
(HANDBOOK OF CURRICULUM EVALUATION
                                            )

DATE: (1977)    PUB: (WILEY              )

CALL NO: (375.001            )


+ =  ADD   COPY & LOCATION DATA FIRST
R =  REVISE  INPUT DATA ON THIS SCREEN
A =  ADD   RECORD TO WISC DATA BASE
D =  DELETE   THIS DATA (IGNORE INPUT)
O = GO TO  OPTION  SCREEN

      OPTION CODE: (+)
```

Fig. 3. MARC Search Screen Filled in by User (User's Input Data Shown in Bold).

225

coordinator. The database coordinator will copy the data from all of the floppys onto a computer tape, and send the tape to the COM vendor. In some cases, there may not be a database coordinator, and the libraries will send the floppys directly to the COM vendor.

In any case, when the data are copied to a tape, the floppys are sent back to the originating library. The floppys can then be used to record new data, and the cycle is repeated until retrospective conversion is completed. By using several sets of floppy disks, the library may continually enter data with the alternate sets.

The COM Vendor,
the Bibliographic Resource File,
and the Library's File

Upon receipt of the computer tape from the database coordinator (or the floppys from the library), the COM vendor will process each MITINET/retro record one at a time on the vendor's computer. For each record, the vendor will match the LCCN against the LC MARC file (the bibliographic resource file) and extract the proper MARC bibliographic record. To this 600–750 character full bibliographic record, the vendor will attach the library's call number and copy/location data for any or all copies of that title.

Something for (Almost) Nothing

Using figure 2 as an example, the result of the library's entering 15–30 characters (LCCN, call number, and holdings data) on the Apple is that the library will receive a 600–750+ character record of bibliographic data cataloged and entered in machine-readable form by LC, and also the local library data (call number, copy, and location data) entered by the library.

When all retrospective conversion titles have been submitted by the library and processed by the COM vendor, the library may order a local library COM catalog, a union COM catalog, or a MARC tape for use in other automated library systems. Many other automated library systems, such as circulation systems, are able to read the LC MARC format tapes generated by the COM vendor.

Hit Rate

In most cases, the library will find 70–95 percent of the current and retrospective titles on the LC MARC database, using the LC MARC-MITINET/retro fiche. The library would then be able to obtain a copy of LC's cataloging and keying (data entry) for 70–95 percent of the library's titles.

Libraries with older collections and large audio collections should have a lower hit rate, toward the 70-percent range. Libraries with newer (1968+) material and large film and video collections should have a much higher hit rate, closer to the 95-percent range. Most libraries will fall somewhere between the two extremes.

Library Costs

MITINET/retro is one of the least expensive methods of retrospective conversion. The major costs to the library are the costs of:

1. Staff time, to: (a) search and identify the correct titles in the LC MARC fiche (approximately 60–100 titles per hour), and (b) key in the brief local library data and LCCN (approximately 40–100 titles per hour). (Note: The combined searching and keying activities result in a total staff time of 24–50 titles per hour. In Wisconsin, where the system was tested, the 11 pilot-test school, public, and special libraries processed an average of 36 titles per hour, using both student and staff labor. The labor costs ranged from seven to twenty cents per converted title.)

2. The Apple microcomputer (which can also be used for other purposes in the library).

3. The microfiche reader (which can also be used for other purposes in the library).

4. Obtaining a copy of the 1.1 million title LC MARC–MITINET/retro custom edition fiche catalog (approximately $90; libraries in Wisconsin will receive a copy of the Wisconsin statewide fiche union catalog – WISCAT).

5. Obtaining a copy of the MITINET/retro software and user manual ($85 per installation, outside of Wisconsin; selected Wisconsin libraries will receive a copy of MITINET/retro). (An installation may be a single institution such as a school, public, or special library with its own card catalog. An installation may also be a multi-institution such as a school district, region, or library system with an accurate union card catalog. Each installation may obtain local COM products for the institution, or may merge several installations to form union catalogs. In this way each library in a school district can perform retrospective conversion separately using data from its local card catalog. When completed, the district can order a single union COM catalog or MARC tape for the entire district. Multibranch public libraries

could follow the same procedures.)

6. Obtaining a copy of the library's database on MARC tapes or COM products from the COM vendor, when retrospective conversion is complete. Prices vary with products requested.

MARC Tape Costs
for LC MARC Fiche Users

The COM vendor (Brodart, Inc.) prices for extracting LC MARC records, adding the library's holdings data (call number, copy, and location) to the library's copy of the MARC records, and processing a MARC tape are approximately eight to ten cents per title for libraries ordering both MARC tapes and some COM catalog products, and twenty to twenty-three cents per title for libraries ordering MARC tapes and no COM products.

Wisconsin Statewide Database
and Local MARC Tape Costs

In the Wisconsin contract, the COM vendor (Brodart) does not charge for adding a library's holdings to an existing title in the statewide database. The addition of a new title, with the first library's holdings, to the statewide database (caused by adding an LC MARC title or a library-supplied full MARC record) costs seven cents per new title. The Wisconsin state library agency (Department of Public Instruction/Division for Library Services) will pay the seven cents per new title for each title not on the 1.4 million title statewide database, regardless of which library added the new title. Libraries that wish to extract their data from the Wisconsin database and obtain a MARC tape pay six and three-tenths cents per title.

Different COM vendors have different price lists, and prices may vary from contract to contract, so the unit and total costs to libraries in other states will vary.

Conversion from a Card
Catalog to a COM Catalog

For a library converting to a microfilm or microfiche catalog (for a single library or a union catalog), MITINET/retro is one of the least expensive methods of obtaining current and retrospective cataloging information. The costs involved with a COM catalog involve the retrospective conversion costs described above, plus the one-time costs of the microform readers, and the on-going costs of producing the COM catalog.

228

In order to introduce the use of the MITINET/retro system, this portion of the text will describe the system as the user would see it.

The MITINET/retro user deals with three kinds of floppys: a "program" floppy (where the MITINET/retro programs are stored), "custom-data" floppys (where permanent information about the library is stored), and "library-data" floppys (where the library's holdings and matching data are stored). The "program" floppy contains a series of programs that perform the separate functions listed below:

---- creation of "custom data" for the library, based on the user's one-time input of branch names and other permanent data;

---- creation of the library's "data" floppy disks, based on the user's input of the matching, searching, and holdings data;

---- duplication of the floppys to provide a "backup" copy of the input file for the library.

The user does not need to understand the programming in order to use MITINET/retro. The system asks the user to select options from a menu on the Apple screen, insert certain floppys in the disk drive, and input specific data when requested. By performing these activities the user can take full advantage of the system.

The first time the system is used, the library will input customized data (such as library name, classification scheme, number and names of branches, etc.) for future use. After the custom data are entered and saved on the disk, the library will automatically bypass this step unless the user specifically requests to change some of the custom data.

When beginning a data input session, the user describes the options required for this session. After choosing an option from the menu screen, the user will enter the data for one title. The MITINET/retro system will collect the data, copy the information on to the floppy disk in the form of a partial MARC record, and prompt the user for data for the next title. The user continues this process until another option is required, or the user ends the session.

Holdings Input

The most heavily used activity in the MITINET/retro system is the addition of a library's holdings to an LC MARC record (or to the union catalog database). This will account for 75--90 percent of a library's transactions, depending on the type of library and the size of the collection. If a title has been found on the LC MARC or union COM fiche catalog and the user wishes to add the library's holdings to the database record, this can be accomplished by using a single screen (screen 13, see figure 2).

For purposes of the system walk-through, a library with fifteen branches or locations will be used as an example.

The first step in the retrospective conversion process is to search the LC MARC fiche or a union microfiche catalog for titles owned by the library. Assume the library has completed searching several hundred titles and written the LCCN number and check digit, which identifies a particular title in the LC MARC database, on the catalog card for each title found. (Libraries using a fiche union catalog would copy the vendor's record number instead of the LCCN.)

The user is now ready to enter the holdings information in MITINET/retro. The user fills in the unique fiche record number and the local call number. If the library elects to enter the copy and location information, this information is entered on the screen. In this walk-through example, the library will enter copy and location information in order to obtain a local library database containing detailed holdings data. These detailed holdings data could be used for a future automated circulation system file or a future COM catalog.

The branches or locations presented on the screen are part of the custom data that were initially entered by the library. In this example, the codes for each of the branches (ART, BANT, etc.) are displayed.

Once the custom data are defined during the first use of the system, the user need only input the information requested between the parentheses. In figure 2, the user has entered the entire input to add the library's call number and holdings for six (of their fifteen) branches to a particular LC MARC title. The user input the data shown in bold, a total of twenty-seven characters.

When the fiche record number (LCCN or vendor's number) was entered by the user for the unique title desired, the system immediately verified the check digit. If the user had entered the record number incorrectly, the system would have requested that the user reenter the record number.

The library's call number will be added to the database exactly as the user enters it on the screen. For each branch holding one or more copies of the title, the user enters the number of copies. For branches with no copies of the particular title, the user enters no information.

That's it. That is all the user needs to do to enter the library's holdings into the database. The MITINET/retro system will record the information on the floppy disk in a format that the COM vendor's computer can read and will add MARC tagging to each of the data fields.

Union Catalog Users:
MARC Search Input

Some libraries will use a fiche union catalog, such as a regional or statewide union catalog, instead of the LC MARC fiche. For titles found on the union catalog fiche, the library would follow the process described above, using the vendor's record number instead of the LCCN on screen 13.

In the event that these users were unable to find a particular title in the statewide or union catalog, there is still an additional excellent source for obtaining a full bibliographic record: the vendor's LC MARC file. If these libraries do not also have a copy of the LC MARC fiche, they cannot provide a unique fiche ID number (LCCN with check digit). In this case, the user must request the vendor to search the vendor's copy of the LC MARC file, using only the data available from the catalog card or the title page of the book. All major COM vendors subscribe to the LC MARC tapes and maintain their own copy of the LC MARC file.

Screen 15 (figure 3) requests that the vendor search the LC MARC file, and screen 16 (figure 4) adds the library's holdings information (local copy/location data) to the request. The user would fill in the data including the LC card number, if known, the author's name, a portion of the title, the publication date, and the library's local call number.

Following this input of the search request, the system provides a second screen for the input of the copy/location data, if required by the library. This screen "Screen 16: MARC COPY INPUT" is shown in figure 4. Note that the user input data from screen 15 is repeated in condensed format on screen 16 to remind the user which title is being processed. The user then enters the copy and location data as shown. The system will store the information on the floppy for later processing by the vendor.

As a result of the search request, the vendor will search the MARC file and, if a match to the record is found, he/she will add

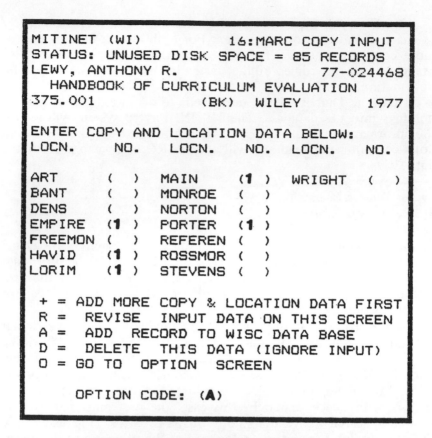

```
MITINET (WI)          16:MARC COPY INPUT
STATUS: UNUSED DISK SPACE = 85 RECORDS
LEWY, ANTHONY R.                    77-024468
  HANDBOOK OF CURRICULUM EVALUATION
375.001          (BK)  WILEY         1977

ENTER COPY AND LOCATION DATA BELOW:
LOCN.      NO.   LOCN.     NO.  LOCN.     NO.

ART       (  )   MAIN     (1 )  WRIGHT   (  )
BANT      (  )   MONROE   (  )
DENS      (  )   NORTON   (  )
EMPIRE    (1 )   PORTER   (1 )
FREEMON   (  )   REFEREN  (  )
HAVID     (1 )   ROSSMOR  (  )
LORIM     (1 )   STEVENS  (  )

  + = ADD MORE COPY & LOCATION DATA FIRST
  R =   REVISE   INPUT DATA ON THIS SCREEN
  A =   ADD   RECORD TO WISC DATA BASE
  D =   DELETE   THIS DATA (IGNORE INPUT)
  O = GO TO   OPTION   SCREEN

      OPTION CODE: (A)
```

Fig. 4. MARC Copy Input Screen Filled in by User (User's Input Data Shown in Bold).

the title and the library's holdings to a temporary file. The vendor will send a computer printout (an edit list) to the statewide database coordinator, who will in turn mail each library's portion of the edit listing to the proper library.

The library will be requested to verify that the title selected by the vendor accurately represents the title owned by the library, a process called "validation editing." If the title is correct, the user will enter a validation (or release code) on a new floppy. The vendor will then release the new title and the library's holdings from the temporary file and transfer all of this data to the union database. When the new edition of the union catalog is produced, the new title and the library's holdings will appear on the catalog.

It is important for the library to verify the title because there is no check-digit validation on an LC card number in this instance. Keying errors of LCCNs could therefore cause an incorrect record to be added to the library's database. The validation step is an opportunity to prevent the inadvertent addition of an incorrect title to the union database and to the local library's database.

End of Session Activities

As the user completes each record throughout the day, the data is stored on the floppy. The same floppy can be used to add additional data, which could be input at a future session. When the floppy is full, or the established weekly or monthly mailing cycle becomes due, the library will send the floppys to the MITINET/retro coordinator or directly to the vendor.

The coordinator will copy the data from the floppys onto a magnetic tape, reproduce the tape, and send one copy of the tape to the COM vendor. The coordinator will also return each of the floppys received during the latest cycle to the originating libraries. Each library will receive the specific floppys that it submitted to the statewide coordinator. The floppys can be used again for new library input data.

Current Status

The MITINET/retro system is now operating in public, school, school district, academic, special, and state libraries, as well as multi-type library systems and library schools in the U.S. and Canada. In Wisconsin, projects using MITINET are underway at 32 libraries to convert 621,000 titles. The projects range in size from 3,200 to 46,000 titles. One multi-type library system is converting 97,000 titles.

The current version includes: (1) the addition of a library's holdings to an LC MARC record (or an existing record on a statewide or other union database), and (2) the addition of the LC MARC records and the library's holdings to a union database (for those records not currently on the union database).

The first edition of the Wisconsin COM union catalog (WISCAT) contains approximately 1.4 million titles (the largest statewide union catalog produced to data), mostly from Wisconsin OCLC tapes and some tapes from local systems. The MITINET/retro system and the special edition LC MARC fiche catalog has been distributed to libraries in other states and Canada.

The average school or small to medium public library will only require the use of the Apple for about one hour per week after the initial retrospective conversion is completed. Thus, it is possible for a library to share an Apple with another department or library, or use it for other internal applications.

233

Development Status

While this paper has limited itself to reporting current functions and capabilities, there are two further applications in early stages of development. The first would allow MITINET libraries to enter original cataloging for titles not found on the fiche database or the LC MARC file (MITINET/marc). The second application would permit libraries to transmit, receive, file, and update ILL requests (MITINET/interloan). These requests would be transmitted between two libraries, or between a library and a regional library system, in a hierarchical interloan protocol.

PROBLEMS AND SOLUTIONS IN A RETROSPECTIVE SERIALS CONVERSION PROJECT

Sandra Card

In the late summer of 1978, the University of California, Berkeley, the University of California, Los Angeles, and Stanford University were awarded a joint federal grant under the Title IIC program. The grant was for one year, with potential renewal for up to an additional two years, and was awarded for the conversion of serials bibliographic records into machine-readable form at all three institutions. This paper covers the experience with the project at UCLA during a three-year period from October 1978 through September 1981.

UCLA Project

During the spring of 1978, preliminary work took place at UCLA to design the local segment of the conversion project. Certain general decisions were made about the quantities and types of records involved, since it was necessary to include such information in the grant proposal. It was originally estimated that UCLA would need to convert about 80,000 live and dead serials into machine-readable form during the three-year period. This estimate was later revised downward, due to unforeseen problems during the first year. General policy decisions made at this time included: use of OCLC as a conversion tool; participation in CONSER upgrade of bibliographic records through the University of California's system-wide office's membership in CONSER; conversion of all records into MARC-s at full level (level I); following the then draft ANSI Z39 standards for holdings at the summary level; using successive entry for title changes from 1967 on; central control of corporate name headings used and placement of the conversion staff within the Serials Department.

During the summer of 1978, additional preparation took place while UCLA awaited approval for the grant. The Head of the Serials Department set up a tentative staff organization for the conversion project and drafted job descriptions for the coders (hired at the paraprofessional level) and the Project Coordinator (a librarian). She also drafted a task sequence for the coming year. As soon as the grant was approved, the job descriptions and scheduling were completed. Recruitment and hiring of staff did not begin until after October 1, which was the official beginning date of the grant funds. While interviews were being conducted, trial runs of data collection methods were made by using existing student assistants, who were already trained in pre-order searching on OCLC. The first members of the coding staff were hired to start at the beginning of November.

Several unexpected problems arose in the first few months. Not all staff positions were filled until February. Purchase orders for OCLC terminals were delayed on campus, and, until March 1979, the project staff had to borrow hours on already heavily used cataloging terminals. This greatly slowed down both training and input of records. A reasonable working level of productivity was not reached until six months of the first year had already passed because of lack of sufficient terminal time for data collection and keying. Data collection and coding of records had been done from November through March. This had one slight advantage, although it did not offset the lack of productivity. The earlier staff had a longer training period than had originally been planned.

Project Speeded Up

During the following three years the procedures and training programs were revised. Initially data collection had been done in the card catalog by copying by hand on a data collection form the information in the record. The card catalog was heavily used as a public file. Towards the end of the first year the project staff received permission to remove cards temporarily from the public card catalog and photocopy them, on condition that we kept the cards out no more than an hour or two and never kept them out overnight. This single change greatly increased the speed and accuracy of data collection.

Extensive searching for ISSNs in printed sources (such as NST), as well as in OCLC, was performed at the beginning of the project. Since OCLC was the single greatest source for ISSN information and those records without ISSNs seldom had an ISSN located in a printed source, we discontinued the special ISSN searching during the second year. The average manual search for an ISSN not found on OCLC took 6 minutes, and the hit rate was only 2%. Hit rates for ISSNs on OCLC were 55% for dead serials and 80–95% for live serials (varying with the country of origin; U.S. titles had 95%).

Name headings had to be verified laboriously in the card catalog, which acted as an authority file for about two-thirds of the campus libraries. After AACR2 was implemented, this step was discontinued, since name headings were being changed. Constant fine tuning was done to the data collection procedures as situations and types of records changed. The main object was to be flexible about procedures when a better way was found.

Training Procedures Improved

Similarly, training procedures were improved as time went on. Originally we had started training coders with OCLC copy which required editing. Then we began to use some training exercises, since the records with which we actually worked did not always have a representative sampling of fields. As the project progressed, it became clear that it was best to start people with a few exercises concentrating on selected fields and then proceed to the creation of OCLC workforms for original input. If no OCLC copy existed, then the UCLA copy could be tagged on a workform with little effort. After the coder was familiar with the fields and their contents, she/he could then begin the comparison of OCLC and UCLA records and edit the OCLC copy for input according to local guidelines. We also found that training worked best if the coders first worked in the areas of data collection and keying before they learned how to code. Training is now so effective that we can have a productive coder within three weeks of the beginning of the training period.

Procedures Documented

With all the changes in procedures and workflow, current written documentation of procedures and decisions on policy implementation were vital. From the first month of the project we began writing down procedures. Each coder kept a looseleaf notebook with copies of procedures. Pages and sections could be updated or replaced as changes occurred. The staff themselves were involved in the early notebook; one staff member wrote the ISSN searching procedure, another wrote the keying procedure, and so on. The CONSER editing guide was used as the standard for the contents of fields and correct coding. However, local practices needed to be explained and decisions recorded. When staff increased, the amount of supervisory time also increased. This, in turn, led to more documentation in order to answer common questions and resolve common problems. Thus, we reduced the originally increased time needed for questions and problem referral. Gradually a set of guidelines for resolving conflicts came into being.

At the beginning of the project the library owned a small, old computer. Existing staff in the library worked with the Project Coordinator and the Head of the Serials Department on several tasks for the project. The first need was to be able to access the local OCLC records in some way. We had been receiving archive tapes from OCLC for some time. If we needed to revise records already done by a cataloger in order to add holdings statements, we needed to know exactly what other coding had been done in the record, since the cards never reflected the entire set of MARC tags and codes. An online sytem was the ideal, but it was not immediately available. Therefore, a batch system was devised as a temporary measure. In this system the OCLC weekly tapes were printed out in a register format with a cumulative index. This allowed us to look up a main entry in the index, find the register number (which was sequential), and check the register dump of the record. The size of the file and the sorting of the cumulated index was too large for the library's computer; so most of the work was done in several batch jobs on the large campus academic computer.

Towards the end of the first year, work began on planning the online updating system, using the expertise of the programmer who had been working for many years on the Biomedical Library's serials control system. In the fall of 1979, approximately 11,000 records were loaded from the OCLC tapes into a file in the campus computer. At that time they were indexed by title (245 field) only. The programming included the loading of the weekly OCLC tapes to add new records; the batch system was discontinued. Once this file was online, we immediately began editing and updating records, and work proceeded on improving the indexing, filing, and maintenance capabilities of the online file.

By the following February, sophisticated searching, tape loading, keying, and automatic file maintenance capabilities had been added to the online system. This, of course, led to the need for additional documentation for the local online editing system, which at this point was used only by the conversion staff and a few catalogers. The online editing system also began to generate changes in workflow between the OCLC keying, local input, and manual files and procedures. For example, different cataloging centers can see for the first time what other locations on campus have cataloged a title and how they have cataloged it. Changes in data, such as call number changes, are done locally. Initial cataloging is still keyed into OCLC, but cards are no longer produced for serials. These are only a few examples of the changes created by what began as an online editing mechanism and has grown into an extensive serials control system.

One of the earlier policy decisions had also included centralized control of corporate name headings. There was no central authority file on campus (UCLA has 19 libraries), even though there were five different cataloging centers. This meant that it was theoretically possible to have a corporate name appear in as many as five different ways. There had been a precedent for a single form of name. The old title/holdings serials list, which preceded the conversion project, had been manually edited to reduce name conflicts; a single form of name was chosen, with cross references from the conflicting forms of names. Therefore a unit's cataloging did not necessarily match the entry as it appeared in the serials holding list. The conversion project started keeping records of forms of name used, with cross references when appropriate. This frequently reflected divergences from the names used within the catalog of a single unit.

A batch system was created to maintain records of names and to create name cross references and record-specific cross references for the serials lists. In May 1979, this batch file was also loaded online, greatly reducing the maintenance time and increasing the currency of the records. It was loaded in a highly simplified version of the MARC authorities format. Records could be added, deleted, and changed online with immediate results. This also meant the headings were available across the entire campus. For the following years this file continued to be maintained for corporate names and for cross references. With AACR2 the file also enabled conversion staff to record which headings had been changed to AACR2 form and which still needed review. During the summer of 1982, the record-specific cross references were replaced by a new version of the serials list which automatically generated the "see" references. The file was also expanded to include personal, conference, and geographic names. It is now being used by the different cataloging centers for input of authority names with cross references. Again workflow was changed, since manual authority records were no longer produced.

Editing of Records Pared

One of the major types of problems that the project encountered during its three years was the lack of established standardized policies and guidelines for cataloging. Since there were different cataloging centers and subsections, there was a lack of information about cataloging practices both across campus and over time. Most information about such practices was passed on through the "oral history" method of tradition. Initially the project created its own procedures, guidelines, and standards after some discussion with the major cataloging center, and this information was passed on in written form.

When the first records were coded, very extensive editing of the records was done in order to combine data from OCLC and from UCLA's cataloging and processing records (which often contained bibliographic information not available elsewhere). After the first few months, decisions were made to ignore certain fields when editing copy. For example, the 300 (collation) and 321 (former frequency) fields were left as they appeared in OCLC without any changes or additions. As time went on, additional fields, such as the 570 and 700 fields (editor notes and added entries), were added to the "do not add/edit" list. This was a first step in speeding up data conversion, while still controlling quality, and in accepting more copy as it appeared. Since the project was never just adding a holdings symbol to a record, conversion was expensive and time-consuming. The more extensive the editing, the more expensive the record. We had started by almost completely redoing the descriptive cataloging of the record.

After certain fields had been placed in the "do not add/edit" list, other fields required certain levels of decision. Frequently the imprint and the issuing body information were different in the OCLC and UCLA records. Where such discrepancies existed, the coders were instructed to accept the OCLC record imprint (260 field) as it appeared. For 550's (issuing body notes) OCLC copy was accepted "as is", unless the local cataloging was more recent and had more detailed information. In many cases where there was outright disagreement between fields, coders were instructed to accept the most recent data. This considerably reduced questions about conflicts while still retaining quality control, since, if the cataloging were more than twenty years old, the UCLA records which disagreed with OCLC were often the erroneous ones. Similar rules were created for title changes and for handling ceased titles. (OCLC information about cessation was accepted unless our kardex showed receipt of an issue after the cessation date.)

Conversion versus Cataloging Controversy

Gradually while this was going on, it became apparent that there were two schools of thought on campus as to what was to be considered conversion of a record and what was to be considered cataloging. The Project Coordinator took one point of view: anything that involved editing OCLC records or creating workforms from existing manual records (including records for uncataloged material) was "conversion"; this included breaking out latest entry records into successive entry records without copy. Most of the catalogers took the opposite viewpoint: creating workforms for uncataloged material or for successive entry records or anything that involved changes in issuing bodies, main entries and added entries, or closing ceased titles was "cataloging" and should not be done by the conversion staff (who were all paraprofessionals, with the exception of the Project Coordinator). There was also a range of views between these two extremes.

The Project Coordinator then did an extensive study of the discrepancies between the manual files and the machine-readable files and the diverging directions that these files were taking. The discrepancies ranged from filing errors and call number typographical errors in the manual files to changed name headings in the machine files. At the same time she developed a recommended standard for editing records: what items should be left as is, what should be edited, and what the level of work on the manual files should be when discrepancies arose. These documents, based on the practices of the conversion project at that time, were distributed for discussion.

When the project began, the position of Associate University Librarian for Technical and Bibliographic Products and Services was in the process of being filled. When the new Associate University Librarian started in April 1979, he reinstituted an informal group, which had once met, consisting of the heads of the four main cataloging centers. This group, under his instigation, became formally constituted as the Advisory Committee for Cataloging Policy (ACCP). Memos flew back and forth between the Associate University Librarian, the committee, and the Project Coordinator on the editing of records and the standards for input. Meetings were held, at which the temperature ranged from mild to stormy. Finally, the Associate University Librarian produced what is locally known as the "treaty."

This document laid out the local definitions of conversion and cataloging; it defined, for practical purposes, what types of activities and what kinds of records are covered in each area. It also stated that the IIC project (i.e., retrospective serials conversion) was, de facto, a copy cataloging unit for descriptive cataloging. At the same time, it laid out several compromises on particular topics, which also had the practical effect of more widely distributing the workload.

Project staff could change latest entry records to successive entry if there were successive copy in OCLC; if there were no successive copy in OCLC, the project referred the record to a cataloging unit to be recataloged for successive entry input into OCLC. Uncataloged titles, without OCLC copy, were not input into OCLC until they were cataloged; but the project could convert an uncataloged serial if there were OCLC copy. It was also agreed that many kinds of changes would be reflected in the online file only, e.g., ceased

241

titles and changes in issuing bodies. Cards were not redone unless a main entry was changed or a linking note for a title change was added. Title changes could be converted by the project and later checked by a cataloger for call number and subject headings.

However, this entire process was still not resolved to everyone's satisfaction. Project staff continued to feel that they could do more "conversion," and catalogers continued to feel that the project should do less "cataloging." The controversy did lead to a number of positive developments. First, it became obvious that informal communication mechanisms were inadequate for distributing policy and procedures. Gradually a more formal referral and decision-making mechanism came into being under the Associate University Librarian's direction. The Advisory Committee for Cataloging Policy could examine topics as they arose and make a recommendation for a campus-wide policy or procedure; the Associate University Librarian made the final decision. This meant that all cataloging centers would follow the same guidelines for the first time. Decisions were being made regularly for the first time. If cataloging centers could not agree on a recommendation, the Associate University Librarian could act as arbitrator and had the authority to make the final decision. This was very important for the continuance of conversion work after the project's completion, as well as for future cataloging, and it has resulted in more consistency in the records.

There are still problems: one of the most difficult tasks has been getting copy to be accepted with less editing and to have paraprofessionals more involved in copy cataloging. Most paraprofessionals are still being restricted to LC copy. In addition, we wish to have LC copy done at the receiving point: the acquisitions department for monographs. The conversion staff are still editing records far more than I think they need to. Additional restrictions are required on how much editing is done. We have started to accept AACR2 copy "as is," adding only local subject headings, call numbers, and holdings. More records should be treated in this way.

The entire experience made what should have been obvious from the beginning very clear. It is necessary, especially in such a large environment as UCLA, to formalize and standardize policies and implementation of policies to ensure consistencies in standards and practices. The policies and procedures must be written down, yet subject to change as needed. Practices should be documented and periodically reviewed. UCLA had been acting as if it were a small library where all the staff knew what each other was doing in detail; that had not been the case for many, many years. The "oral tradition" method of training and documentation had fallen apart over time without any notice being taken.

Holdings

Holdings statements were another problem area. It had been decided to enter a volume-level summary holdings statement following what was then a draft of the ANSI Z39 standard (since completed and issued). It soon became apparent that the holdings in the central catalog were very inaccurate for other units; this meant the holdings statements frequently had to be redone when we did data collection in another unit. Furthermore, when conversion of processing information was later started at UCLA, all the work of collecting information about holdings had to be redone, because the processing system required a detailed issue-specific holdings statement which also distinguished between bound and unbound volumes. A way around this problem was never found. If we had encoded the detailed holdings statement in place of, or in addition to, the summary holdings statement, it would have required almost daily update as volumes were bound or new issues received, since we did not have the serials control system from the beginning. Eventually we do plan to drop the summary holdings statement completely and to derive a summary holdings statement from a collapsing of the detailed holdings statement. However, at the time the project was started, we did not know exactly how the records would be used in the future.

Project Results

The original project allowed for the machine database to produce a serials list in order to replace our old title/holdings serials list, which had been laboriously batch produced. It also allowed for the coding of detailed holdings information and for a study of the existing Biomedical Library serials control system to see if that system could be expanded for the entire campus. But, from the beginning, we had to code bibliographic and holdings records without an actual decision on the future uses of the records or the fate of the serials control system. Therefore, we tried to code complete detailed records which could serve a variety of purposes and had a high degree of accuracy, so that future maintenance of records could be reduced. At the same time, we tried to design our online edit system to be flexible and to accommodate a wide range of potential uses.

Precarious though second-guessing can be, we succeeded in both goals. The error rate in "public fields" (those that would display on a card or serials list or as an access point) is less than 1%. The online system has since been expanded to cover a wide range of processing activities and record and file structures. Not only did the online editing system become the trigger for the full campus serials control system, it also became the grandfather of the eventual monographic acquisitions system. The serials lists produced from the file continually become more sophisticated. We can combine a selection of files into one list. We can manipulate various data elements in a variety of ways for retrieval in batch lists or online. We can produce tapes for the local union list (CALLS) in the required format. What we have tried to avoid doing is locking out any future possibilities by the way we code our records.

Impact of the Project Campuswide

The project had a strong impact on workflow across the campus. We no longer have cards for serials but rely on the serials lists and online access. We have the same single record for all copies in all units of a given serial, and this record is used for all processing purposes (except circulation). A record no longer belongs to a unit; it belongs to the system, but within that record is contained highly local information, which units add and update. Staff is becoming more transferable between units; record structures are more consistent, and procedures are more widely known and understood. There have been impacts on the training and organization of staff within processing units. Not all the results are "in" yet. Changes are still happening.

Areas which are still sensitive include the question of "territoriality," which first arose in the cataloging versus conversion controversy. A unit can no longer record replies to claims in any old way, changing their abbreviations each time a different staff member records a note. Now everyone will see and use the same notes, including the public. Everyone will be using each other's records and will need to be able to interpret them.

The question of quality versus quantity is also difficult. Records need to be accurate in order to supply patrons with correct information, yet we need to update records in large quantities. Both can be done; we have found it requires a heavy initial investment in training. If staff are thoroughly trained in the beginning, you can achieve both high quality and high quantity.

Conclusion

If you are planning a conversion project:

— follow national standards where they exist;

— decide in advance possible uses of the records, including ten years from now, and make decisions accordingly;

—— make in advance as many decisions about editing policy as you can;

—— have standardized policies and procedures for conversion and cataloging, but be willing to alter them;

—— staff training programs should be ready to go immediately; have some staff specialize in training (make sure they are good at training) and release them from other duties accordingly;

—— write procedures and decisions down as soon as they are formulated; see that everyone knows them;

—— have one single person with full authority to make a final decision on a policy or on conflicts in interpretation of policy; preferably, this person should be at a high administrative level and have the authority to enforce the decisions.

RETROSPECTIVE CONVERSION OF MUSIC MATERIALS

Donald T. Green
and
Dean W. Corwin

For any library with a substantial music collection, retrospective conversion of music materials is a major problem when that library wants to utilize an online public access catalog for its collection. With different cataloging rules, access points, and subject and name authority needs (and many changes to those authorities in recent years), music materials often become the step-child of the collection, put off until the tail end of any conversion project.

We do not want to suggest that music materials are any more problematic in online cataloging, or in an online system, than any of the other special formats, such as maps, audio-visual materials, and especially serials. However, there are cataloging problems that are unique to music materials and that have to be resolved in some manner in the course of a conversion project. To ignore those materials, in the hope that they will somehow convert themselves, seems to be an almost universal, if not quite realistic, response to the problem. While there are many collections involved in conversion projects, we are unaware of any major collection of music materials that is currently undergoing retrospective conversion.

At Rice University, this was also the route chosen from the very beginning of the retrospective conversion (Recon) project. All music materials would be converted sometime toward the end of the project, probably when the projected online system was up and running. At least, that was the plan until two Friday-night slots opened up on the Recon team, and the Music Cataloger and the Assistant Music Librarian (formerly the Music Cataloger) jumped at the chance to earn some extra money at a very convenient part-time job. While others of the professional library staff had worked on the Recon project converting monographs, it was felt that the special subject expertise offered by the music librarians should not be ignored. So, the music conversion began at Rice considerably earlier then had been expected.

Collection Background

Fondren Library's music collection is relatively young. Prior to 1953, most of the music titles in the collection were acquired as gifts. These gifts were comprised largely of biographies of composers and performers and popular editions of standard piano music. At that time there were no music courses taught at Rice.

In 1953, however, a department of music was established at Rice. A faculty member was hired, and, later, a music librarian was hired. Music acquisitions began to be supported on a continuing basis by the library. The money was initially spent on backruns and standing orders of historical sets and complete editions, including such standard titles as *Denkmaeler der Tonkunst in Oesterreich, Das Chorwerk, Anthology of Music, Hortus Musicus,* the *Neue Bach-Ausgabe,* the Beethoven *Werke,* and the *Saemtliche Werke* of Brahms. Study scores of selected works by Bach, Beethoven, Brahms, etc., were also added. The music collection grew slowly at this time, because the size of the department did not justify a large allocation.

Shepherd School of Music

Beginning in 1950 and continuing over the next 20 years, Sallie Shepherd Perkins and her family made several donations to Rice to establish a music school, to be named in honor of her grandfather, Benjamin A. Shepherd. It was not until 1971 that the university began a search for a dean to lay the groundwork for the music school. In 1973, Sam Jones was appointed to that position, coming to Rice from the Rochester Philharmonic, where he had been Music Director.

When the Shepherd School of Music officially opened in 1975, its stated objective was the training of orchestral musicians. All other areas (piano, organ, musicology, theory, composition, voice) were peripheral, although the conducting program was emphasized because of Dr. Jones' interests. As a result of this emphasis on orchestral performance and conducting, the library's collection of study scores of standard orchestral repertoire was expanded considerably during the first two or three years of the school's existence.

The Shepherd School was unique in this country in that all of its programs were five-year Bachelor/Master of Music programs or separate Master of Music programs. It was originally anticipated that the musicology department would be fairly strong and that original research would be an important factor in graduate-level work for most students. Thus, standing orders for many more historical sets and collected editions were established: *Diletto Musicale, Denkmaeler Deutscher Tonkunst,* the various *Recent Researches* series, and collected works of Handel, Berlioz, Telemann, Schoenberg, Schubert, and Gluck, to name but a few.

Another large segment of the collection has been acquired through an approval plan for European music publications through Otto Harrassowitz of Wiesbaden, West Germany. Through this plan, the library receives current European publications of the music of major contemporary composers as well as current publications of older music, much of it relatively obscure. This should give you an idea of the nature of the collection being converted.

Rice Recon Project

The Recon project at the Fondren Library is an in-house program designed to convert the estimated 452,000 titles in the catalog into machine-readable form. All items in the Fondren collection are being converted from the main entry cards in the public card catalog, because that is the only place where the complete bibliographic record and full holdings information for items is to be found. The only exception to this is sound recordings, which are to be converted from the separate music card catalog.

The first sweep through the card catalog by the Recon staff is for the conversion of monographs only. All entries in the card catalog for serials, maps, scores, certain analytics, and non-Roman items are flagged with color-coded sleeves for later input. This was determined to be the fastest and most cost-effective method for putting the major portion of the collection into machine-readable form.

With the current, much revised specifications, each of the 10 to 15 monograph Recon assistants is able to convert 5 to 7 records per hour shortly after joining the staff. With experience, staff members work up to a figure averaging between 12 and 17 records per hour and are able to work, for the most part, without revision.

Music Recon

Not so with music! Although both of us are library professionals and musicians and are very familiar with the OCLC system, cataloging codes, and cataloging systems used, the conversion rate for music scores has remained at between 3 and 4 per hour. The reasons for this disparity in the conversion rates form the crux of the problems of music conversion in general.

The nature of music materials is substantially different from that of many other fields. Most of the materials collected by libraries have some fairly unique characteristic: unique title, unique title/author, unique title/author/date, etc. Some form of distinction

Figure 1

```
Rec stat: n Entrd: 821221 Used: 821221
Type: z Bib lvl: t Govt Agn:   Lang:     Source:
Site: 003 InLC: a Enc lvl: n Head ref: a Head:
Head status: a Name: a Mod rec:   Auth status: a
Ref status: a

1 010   n   82111258
2 100 10  Strauss, Johann, _d 1825-1899. _t An der schönen, blauen Donau _w
n00182112Øaacann---nnn-
  3 400 10  Strauss, Johann, _d 1825-1899. _t On the beautiful blue Danube _w
n00282112Øaanann---nnn-
  4 400 10  Strauss, Johann, _d 1825-1899. _t Blue Danube _w n00382112Øaanann-
---nnn-
```

250

generally exists that will make construction of a search key for an item fairly easy to accomplish. Music scores, on the other hand, are most often found in multiple editions, often with a generic title, very often without date or distinguishing, unique characteristic of any kind. This makes the formulation of a distinctive search key difficult to achieve and turns the search procedure into a lengthy, tedious process.

Access points assume somewhat different levels of importance for music materials than for other materials. The uniform title, that device of librarians which allows for the grouping of all the different realizations of a particular work, is much more important. Even for such well-known works as Strauss' Blue Danube waltz (figure 1), the correct German language uniform title is required in order to have a single grouping of all representations of the work. Coded access points can be invaluable for the researcher dealing with a large archival music collection. Indications of instrumentation, chronological period of composition, composition type, even if only through very "rough" codes, can aid tremendously in computer searches for special materials. The inclusion of these fields in the catalog record is potentially very important for the online public access catalog.

Editing Music for Recon

Editing of Recon music records has evolved from a combination of Recon policies and cataloging policies. In general, we try to follow the basic cataloging policies for music materials established by the library. This means updating all access points to AACR2 choice and form of entry. We leave if correct or delete if incorrect the following 0xx fields: 041, 043, 045, 047, 048. We input complete available information into the 028 field, whether that information is included in the OCLC record or not. Of course, local call numbers and holdings information are input exactly as found on the catalog card. For the mandatory and required fields, fixed fields are edited to match the card exactly and, for the optional fields, they are edited if they can be easily determined by us. The description of the record is edited only to match the information that is contained on the RUL catalog card. No attempt is made to match punctuation style or form of description as long as the content is the same. The description will be edited, though, in order to make the record consistent within itself, and all fields are checked for proper tagging.

As we previously suggested, the biggest slowdown in the conversion of music materials is not the editing of the records, but rather the difficulty of the online searching that must be done for each record. That was our basic feeling from the beginning of the project and is a basic feeling of music catalogers in general. It should be pointed out, however, that a recon project for music materials utilizing OCLC would have been much more impractical if OCLC had not implemented their search enhancements in 1980. The problems with searching are corroborated through the Rice Recon statistics and by a paper written by Allen Hoffman, formerly at the Fondren Library, now at Indiana University.[1]

Comparative Statistics for Searching

Mr. Hoffman's paper, which appears in the November 1982 issue of the Music OCLC Users Group Newsletter, is a detailed comparison and analysis of searching for scores and books on music in OCLC's online union catalog. Several of his observations and conclusions are relevant to our topic. He found that, while 100% of the monographs selected had imprint dates, only 73.5% of the scores had any date which could be used to qualify a search. Of greater importance is the fact that 93% of the monographs had a searchable LCCN or ISBN number in them, but only 1.7% of the scores had any such number. Interestingly enough, however, 83.5% of the scores did contain a (currently unsearchable) plate and/or publisher's number of some kind. Obviously, when working from catalog cards, the rate of LCCN searches for scores will increase, but there is still a large difference in the number of numeric search key requests that can be made. We have found that 70.12% of all monographs conversion can be effected through a numerical search of LCCN. By contrast, this number drops to only 52.84% of the scores that may be found with LCCN.

Of even more significance for music searching are Mr. Hoffman's results for the numbers of commands needed for retrieval. Monographs were found to need a mean of 1.5 commands per record searched, while scores were found to require 2.8 commands per record. (This does not include the mean of 9.6 commands that were required to determine that 18.3% of the scores were indeed not in the Online Union Catalog, or OLUC.) Mr. Hoffman puts these figures into real terms thus: "In searching a stack of 20 books, for instance, about 30 commands would be expected, whereas the same number of scores would probably require about 56 commands."

It should be explained that Mr. Hoffman's use of the word "command" does not involve any measurement of the expenditure of work done for that command. If, for example, you need to search

----

[1] Hoffman, Allen. "Searching Scores and Books on Music in the OCLC Online Union Catalog: A Comparison of Retrieval Characteristics," *Music OCLC Users Group Newsletter,* no. 16 (November 1982): 5--8;

the online name authority file for the prelude to Act 3 of Verdi's Traviata, it is a simple enough command to enter the search key "verd,giu,", with little expenditure of time or effort. The response is found in figure 2. It again takes very little time or effort to decide that, yes, you do want that authority record and input "yes." Given the response found in figure 3, it now takes more brain effort and time to scan the screen and find that there are 17 hits that will match Traviata in the display. Again, keying the command "19" requires little time or effort. The response, found in figure 4, indicates 11 hits for various parts of Traviata. Evaluation, and in this case, the paging through of every screen for Traviata is required before the correct authority record has been called up on the screen. (The correct record is the 11th screen; see figure 5.) As you can see, even though the command ratio is not quite twice as high for scores as it is for monographs, the actual work expended and the amount of time taken for the search can easily be four times as much or more for scores.

There are essentially no DLC/DLC music score records in the OLUC, and the quantity and accuracy of many DLC/member records leave something to be desired. Historically, a lack of standardization in the cataloging of music materials has led to a wide variety of catalog entries, even in a music collection as young as the one at Fondren. Taken with the number of duplicate records or near duplicates found in the system, the hunt for a particular matching record in the OLUC can indeed be an arduous journey.

This is perhaps best illustrated by showing a few searches for works of standard composers.

Beethoven Concertos Search

The first set of searches is for Beethoven piano concertos numbers 1–4 in Eulenburg miniature score editions. All of these records have common problems of prolific composer, generic titles and uniform titles, no editor, uncertain dates, and no LCCN or other numeric key to search.

Figure 6 is a reproduction of the Fondren catalog card for the first concerto. Using the transcribed title search key (the one suggested by OCLC and other documentation as the most specific derived search key) and qualifying by score format and date (in this case a range of dates because of a distrust of the date on the card), the results in figure 7 are retrieved. By choosing the record with the matching date, we indeed find the record that was used for the Fondren Recon project (figure 8).

With confidence, we move to the second concerto and repeat the process. (Figures 9 and 10.) Again picking the record with the

253

Figure 2

[verd,giu,\

YES OR NO
[VERD,GIU, produces more than fifty entries.
Do you wish to continue your search?

Figure 3

To see title for a COLLECTIVE ENTRY, type line#, DEPRESS DISPLAY RECD, SEND.

```
 1  Verdi, Giuseppe, 1813-1901.
 2  VERDI GIUSEPPE 18131901 A (5)
 3  VERDI GIUSEPPE 18131901 BA (7)
 4  VERDI GIUSEPPE 18131901 D (8)
 5  VERDI GIUSEPPE 18131901 ERNANI (3)
 6  VERDI GIUSEPPE 18131901 F (7)
 7  VERDI GIUSEPPE 18131901 I (3)
 8  VERDI GIUSEPPE 18131901 L (4)
 9  VERDI GIUSEPPE 18131901 MACBETH (3)
10  Verdi, Giuseppe, 1813-1901. Operas.
11  VERDI GIUSEPPE 18131901 OTELLO (2)
12  Verdi, Giuseppe, 1813-1901. Poveretto
13  Verdi, Giuseppe, 1813-1901. Quartet,
14  VERDI GIUSEPPE 18131901 REQUIEM (2)
15  VERDI GIUSEPPE 18131901 RIGOLETTO (6)
16  Verdi, Giuseppe, 1813-1901. Romances,
17  Verdi, Giuseppe, 1813-1901. Simon Boccanegra.
18  VERDI GIUSEPPE 18131901 STIFFELIO (2)
19  VERDI GIUSEPPE 18131901 TR (17)
20  VERDI GIUSEPPE 18131901 VE (4)
```

Figure 4

```
 1  Verdi, Giuseppe, 1813-1901. Traviata.
 2  Verdi, Giuseppe, 1813-1901. Traviata.
 3  Verdi, Giuseppe, 1813-1901. Traviata.
 4  Verdi, Giuseppe, 1813-1901. Traviata.
 5  Verdi, Giuseppe, 1813-1901. Traviata
 6  Verdi, Giuseppe, 1813-1901. Traviata.
 7  Verdi, Giuseppe, 1813-1901. Traviata.
 8  Verdi, Giuseppe, 1813-1901. Traviata.
 9  Verdi, Giuseppe, 1813-1901. Traviata.
10  Verdi, Giuseppe, 1813-1901. Traviata.
11  Verdi, Giuseppe, 1813-1901. Traviata.
12  Verdi, Giuseppe, 1813-1901. Trovatore.
13  Verdi, Giuseppe, 1813-1901. Trovatore.
14  Verdi, Giuseppe, 1813-1901. Trovatore.
15  Verdi, Giuseppe, 1813-1901. Trovatore.
16  Verdi, Giuseppe, 1813-1901. Trovatore.
17  Verdi, Giuseppe, 1813-1901. Trovatore
```

Figure 5

```
Rec stat: c Entrd: 801122 Used: 820417
Type: z Bib lvl: t Govt Agn:   Lang:    Source:
Site: 005 InLC: a Enc lvl: n Head ref: a Head: cc
Head status: a Name: a Mod rec:   Auth status: a
Rec status: a

 1 010     n  79051106
 2 100 10  Verdi, Giuseppe, _d 1813-1901. _t Traviata. _n Atto 3o. _p
Preludio _w n003820226aacann----nnnn
 3 400 10  Verdi, Giuseppe, _d 1813-1901. _t Traviata. _p Prelude, act 3 _w
n004820226aaaana----nnnd
 4 400 10  Verdi, Giuseppe, _d 1813-1901. _t Traviata. _n Atto 3o. _p Prelude
_w n005820226aanann----nnnd
 5 670     His Violetta, 1944: _b t.p. (Violetta) _w n002790619aanann----nnnn
```

255

Figure 6

```
M        Beethoven, Ludwig van, 1770-1827.
1010        ⌜Concerto, piano, no.1, op.15, C major⌝
.B41        Concerto, no.1, C major, for pianoforte
op.15    and orchestra.  Op. 15.  With the composer's
E8       original cadenzas.  London, E. Eulenburg
         ⌜foreword 1935⌝
            miniature score (120 p.)  19 cm.  (Edition
         Eulenburg, no.724)

            1. Concertos (Piano)--Scores.
```

Figure 7

con,no,1^,c/sco/1900-1935\

  1 Concerto, no. 1, C major for pianoforte and orchestra, op. 15.
Beethoven, Ludwig van,   London : New York :   1935 [Score]
  2 Concerto, no. 1, C major, op. 15, for pianoforte and orchestra.
Beethoven, Ludwig van,   London, New York,   1934 [Score]

Figure 8

Screen 1 of 2
RCE - FOR OTHER HOLDINGS, ENTER dh DEPRESS DISPLAY RECD SEND
 OCLC: 5909476   Rec stat: c Entrd: 800124   Used: 830121
Type: c Bib lvl: m Lang: N/A Source: d Accomp mat:
 Repr: Enc lvl: I Ctry: enk Dat tp: s MEBE: 0
          Mod rec: Comp: co Format: b Prts:
 Desc: Int lvl: LTxt: n   Dates: 1935,
  1 010
  2 040   NQA _c NQA _d OCL _d m.c.
  3 090   M1010 _b .B41 op. 15, E7
  4 090   _b
  5 049   RCEA
  6 100 10   Beethoven, Ludwig van, _d 1770-1827. _w cn
  7 240 10   Concertos, _m piano, _n no. 1, op. 15, _r C major _w nm
  8 245 0   Concerto, no. 1, C major for pianoforte and orchestra, op. 15. _c
With the composer's original cadenzas. Revised from the original edition and
with foreword by Wilhelm Altmann.
  9 260 0   London : _b E. Eulenburg; _a New York : _b Edition Eulenburg, _c
1935. _d Pl. no. E. E. 3815.
 10 300   miniature score (120 p.) _c 20 cm.

Screen 2 of 2
 11 500   "I. H. der Fhürstin Odescalchi geb. Gräfin Keglevics gewidmet."
 12 650 0 Concertos (Piano) _x Scores.
 13 873 09   _j 240/1 _a Concerto, _m piano, _n no. 1, op. 15, _r C major

Figure 9

```
M        Beethoven, Ludwig van, 1770-1827
1010       (Concerto, piano, no.2, op.19, Bb major)
.B41        Concerto, no.2, Bb major, for pianoforte
op.19    and orchestra.  Op.19.  With the composer's
A4       cadenza.  Edited by Wilhelm Altmann.  London,
         E Eulenburg (foreword 1954)
            miniature score (84 p.)  19cm.  (Edition
         Eulenburg, no.725)

            1. Concertos (Piano)--Scores.  I. Altmann,
         Wilhelm, 1862-1951, ed.
```

Figure 10

con,no,2^,b/sco/1900-1934\

1 Concerto, no. 2, B) major : for piano and orchestra, op. 19, with the composer's cadenza / Beethoven, Ludwig van, London : New York : 1900 [Score]

2 Concerto no. 2, B) major, for pianoforte and orchestra, op. 19. Beethoven, Ludwig van, London, New York, 1934 [Score]

3 Concerto, no. 2, B) major for pianoforte and orchestra, op. 83. Brahms, Johannes, London, New York, 1905 [Score]

matching date, we find the correct record (figure 11).

The third concerto (figure 12) appears to have the same characteristics, so the same search strategy is applied. Our confidence in the ease of searching diminishes with the response of figure 13. Undaunted, we try a slightly truncated search key in the expectation that the title field in the record was subfielded differently from the others we have searched. This new search key retrieves four hits (figure 14), and the one with the matching date is the correct record (figure 15). Note that the inputting library decided to put the musical key into the unsearchable subfield "b".

By applying the same strategies to the fourth concerto (figures 16–18), we retrieve what seems to be a matching record. However, there are no holdings for Rice listed on this record. Since we know that this record has already been converted in our Recon project, we can safely make the assumption that there is a duplicate record for this item in the system that is not retrieved by the search keys used so far. By revising the search strategy (figure 19), we retrieve both the unused record (figure 20) and the record (figure 21) that is to be used according to OCLC documentation. In this case, the record in figure 21 is to be used because it has more holdings symbols attached to it than the more recent record in figure 20.

These four concertos illustrate several of the basic problems in searching for music. Lack of a numeric search key forces title searches. Generic titles have not been tagged in a consistent manner in the OLUC, forcing a variety of search key strategies for similar records. Duplicate records exist in the OLUC and appear to be more evident in music materials than in monographic materials. It is often not enough to find a matching record in the OLUC. Several possibilities may have to be eliminated before the correct record (i.e., the one OCLC says is to be preferred) is retrieved.

Beethoven Recording Search

Suppose now that you have a catalog entry for the 1980 Deutsche Grammophon recording, no. 2531 311, of Beethoven's Symphonie Nr. 5 c-moll op. 67. The performance is by the Wiener Philharmoniker with Leonard Bernstein conducting. Because you have a good transcribed title, you try a title search with, unfortunately, no results (figure 22). Similarly, a slightly truncated title retrieves no entries (figure 23). A search for Beethoven symphony recordings for 1980 retrieves 16 entries, but not the one we are looking for (figure 24). A search for Bernstein (the conductor) and symphonies retrieves 8 more hits (figure 25), but none for this recording. In fact, it turns out that any search for this record that includes a qualification of a date within five hundred years on either

Figure 11

```
RCE - FOR OTHER HOLDINGS, ENTER dh DEPRESS DISPLAY RECD SEND
  OCLC: 1215591       Rec stat: c Entrd: 750314        Used: 820529
Type: c Bib lvl: m Lang:  N/A Source: d Accomp mat:
  Repr:    Enc lvl: I Ctry:  enk Dat tp: s MEBE: 0
           Mod rec:   Comp:  co Format: b Prts:
  Desc:    Int lvl:   LTxt:  n   Dates: 1934,000_
   1 010
   2 040     AKR _c AKR _d OCL _d m.c.
   3 090     M1010 _b .B41 op. 19, .E8, 1934x
   4 090     _b
   5 049     RCEA
   6 100 10  Beethoven, Ludwig van, _d 1770-1827. _w cn
   7 240 10  Concertos, _m piano, _n no. 2, op. 19, _r B) major _w nm
   8 245 0   Concerto no. 2, B) major, _b for pianoforte and orchestra, op. 19.
_c With the composer's cadenza. Edited by Wilhelm Altmann.
   9 260 0   London, _b Ernst Eulenburg; _a New York, _b Edition Eulenburg _c
[1934]
  10 300     miniature score (84 p.)
  11 490 0   Edition Eulenburg, no. 725
  12 500     Pl. no. E. E. 3816.
  13 650  0  Concertos (Piano) _x Scores.
```

Figure 12

```
  M         Beethoven, Ludwig van, 1770-1827.
  1010          [Concerto, piano, no.3, op.37, C minor]
  .B41          Concerto, no.3, C minor, for pianoforte and
  op.37     orchestra.  Op. 37.  With the composer's cadenza.
  A4        From the original autographed ms., rev. and
            with foreword by Wilh. Altmann.  London, E.
            Eulenburg [Revisionsbericht 1933]
                miniature score (120 p.)  19 cm.  (Edition
            Eulenburg, no. 704)

                1. Concertos (Piano)--Scores.   I. Altmann,
            Wilhelm, 1862-1951, ed.
```

Figure 13

con,no,3^,c/sco/1900-1933\

CON,NO,3^,C/SCO/1900-1933 is not in TITLE index.
If you have already tried the other index search keys,
Please request a workform.

Figure 14

con,no,3^,/sco/1900-1933\

 1 Concerto no. 3, C minor for pianoforte and orchestra, op. 37.
Beethoven, Ludwig van,   London, New York,   1933 [Score]
 2 Concerto no. 3 : for cello and piano : in B minor, opus 51 /
Goltermann, Georg Eduard,   New York :   1900 [Score]
 3 Concerto no. 3 : op.51 /   Goltermann, Georg Eduard,   London :   1920
[Score]
 4 Concerto no. 3 : pour piano avec accompagnement d' orchestre ; op. 75 /
Tchaikovsky, Peter Ilich,   New York :   1900 [Score]

Figure 15

```
RCE - FOR OTHER HOLDINGS, ENTER dh DEPRESS DISPLAY RECD SEND
  OCLC: 1215577       Rec stat: c Entrd: 750314         Used: 820721
Type: c Bib lvl: m Lang:  eng Source: u Accomp mat:      __
Repr:     Enc lvl: I Ctry:  ___ Dat tp: _ MEBE: _
          Mod rec:  Comp:      Format:  Prts:
 Desc:    Int lvl:  LTxt:  __ Dates: 1933,____
  1 010
  2 040      _c AKR _d OCL _d m.c.
  3 090      M1010 _b .B41 op. 37, .E8, 1933x
  4 090      _b
  5 049      RCEA
  6 100 10  Beethoven, Ludwig van, _d 1770-1827. _w cn
  7 240 10  Concertos, _m piano, _n no. 3, op. 37, _r C minor _w nm
  8 245 0   Concerto no. 3, _b C minor for pianoforte and orchestra, op. 37.
_c With the composer's cadenza. Edited by Wilhelm Altmann.
  9 260 0   London, _b Ernst Eulenburg; _a New York, _b Edition Eulenburg _c
[1933]
 10 300     miniature score (120 p.)
 11 490 0   Edition Eulenburg, no. 704
 12 500     Pl. no. E. E. 3804.
 13 650  0  Concertos (Piano) _x Scores.
```

Figure 16

```
M          Beethoven, Ludwig van, 1770-1827
1010          [Concerto, piano, no.4, op.58, G major]
.B41          Concerto, no.4, G major, for pianoforte and
op.58      orchestra. Op.58. With the composer's cadenzas
A4         Rev. from the original ed., and with foreword by
           Wilhelm Altmann. London, E. Eulenburg; New
           York, Eulenburg Miniature Scores [Revisionsbericht
           1934]
              miniature score (141 p.) 19cm. (Edition
           Eulenburg, no.705)

              1. Concertos (Piano)--Scores. I. Altmann,
           Wilhelm, 1862-1951 ed.
```

Figure 17

con,no,4^,g/sco/1900-1934\

    1 Concerto no. 4, G dur /   Bach, Johann Sebastian,   Wien :   1900
[Score]
    2 Concerto no. 4, G dur, G major.   Bach, Johann Sebastian,   Wien,   1900
[Score]
    3 Concerto no. 4, G major : for pianoforte and orchestra : op. 58 : with
the composer's cadenzas /   Beethoven, Ludwig van,   London : New York :   1934
  [Score]
    4 Concerto, no. 4, G major, for pianoforte and orchestra, op. 58, with the
composer's cadenzas /   Beethoven, Ludwig van,   London :   1934 [Score]

Figure 18

 Screen 1 of 2
NO HOLDINGS IN RCE - FOR HOLDINGS ENTER dh DEPRESS DISPLAY RECD SEND
 OCLC: 5248267   Rec stat: n Entrd: 790807   Used: 830104
Type: c Bib lvl: m Lang: N/A Source: d Accomp mat: hi
Repr: Enc lvl: I Ctry: enk Dat tp: s MEBE: 1
          Mod rec: Comp: co Format: b Prts:
 Desc: r Int lvl: LTxt: n   Dates: 1934,
  1 010
  2 040   DHU _c DHU _d m.c.
  3 041 0   _e engger
  4 045   w0w0
  5 048   oa _b ka01
  6 090   M1010 _b .B4 op.58, 1934
  7 090   _b
  8 049   RCEA
  9 100 10 Beethoven, Ludwig van, _d 1770-1827. _w cn
 10 240 10 Concertos, _m piano, _n no. 4, op. 58, _r G major _w nm
 11 245 00 Concerto no. 4, G major : _b for pianoforte and orchestra : op. 58
: with the composer's cadenzas / _c by Ludwig van Beethoven ; revised from the
original edition and with foreword by Wilhelm Altmann.
 12 260 0   London : _b E. Eulenburg ; _a New York : _b Edition Eulenburg, _c
[pref. 1934]

263

Figure 19

beet,conc/sco/1934\

1 Beethoven, Ludwig van,   Concerto, no. 1, C major, op. 15, for pianoforte
and orchestra.   London, New York,   1934 [Score]
2 Beethoven, Ludwig van,   Concerto no. 2, B) major, for pianoforte and
orchestra, op. 19.   London, New York,   1934 [Score]
3 Beethoven, Ludwig van,   Concerto no. 4, G major : for pianoforte and
orchestra : op. 58 : with the composer's cadenzas /   London : New York :
1934 [Score]
4 Beethoven, Ludwig van,   Concerto, no. 4, G major, for pianoforte and
orchestra, op. 58, with the composer's cadenzas /   London :   1934 [Score]
5 Beethoven, Ludwig van,   Concerto, no. 4, G major, for pianoforte and
orchestra, op. 58; with the composer's cadenzas.   London, New York,   1934
[Score]
6 Beethoven, Ludwig van,   Concertos,   Leipzig,   1934 [Score]
7 Beethoven, Ludwig van,   Concertos,   Leipzig,   1934 [Score]

Figure 20

```
Screen 1 of 2
NO HOLDINGS IN RCE -  FOR HOLDINGS ENTER dh DEPRESS  DISPLAY RECD SEND
OCLC: 5248267      Rec stat: n Entrd: 790807        Used: 830104
Type: c Bib lvl: m Lang: N/A Source: d Accomp mat: hi
Repr:    Enc lvl: I Ctry:  enk Dat tp: s MEBE: 1
         Mod rec:   Comp:  co Format: b Prts:
Desc: r Int lvl:   LTxt: n   Dates: 1934,
 1 010
 2 040     DHU _c DHU _d m.c.
 3 041 0     _e engger
 4 045     w0w0
 5 048     oa _b ka01
 6 090     M1010 _b .B4 op.58, 1934
 7 090      _b
 8 049     RCEA
 9 100 10  Beethoven, Ludwig van, _d 1770-1827. _w cn
10 240 10  Concertos, _m piano, _n no. 4, op. 58, _r G major _w nm
11 245 00  Concerto no. 4, G major : _b for pianoforte and orchestra : op. 58
: with the composer's cadenzas / _c by Ludwig van Beethoven ; revised from the
original edition and with foreword by Wilhelm Altmann.
12 260 0   London : _b E. Eulenburg ; _a New York : _b Edition Eulenburg, _c
[pref. 1934]
```

Figure 21

```
Screen 1 of 2
RCE - FOR OTHER HOLDINGS, ENTER dh DEPRESS DISPLAY RECD SEND
 OCLC: 414932       Rec stat: c Entrd: 720926        Used: 830104
Type: c Bib lvl: m Lang:  N/A Source: d Accomp mat:
Repr:    Enc lvl: I Ctry:  enk Dat tp: s MEBE: 0
         Mod rec:  Comp:  co Format: b Prts:
 Desc:   Int lvl:  LTxt:  n   Dates: 1934,
  1 010
  2 040     WOO _c WOO _d OCL _d m.c. _d OCL
  3 090     M1010 _b .B41 op.58, E8, 1934
  4 090       _b
  5 049     RCEA
  6 100 10  Beethoven, Ludwig van, _d 1770-1827. _w cn
  7 240 10  Concertos, _m piano, _n no. 4, op. 58, _r G major _w nm
  8 245 00  Concerto, no. 4, _b G major, for pianoforte and orchestra, op. 58;
 with the composer's cadenzas.
  9 250     Rev. from the original ed. _b and with foreword by Wilhelm
 Altmann.
 10 260 0   London, _b E. Eulenburg; _a New York, _b Edition Eulenburg _c
 [1934]
 11 300     iv. p., miniature score (141 p.) _c 19 cm.
 12 490 0   Edition Eulenburg, no. 705
```

Figure 22

sym,nr,5^,c/rec/1980\

SYM,NR,5^,C/REC/1980 is not in TITLE index.
If you have already tried the other index search keys,
Please request a workform.

Figure 23

```
sym,nr,5,/rec/1980\
```

```
SYM,NR,5,/REC/1980 is not in TITLE index.
If you have already tried the other index search keys,
Please request a workform.
```

Figure 24a

```
beet,symp/rec/1980\
```

Figure 24b

```
 Screen 1 of 2
   1  Beethoven, Ludwig van,   Symphonie Nr. 2 D-dur op. 36 ; [Overture to the
ballet] "Die geschhopfe des Prometheus" op. 43   West Germany :   1980  [Music
recording]
   2  Beethoven, Ludwig van,   Symphonie Nr. 6 F-dur op. 68 "Pastorale."   West
Germany :   1980  [Music recording]
   3  Beethoven, Ludwig van,   Symphonie Nr. 9 d-moll op. 125.   Holland :
1980  [Music recording]
   4  Beethoven, Ludwig van,   Symphonies   West Germany :   1980  [Music
recording]
   5  Beethoven, Ludwig van,   Symphonies,   West Germany :   1980  [Music
recording]
   6  Beethoven, Ludwig van,   Symphonies   Germany :   1980  [Music recording]
   7  Beethoven, Ludwig van,   Symphonies.   1980  [Music recording]  DLC
   8  Beethoven, Ludwig van,   Symphony,   1980  [Music recording]
   9  Beethoven, Ludwig van,   Symphony no. 1 in C, op. 21. "Leonore" overture
III.   1980  [Music recording]  DLC
```

(continues)

(continued from previous page)

```
Screen 2 of 2
10  Beethoven, Ludwig van,   Symphony no. 3 in E-flat major, op. 55,
"Eroica".   New York :   1980  [Music recording]
11  Beethoven, Ludwig van,   Symphony no. 3 in E-flat major, op. 55 :
(Eroica) /   [New York] :   1980  [Music recording]
12  Beethoven, Ludwig van,   Symphony no. 3 in E-flat major, op. 55, "Eroica"
.   New York :   1980  [Music recording]
13  Beethoven, Ludwig van,   Symphony no. 3 in E-flat, op. 55 "Eroica"
[Berkeley, Calif.?] :   1980  [Music recording]
14  Beethoven, Ludwig van,   Symphony no. 6 in F major, op. 68 (Pastoral) /
New York :   1980  [Music recording]
15  Beethoven, Ludwig van,   Symphony no. 6, in F major, op. 68 (Pastoral
symphony).   1980  [Music recording]
16  Beethoven, Ludwig van,   Symphony no. 7 in A, op. 92 /   Minneapolis,
Minn. :   1980  [Music recording]
```

Figure 25a

```
bern,symp/rec/1980\
```

Figure 25b

```
1  Bernstein, Leonard   Symphonie Nr. 2 D-dur op. 36 ; [Overture to the
ballet] "Die geschhopfe des Prometheus" op. 43   West Germany :   1980  [Musi
recording]
2  Bernstein, Leonard,   Symphonie nr. 3, a-moll, op. 56, "Schottische" /
West Germany :   1980  [Music recording]
3  Bernstein, Leonard,   Symphonie nr. 3, a-moll, op. 56, "Schottische" ;
Ouverthure "Die Hebriden" op. 26 /   [New York] :   1980  [Music recording]
4  Bernstein, Leonard,   Symphony no. 5, op. 47.   New York :   1980  [Music
recording]
5  Bernstein, Leonard.   Symphony : no. 5, op. 47 /   New York :   1980
[Music recording]
6  Bernstein, Leonard,   Symphony no. 97 in C major.   1980  [Music
recording]
7  Bernstein, Leonard,   Symphony no. 98 in B) major.   New York :   1980
[Music recording]
8  Bernstein, Leonard,   Symphony no.5   [New York] :   1980  [Music
recording]
```

267

side of the present will not retrieve this record.

Figure 26 is the correct OLUC record for this recording and is an illustration of how improper subfield coding can create problems in the OLUC. Because the record number was incorrectly input in subfield "c" of the 262 field, the date was placed into subfield "d," and no date was placed in the fixed fields by the cataloging agency, the system supplied the first four digits of subfield "c" as the searchable date. This makes this record retrievable with a qualification of date of the year 2531, or with any open ended date qualification.

While this problem has more general applicability than just to a conversion project, it illustrates what can happen when incorrect information is input and is illustrative of the type of problem we have experienced doing the scores conversion at Rice.

Haydn Symphony Search

Here is an extreme example of a searching problem. This catalog entry (figure 27) looks innocent enough at first glance. Let's look at what we do know about this item and this record. We have an unambiguous main entry; we have a legitimate uniform title; the first word of the title looks OK; we have an editor; we have an unambiguous place of publication; and we know beyond any reasonable doubt that it is a score and that the record in the database, if indeed it is in the database, should be on the scores format. Also, we know the plate number of the publication, which would be a lovely access point if the item were in the database, if the plate number were recorded in the 028 field of the record, and if the 028 field were searchable.

Next, and just as importantly, let's look at what we don't know about this item and this record. We don't know if the composer's name is spelled correctly in the record in the database; we don't know if the record in the database includes a uniform title or, if so, if the uniform title is subfielded properly; we don't know where the bracketed information in the title is taken from. Presumably, it doesn't come from the title page, since it is in brackets. (This is assuming, of course, that the primary source of information for the description is a title page, since there is no indication to the contrary.) It could, however, come from the cover. It is not at all unusual for the title information on the cover to differ substantially from that on the title page. The title on the cover could read something like: "Symphonies numbers one through twelve for piano solo," or the French or German equivalent of that. And it's possible that the music cataloger at some other member institution of OCLC decided that the cover should be the chief source of information. So, while

268

Figure 26

```
NO HOLDINGS IN RCE -  FOR HOLDINGS ENTER dh DEPRESS  DISPLAY RECD SEND
OCLC: 9067621       Rec stat: n Entrd: 821218       Used: 821218
Type: j Bib lvl: m Lang:  N/A Source: u Accomp mat:
Repr:    Enc lvl: K Ctry:   xx  Dat tp: u MEBE: 0
         Mod rec:  Comp:       Format: n Prts: n
Desc:    Int lvl:  LTxt:       Dates: 2531,
 1 010
 2 040      _c SXP
 3 090      _b
 4 049      RCEA
 5 100 10   Beethoven, Ludwig van, _d 1770-1827.
 6 245 00   Symphonie Nr. 5 c-moll op.67. _h Sound recording.
 7 262      West Germany, _b Deutsche Grammophon _c 2531 311 _d 1980.
 8 300      1 sound disc : _c 33 1/3 rpm. _e stereo _b 12 in.
 9 511      Wiener Philharmoniker; Leonard Bernstein, conductor.
10 650  0   Symphonies.
11 705 11   Bernstein, Leonard
```

Figure 27

```
M        Haydn, Joseph, 1732-1809
35         [Symphonies. Selections; arr.]
.H3        Symphonies [no.1-12] arrangees pour piano
W5       seul par R. Wittmann. Leipzig, C. F. Peters
         [n. d.] Pl. no. 4983.
             score (179 p.) 30cm. (Edition Peters)




         1. Symphonies arranged for piano.
```

269

the bracketed information in the 245 field, subfield "a," is disregarded by the OCLC searching program, we cannot disregard the possibility that the information that appears in brackets on our card might not be in brackets in a record in the database.

Also, we do not know whether this mythical music cataloger was considerate enough to leave a space between the period and the "one" in the "numbers one to twelve." This, of course, would affect the search keys that must be tried. We also do not know where our cataloger decided that subfield "a" of the 245 field should end: after "Symphonies"; after "12"; or after "piano seul". While we do know the editor's name, we do not know whether our cataloger was considerate enough to make an added entry for him. Very importantly, we do not know a date of publication. We do not even know for sure that the cataloger put this record on the scores format (type C). Finally, we do not know for sure that this title is represented in the database at all.

Now that we've analyzed the elements of the description to look for possible search keys, we begin our search in the OLUC. Figure 28 displays the possible search keys. We know that we've already worked with several entries in the card catalog for Haydn symphonies, and upon thumbing through the following entries, we see many, many more, so we decide that "HAYD, SYMP/SCO" will be our last-resort search key. We hope for the best and try the first search key listed, the editor/title search. Although this search key strategy has often worked for us in the past, it retrieves only three records this time, none of them for a Wittmann.

Undaunted, we decide to try a variety of title searches from the transcribed title (245 field). We know that, if subfield "a" of the 245 field of the record we're looking for contains just the word "Symphonies," a title search is hopeless. So we assume that there is more information in subfield "a". We try the second search key, assuming that the title is input as on our card and that subfield "a" ends after the word "seul". Nothing. For the rest of the searches involving the 245 field, we assume that "numbers one to twelve" is not in brackets. First, we try the third search key with no space between the period and the one, with subfield "a" ending after the 12, and we get the results shown in figure 29. One hundred and three entries, but none of them is a Haydn entry published in Leipzig. Then we try the fourth search key, which is the same as the third, except with a space between the "period" and the "one", and we get figure 30.

We're beginning to get a little worried, but we're not panicking yet. Next we assume that the phrase "arrangées pour piano seul" is also in subfield "a" of the 245 and try search keys five and six: with a space between the "period" and the "one" and without a space. Again, nothing. Our palms are beginning to sweat in

270

Figure 28

	Search Key	Type of Search	Fields Searched
1.	WITT, SYMP/SCO	Author/Title	700/245 (Wittmann .../ Symphonies)
2.	SYM,AR,PO,P/SCO	Title	245 (Symphonies arrangées pour piano ...)
3.	SYM,NO,,/SCO	Title	245 (Symphonies no. 1-12.)
4.	SYM,NO,11,/SCO	Title	245 (Symphonies no. 1-12.)
5.	SYM,NO,11,A/SCO	Title	245 (Symphonies no. 1-12 arrangees ...)
6.	SYM,NO,AR,P/SCO	Title	245 (Symphonies no. 1-12 arranges pour ...)
7.	SYM,SE,AR,/SCO	Title	240 (Symphonies. Selections; arr.)
8.	WITT,R	Author	700 (Wittman, R ...)
9.	HAYD,SYMP/BKS	Author/Title	100/245 (Haydn ... Symphonies ...)
10.	HAYD,SYMP/SCO	Author/Title	100/245 (Haydn ... Symphonies ...)

Figure 29

```
SYM,NO,^^,^/SCO
   1  Music Scores      1900          7
   2  Music Scores      1909-1938    10
   3  Music Scores      1939-1947    11
   4  Music Scores      1950-1955    12
   5  Music Scores      1956-1962    11
   6  Music Scores      1963-1966    10
   7  Music Scores      1967-1969    14
   8  Music Scores      1970-1972    10
   9  Music Scores      1973-1981    11
  10  Music Scores      NO DATE       7
                                   ____
                                    103
```

Figure 30

Screen 1 of 2
1 Symphonie no. 11 (Milithar-Symphonie) (Symphonie militaire), G major;
Haydn, Joseph,   Bruxelles,   [Score]
2 Symphony no. 11, in G major (Military)   Haydn, Joseph, New York,
[Score]
3 Symphony no. 11 /   Haydn, Joseph,   London :   1900 [Score]
4 Symphony, no. 11   Milhaud, Darius,   Paris,   1962 [Score] DLC
5 Symphony, no. 11   Milhaud, Darius,   Paris :   1962 [Score]
6 Symphony no. 11 : the year of 1905 : op. 103 /   Shostakovich, Dmitri
Dmitrievich,   New York :   1950 [Score]
7 Symphony no. 11 : "The year of 1905" : op. 103 /   Shostakovich, Dmitrifi
Dmitrievich, Melville, N. Y. :   1950 [Score]
8 Symphony no. 11 : "The year of 1905": Op. 103 /   Shostakovich, Dmitrifi
Dmitrievich,   New York : 1957 [Score]
9 Symphony no. 11 : the year 1905, op. 103 /   Shostakovich, Dmitrifi
Dmitrievich,   New York,   1958 [Score]

272

apprehension of the possibility of having to search by "Haydn/Symphonies/Score", unqualified by date. We try a title search on the uniform title (search no. 7), assuming that it is not subfielded. Still nothing. We try the most basic search we can for the editor, unqualified by date or format (search no. 8). This retrieves three records, none of them for the elusive Herr Wittmann.

We're starting to convulse as we hope against hope that somebody put the thing in on the books format (search no. 9). We get the response found in figure 31. One of the records is indeed a score, but it's not the score for which we're looking. Gloomily, we resume our search with the search key we've been avoiding like the plague, search key no. 10. And it retrieves the display found in figure 32. We go into cardiac arrest as our worst fears are realized: *seven hundred and fifty-one hits* on this search key, and there are really none of them that we can eliminate at this point.

We won't bore you with the displays from each of the 16 lines on the group display, but suffice it to say that it took a total of *eighty-three* separate commands and about *forty minutes* to determine that this title was not in the online union catalog. Even more depressing was the discovery, upon searching for the physical item in the stacks, that the item had been missing since our last music inventory three years ago but had never been withdrawn from the catalog.

Generic Title Searches

In an effort to illustrate the difficulty of generic transcribed title searches, we ran test searches of typical generic titles. The results are found in figures 33–37 respectively.

A title search as distinctive (or as generic) as "sym,no,1-,c/sco" retrieves 24 hits to be evaluated. Taking away the key designation and allowing the system to retrieve anything following the "1", the hit rate zooms to 188 items retrieved. The two concerto form searches had hit rates of 182 items (vi) and 112 items (pi), while the "vi" sonata search yielded 215 hits.

As can be seen, generic title searches, even in full four-element combinations, are generally impractical for scores. The form qualification "/sco" must always be used. A date qualification will obviously reduce the number of hits for each search key, but we have often had no date to use, or the date "[19–]", requiring a search of all the matching records input to date.

Recon and AACR2

When we first started working on the Recon project, we probably had no legitimate reason for updating name headings and uni-

Figure 31

1 Haydn, Joseph,   Symphonie Nr. 92 (Oxford-Symphonie), G dur – G major –
Sol majeur /   Leipzig :   1955
2 Haydn, Joseph,   The symphonies of Joseph Haydn.   New York,   1956

Figure 32

HAYD,SYMP/SCO

1	Music Scores	1774-1896	21
2	Music Scores	1897-1900	97
3	Music Scores	1900	99
4	Music Scores	1901-1910	6
5	Music Scores	1920-1935	35
6	Music Scores	1936-1944	37
7	Music Scores	1946-1950	35
8	Music Scores	1951-1953	38
9	Music Scores	1954-1959	36
10	Music Scores	1960-1962	35
11	Music Scores	1963-1964	59
12	Music Scores	1965-1966	62
13	Music Scores	1967-1968	52
14	Music Scores	1969-1973	43
15	Music Scores	1974-1982	40
16	Music Scores	NO DATE	56

751

Figure 33

```
sym,no,1^,c/sco\

To see title for a COLLECTIVE ENTRY, type line#, DEPRESS DISPLAY RECD, SEND.

  1  Symphonie No. 1, C dur   Beethoven, Ludwig van,   [Leipzig,   1900
[Score]
  2  Symphonie no. 1, C dur, op. 21, /   Beethoven, Ludwig van,   Leipzig :
[Score]
  3  Symphonie No. 1, C major, Op. 21 : Orchestral score with reduction of the
piano placed underneath /   Beethoven, Ludwig van,   [Bruxelles :   1900
[Score]
  4  Symphonie No. 1, C minor, op. 68.   Brahms, Johannes,   [Bruxelles,
[Score]
  5  SYMPHONIE NO 1 C MOLL  (2)
  6  Symphonie Nr. 1, c-Moll (Linzer Fassung)   Bruckner, Anton,   Weisbaden
1949  [Score]
  7  SYMPHONY NO 1 C MAJOR   (7)
  8  SYMPHONY NO 1 C MAJOR OP 21   BEETHOVEN LUDWIG VAN (2)
  9  SYMPHONY NO 1 C MINOR  BR (3)
 10  Symphony, no. 1, C minor, for orchestra, op. 68.   Brahms, Johannes,
London, New York,   [Score]
 11  SYMPHONY NO 1 C MINOR OP  (4)
```

275

Figure 34

```
SYM,NO,1,/SCO
    1   Music Scores        1900        32
    2   Music Scores        1902-1936   10
    3   Music Scores        1938-1940   11
    4   Music Scores        1944-1949   12
    5   Music Scores        1950-1953   14
    6   Music Scores        1955-1958   11
    7   Music Scores        1959-1960   12
    8   Music Scores        1961-1962   12
    9   Music Scores        1963-1969   12
   10   Music Scores        1970-1971   22
   11   Music Scores        1972-1975   12
   12   Music Scores        1976-1980   11
   13   Music Scores        NO DATE     17
```

Figure 35

```
CON,FO,VI,A/SCO
    1  Music Scores        1899-1917  10
    2  Music Scores        1918-1927  11
    3  Music Scores        1930-1938  10
    4  Music Scores        1939-1942  16
    5  Music Scores        1943-1948  10
    6  Music Scores        1949-1950  15
    7  Music Scores        1951-1953  13
    8  Music Scores        1956-1958  10
    9  Music Scores        1959-1960  12
   10  Music Scores        1962-1964  12
   11  Music Scores        1965-1967  15
   12  Music Scores        1968-1969  12
   13  Music Scores        1970-1977  13
   14  Music Scores        1978-1980  15
   15  Music Scores        NO DATE     8
```

Figure 36

```
CON,FO,PI,A/SCO
    1  Music Scores        1900-1939    9
    2  Music Scores        1940-1946   11
    3  Music Scores        1947-1952   10
    4  Music Scores        1954-1957   10
    5  Music Scores        1959-1960   19
    6  Music Scores        1962-1967   10
    7  Music Scores        1968-1970   11
    8  Music Scores        1971-1974   11
    9  Music Scores        1975-1977   10
   10  Music Scores        1978-1981   10
   11  Music Scores        NO DATE      1
```

Figure 37

```
SON,FO,VI,A/SCO
  1  Music Scores        1894         3
  2  Music Scores        1900-1917   12
  3  Music Scores        1918-1923   17
  4  Music Scores        1924-1928   11
  5  Music Scores        1929-1937   12
  6  Music Scores        1938-1942   12
  7  Music Scores        1943-1946   11
  8  Music Scores        1947-1949   11
  9  Music Scores        1950-1952   16
 10  Music Scores        1953-1955   11
 11  Music Scores        1956-1958   10
 12  Music Scores        1959-1960   11
 13  Music Scores        1961-1964   13
 14  Music Scores        1965-1966   10
 15  Music Scores        1967-1968   13
 16  Music Scores        1969-1970   10
 17  Music Scores        1971-1974   10
 18  Music Scores        1975-1979   10
 19  Music Scores        1980-1982   10
 20  Music Scores        NO DATE      2
```

form titles to AACR2 form; it was something we felt compelled to do and had the expertise to do, so why not. However, after working on the project for a few weeks, it became apparent that only a small percentage (probably less than 10%) of the uniform titles in the OCLC records we had worked with were completely correct, in terms of content, subfielding, and indicators, by either AACR2 or by previous codes. Thus, we realized that, since we were having to edit in some manner a very large proportion of the fields that included uniform titles, we might as well change the uniform titles to AACR2 form rather than to the old form as it appeared on the card.

Prior to the implementation of AACR2 in January 1981, the people involved with music at OCLC realized that many of the uniform titles for music existing in the online union catalog could be changed into valid (or nearly so) AACR2 uniform titles by making a few universal changes in all applicable records in the database. Thus, when the OLUC was shut down in December 1980 to run a program that would replace old forms of personal and corporate name headings with AACR2 forms from the LC Name Authority File, it was decided to run simultaneously a program that would make wholesale changes in music uniform titles. Specifically, these changes were: 1) pluralize certain generic terms when there was evidence in the uniform title that the composer wrote more than one work in that form (i.e. the presence of the abbreviation "no."); 2) substitute comma-space for space-ampersand-space in statements of medium of performance; 3) substitute the term "vocal score" for "piano-vocal score"; 4) move a numeral indicating a number of instruments from a position before the name of the instrument to a position following the name, and enclose it in parentheses; and 5) in records for music by J.S. Bach change the abbreviation "S." to "BWV".

By and large, the program worked pretty well, although many elements of uniform titles were not changed that perhaps could have been if the program had been written differently. OCLC consciously decided to err on the conservative side, rather than run the risk of converting an unduly large number of uniform titles incorrectly. Nonetheless, unforeseen problems did arise. Figure 38 illustrates a few examples.

Of course, there were many kinds of changes that could not be effected in OCLC's conversion, such as a change of language of the title or treatment of a work as part of a larger work, rather than as an independent work. Examples of these are shown in figure 39.

LC Name Authority File

We have found the online LC Name Authority File to be invaluable in the conversion of scores as we are doing it. When we begin

Figure 38

La traviata. Piano-vocal score. Italian

changed to

La traviata. Vocal score. Italian

while correct AACR2 form is

Traviata. Vocal score

Airs, 2nd book

changed to

Airs, nd book (2)

while correct AACR2 form is

Ayres, 2nd book

Sonatas, ...

changed to

Sonatass, ...

while correct AACR2 form is

Sonatas, ...

Figure 39

Old Uniform Title	AACR2 Uniform Title
Aus Holbergs Zeit (piano work by Grieg)	Fra Holbergs tid
Le sacre du printemps (ballet by Stravinsky)	Vesna svi͡ashchennai͡a
Gianni Schicchi (opera by Puccini)	Trittico. Gianni Schicchi
Sonata, violin & continuo, op. 5, no. 12, D minor (by Corelli)	Sonatas, violin, continuo, op. 5. No. 12. (converted by OCLC as Sonatas, violin, continuo, op. 5, no. 12, D minor)

282

working on a composer with many entries in the card catalog, we routinely examine the name authority records for that composer and often print out truncated displays that will serve as reminders as we work through that composer's file. We also check the Name Authority File if we have any inkling that a name heading or a uniform title has changed. If we cannot locate a name authority record for a name or uniform title, which we think would be different under AACR2, we leave the heading in the old form. Occasional consulting of the LC Name Authority File slows down our work, but we feel that it considerably enhances the quality and long-range usefulness of the converted records.

Through the use of the LC Name Authority File in Recon, we have also located numerous AACR2 headings which had not yet been found in our regular music cataloging operation. These headings have been added to our in-house music name authority file, and the necessary changes have been made on the catalog cards.

Using the LC Name Authority File is not without its problems, however. As an illustration of this, we will trace the steps involved in searching the LCNAF for the authority record for Antonin Dvorak's *Carnival Overture*. The search key "dvor,ant," retrieves figure 40, including forty-five entries for the composer in question. We know from several entries in the card file that the pre-AACR2 uniform title for the work is "Carneval", so we try entry 3 on the collective display, retrieving figure 41. With the knowledge that AACR2 prescribes that the uniform title be based on "the composer's original title in the language in which it was formulated," we decide to try the Czech spelling "Karneval." We obtained this spelling from the transcribed title information of an entry in the catalog for a Czech edition of the work we are attempting to convert. Returning to the collective display (figure 40), we find no titles listed beginning with "K."

Then we remember that this overture, along with others by Dvorak, was originally conceived by him as part of a larger work, *Nature, Life and Love*. Prior to AACR2, both "Carneval" and "Nature, life, and love" were established as valid uniform titles. Looking again at the collective display, however, we see no titles beginning with "N." Then we seem to recall, with the smattering of Czech language that we know, that the Czech word for nature begins with the letter "P," so we go on to entry 9. (See figure 42.) Upon seeing lines 7 and 8, we are fairly certain that we are on the right track. We call up entry 8 first (figure 43) and find the uniform title for the larger work. Confidently, we call up entry 7 (figure 44) and there, sure enough, is the authority record for the *Carnival Overture*.

This search required eight commands and five minutes of search time. If we had not known as much as we did about the work and/or

Figure 40

To see title for a COLLECTIVE ENTRY, type line#, DEPRESS DISPLAY RECD, SEND.

```
1   Dvo˘r´ak, Anton´in, 1841-1904.
2   Dvo˘r´ak, Anton´in, 1841-1904.
3   DVORAK ANTONIN 18411904 C (5)
4   Dvo˘r´ak, Anton´in, 1841-1904. Drobnosti
5   Dvo˘r´ak, Anton´in, 1841-1904. Instrumental music.
6   Dvo˘r´ak, Anton´in, 1841-1904. Jakob´in
7   DVORAK ANTONIN 18411904 MORAVSKE DVOJZPEVY (4)
8   DVORAK ANTONIN 18411904 P (8)
9   DVORAK ANTONIN 18411904 QUARTETS (2)
10  DVORAK ANTONIN 18411904 R (2)
11  Dvo˘r´ak, Anton´in, 1841-1904. Scherzo capriccioso
12  DVORAK ANTONIN 18411904 SLOVANSKE  (4)
13  DVORAK ANTONIN 18411904 SYM (7)
14  Dvo˘r´ak, Antonin, 1841-1904. Trios,
15  DVORAK ANTONIN 18411904 V  (2)
16  Dvo˘r´ak, Anton´in, 1841-1904. Vodn´ik
17  DVORAK ANTONIN 18411904 WORKS (2)
18  DVORAK ANTONIN 18411904 ZE SUMAVY (2)
19  Dvo˘r´ak, Anton´in, 1920-
```

Figure 41

```
1   Dvo˘r´ak, Anton´in, 1841-1904. ˘Cesk´a suita
2   Dvo˘r´ak, Anton´in, 1841-1904. Cig´ansk´e melodie
3   Dvo˘r´ak, Anton´in, 1841-1904. Cig´ansk´e melodie.
4   Dvo˘r´ak, Anton´in, 1841-1904. Concerto,
5   Dvo˘r´ak, Anton´in, 1841-1904. Concertos,
```

Figure 42

```
1   Dvo˘r´ak, Anton´in, 1841-1904. Piano music
2   Dvo˘r´ak, Anton´in, 1841-1904. Piano music.
3   Dvo˘r´ak, Anton´in, 1841-1904. P´isn˘e milostn´e
4   Dvo˘r´ak, Anton´in, 1841-1904. Polka "Pra˘zk´ym akademik'um"
5   Dvo˘r´ak, Anton´in, 1841-1904. Prague waltzes
6   Dvo˘r´ak, Anton´in, 1841-1904. Pra˘zsk´e val˘c´iky
7   Dvo˘r´ak, Anton´in, 1841-1904. P˘r´iroda, ˘zivot a l´aska.
8   Dvo˘r´ak, Anton´in, 1841-1904. P˘r´iroda, ˘zivot a l´aska
```

Figure 43

```
Rec stat: n Entrd: 820417 Used: 820417
Type: z Bib lvl: t Govt Agn:   Lang:    Source:
Site: 003 InLC: a Enc lvl: n Head ref: a Head: cc
Head status: a Name: a Mod rec:   Auth status: a
Ref status: a


 1 010     n  82010298
 2 100 10  Dvo˘r´ak, Anton´in, ⅄d 1841-1904. ⅄t P˘r´iroda, ˘zivot a l´aska ⅄w
n001820303aacann----nnnn
 3 400 10  Dvo˘r´ak, Anton´in, ⅄d 1841-1904. ⅄t Nature, life, and love ⅄w
n002020303aaaann----nnnd
 4 400 10  Dvo˘r´ak, Anton´in, ⅄d 1841-1904. ⅄t Overtures on nature, life,
and love ⅄w n003820303aaanann----nnnd
```

Figure 44

```
Rec stat: n Entrd: 820417 Used: 820417
Type: z Bib lvl: t Govt Agn:   Lang:    Source:
Site: 004 InLC: a Enc lvl: n Head ref: a Head: cc
Head status: a Name: a Mod rec:   Auth status: a
Ref status: a


 1 010     n  82010299
 2 100 10  Dvo˘r´ak, Anton´in, ⅄d 1841-1904. ⅄t P˘r´iroda, ˘zivot a l´aska.
⅄p Karneval ⅄w n001820303aacann----nnnn
 3 400 10  Dvo˘r´ak, Anton´in, ⅄d 1841-1904. ⅄t Carnival ⅄w n002820303aaaann-
---nnnd
 4 400 10  Dvo˘r´ak, Anton´in, ⅄d 1841-1904. ⅄t Karneval ⅄w n003820303aanann-
---nnnd
 5 400 10  Dvo˘r´ak, Anton´in, ⅄d 1841-1904. ⅄t Carnival overture ⅄w
n004820303aanann----nnnd
```

the Czech language, either the search would have been considerably longer, or we would have simply abandoned the search and converted the record in pre-AACR2 form.

Pre-AACR2 Headings on Our Archive Tapes

Despite the fact that music Recon has been using AACR2 name headings and uniform titles since the beginning of our part of the project and that the regular music cataloging operation has been doing so since January 1981, we still have two years of cataloging records with pre-AACR2 headings on our archive tapes: from January 1979 when Rice went online with OCLC to January 1981. We are unaware of any plans that may have been discussed to convert the old name headings and uniform titles in those records to AACR2 form.

A colleague at the University of Virginia has told us that they are converting all music uniform titles in pre-AACR2 form. Meanwhile, their systems librarian is working on a uniform title conversion program similar to the aforementioned program developed by OCLC for its December 1980 conversion. When Virginia's music retrospective conversion project is complete and their online system is up and running, this program would be run against their database to convert applicable records to AACR2 form. When our music Recon project is complete at Rice, we will have a substantially higher percentage of AACR2 uniform titles in our database than Virginia will have in theirs, and we presumably will not need to develop a special program to convert uniform titles. We will, however, have to convert our two years' of records with pre-AACR2 uniform titles in some manner.

Dating Problems

One of the continuing problems we have had in our project has been the creation of dates for an item by past catalogers. Dates have been "formulated," for example, from numbers found at the bottom of advertising on the back cover. Very often these dates are then put on our catalog card, giving us an indication of date that will retrieve no hits in the OLUC. We are forced to search through many and/or all date combinations in order to find a matching record. If there is sufficient doubt on our part about the accuracy of a match, we will pull the item from the shelf to recheck the search and results. This is probably a library-specific problem, but it is illustrative of the type of problems encountered when dealing with music cataloging retrospectively.

Music MARC

A continuing concern of all catalogers using any of the biblio-graphic utilities for the processing of music materials is the delay in the implementation of the MARC format for music by the Library of Congress. This document was published in October 1976, but there was no timetable set for its implementation until late 1980. Since that time the projected implementation date has been set back several times by LC. Although the availability in OCLC of LC MARC records for music would not have been of great benefit in the con-version of our older materials, LC MARC AACR2 records could have been of benefit to us in establishing name headings and uniform titles. While we frequently consulted the LC Name Authority File available on OCLC, we rarely consulted other bibliographic records in the database for assistance in establishing AACR2 name headings and uniform titles.

Flagging the Card Catalog

The Recon project at Rice is somewhat unique in that the cards in the public card catalog are being used for the conversion. This pro-cess is relatively simple for the monographs Recon staff, because they need only go through every main entry card in the drawers, converting the monographs found and flagging (with the color-coded envelopes) those materials which are to be converted at a later date. However, this is terribly inefficient when dealing with music ma-terials. Because of the difference in the ratio of the number of other materials to music materials in our collection, the music Recon pro-gram quickly outdistanced the monographs Recon staff in the num-bers of drawers completed. So that every card would not have to be examined to determine whether it were a score or not, music Recon established the "quick and dirty flagging" of music materials, using the Schwann guide to recordings as a finding list for music main entries, generally composers' names. This system has worked very well with our collection, with an estimated 90%+ of all score ma-terials caught in the first pass.

028 Field

Our experiences have also indicated the usefulness of an indexed 028 (publisher's and plate number) field. As Mr. Hoffman's paper indicates, a large majority of music scores (83.4%) have at least a semi-unique number supplied by the publisher. Unfortunately, this information is rather new to the format, and is not included in most OLUC records, even when that information is available at another point in the record. We feel that, if this information were to be included in the record and indexed, it would significantly reduce the problems of music searching.

Sound Recordings

You may have noticed that we have said nothing about the conversion of bibliographic records for sound recordings. The principal reason for this is that we have not yet attempted to convert any of the library's collection of recordings. In addition, we anticipate major problems in such a project. These problems arise from several factors.

1. Sound recordings different in nature from other types of library materials in that there is a given amount of space to be filled up, a vinyl disc, generally seven or twelve inches in diameter, with sound encoded on both sides. Most publishers of recordings put at least twenty minutes of music on each side of a standard twelve-inch long-playing record. Thus, if the performance of a given work to be released on an LP is thirty minutes in length, there will usually be a "filler" to take up the rest of the space on the disc. Since a relatively small percentage of the recorded repertoire consists of pieces that are forty to sixty minutes in duration, a relatively high percentage of LP records will be anthologies.

2. In our experience, card catalogs of sound recordings are used differently from those for other formats, even scores. Generally, a user will search for a recording by author/title. Performer, subject, title, and series access are used considerably less often than author/title.

3. Rice's collection of recordings is relatively old. Since the Shepherd School was established, most of the allocation for music materials has been spent on scores. By far the bulk of the collection predates 1970. The age of the collection gives rise to two factors: a) We anticipate that the rate of new input into the OLUC would be considerably higher for recordings than for other materials; and, b) since recordings have been under copyright only since 1972, most recordings issued prior to 1972 will not have a date of any sort given on the label, the container, or elsewhere. As we have pointed out, this is a considerable hindrance to searching.

Prior to the mid-1970s, the Library of Congress did not analyze most recorded anthologies with more than three or four selections. Thus, figure 45 is a rather typical example of LC's former practice in cataloging such collections. The record includes a nondescript collective title, no contents note, a useless subject heading (the music card catalog at the Fondren Library has roughly 700 cards with the heading OPERAS — EXCERPTS), and an added entry for the singer. The cataloging entries for this particular recording are virtually useless. The physical item, therefore, is for all practical purposes lost, even if it is in its proper place on the shelf. If LC, or Rice for that matter, were to catalog that item today, the description would be considerably different. More importantly, there would be author/title access to all works on the record.

There is little point in converting this record as it exists into machine-readable form. If no analytics were to be added, this record would be just as "lost" in an online system as it currently is in the manual file.

A partial solution comes from a group called the Online Music Recordings Analytics Consortium (OMRAC). OMRAC is a small group of OCLC member libraries which makes complete analytics for anthologies and submits that fuller cataloging to OCLC in the form of a change request. OCLC then enters the analytics into its database. OMRAC has upgraded the cataloging of several hundred recorded anthologies in the OCLC database, but there are still many hundreds requiring these analytics.

Figure 45

LP
.T255
2

Opera arias. ₁*Phonodisc*₁ Seraphim 60086. ₁1968₁

2 s. 12 in. 33⅓ rpm. microgroove.

Richard Tauber, tenor, with orchestra; sung in German.
Recorded 1925–32.
Program notes by John Freestone on slipcase; texts, with English translations, (₁4₁ p.), inserted.

1. Operas—Excerpts.   I. Tauber, Richard, 1891–1948.

78–760200

Library of Congress   69 ₁2₁   R

289

Third, every conversion project will be different, and different problems will be encountered in each one. Collections are different in size, makeup, age, and function. Access needs are different. Past cataloging standards, practices, and quality vary within a library and from library to library. The specifications used for each conversion project will vary. Other projects of similar nature are only that – similar. They can only be used as general models by others.

However, for a collection of music materials with any type of research, academic, or performance function at all, it is our feeling that music conversion should not be attempted except by trained music processing personnel. Only those persons who work with music materials on a regular basis and are sufficiently familiar with the rules and changes that are constantly being made, can hope accurately to reflect what is in the collection and to maintain the integrity of the catalog.

What we are doing in music conversion at Rice may be deemed recataloging and out of the scope of a conversion project, but we are convinced that our methods are necessary for the eventual practical applications of the resultant data file.

What, then, should be done with sound recordings in the conversion project? Should they be recataloged? Should a card file for recordings be maintained? Should they be converted "as is," on the premise that on online file of sometimes-unusuable entries is no worse than a manual file of the same entries? The Fondren Library has yet to make a decision on this issue, but different alternatives are being explored.

Conclusions

Several conclusions can be drawn from the work that has been done at Rice. First of all, it is painfully obvious that music conversion is vastly more time consuming, and therefore more costly on a per unit basis, than that for monographic materials.

Second, the younger the collection, the easier the music conversion project will be. As new and retrospective materials are input into the OLUC, it becomes increasingly more likely that a matching record will be found. But the OLUC, as it exists, is not truly representative of the titles held in the music collections of member institutions.

At the Texas Conference on Library Automation held at the University of Houston in the fall of 1982, Jay Clark of the Houston Public Library spoke about HPL's conversion project. One of his points spoke very strongly to all conversion projects and is certainly worth emphasizing here. We are creating catalog entries for the future, ones that should and will outlast the current hardware and software applications packages many times over. This must be taken into consideration when discussing specifications for input into a library's data file via retrospective conversion. There will not be sufficient time or manpower to re-edit the entries in the data file once it is in place and running.

RETROSPECTIVE CONVERSION OF MUSIC MATERIALS—
STREAMLINED

Margaret Ford

As the preceding article indicated, my colleagues at Rice University's Fondren Library have struggled valiantly to convert our music score catalog into machine-readable form, in the hope that one fine day the bibliographic records of all of our music scores would be available online. Because of the many problems, the task seemed Herculean. AACR2 created many changes, especially with revised name and uniform title headings. The proposed MARC format for music has been delayed repeatedly. And OCLC has limited searching facilities for music, as Don Greene and Dean Corwin have described in great detail.

Therefore, Ralph Holibaugh, the Music Librarian, and I began to explore other possibilities. We wanted to make the scores and sound recordings in the backlog available more quickly to the user by means of an automated system and to put all previously cataloged music materials into that same system.

Our New System

We knew we could not increase our staff or buy new equipment, but the library already owned a Philips Micom 2004 Word Processor with sophisticated capabilities, such as sorting, searching, stored operations, merging, etc. Using this computer, we developed a matrix format, with vertical columns for the basic descriptive elements and horizontal lines for the bibliographic data for the individual items (sound recordings and scores). (See example A.)

The descriptive elements we believe to be most necessary for sound recordings are: composer, title, date published, performers, subject headings, call number, label, and label number. Provision is made for adding other notes, such as series and composition dates, as necessary.

The format devised for scores contains composer, title, date published, imprint, editor, subject headings, format, call number, series, and plate and publisher's numbers.

293

Abbreviations are used extensively to save space, but they are fairly common, such as *fl* for flute, *Eng* for English, and *sym* for symphony. A handbook, kept at the terminal for reference, contains all abbreviations used and the name authority lists for composers and performing groups, with cross references from name variants. (See examples B and C.)

The cataloging staff began inputting records into the database early in March, 1983. As of the middle of May, there were approximately 1,200 entries for sound recordings, with 365 items cataloged, and approximately 650 entries for scores.

Time Study

We then began to time different procedures for retrospective conversion. Each procedure was tested on a group of twenty items, with some overlap between these groups. A small portable inputting device was used to input three groups, and the larger machine for two groups.

Input from Shelf List

The first twenty cards of the sound recording shelf list were input with the portable device in 91 minutes. This was was the most convenient for the Music Cataloger, since the shelf list is located in front of her desk. The Recon project could be worked on very easily at odd moments throughout the day.

There were several problems, however. The most crucial was the problem of "with" sets. Before AACR2 each composition on a recording (up to 5) was cataloged separately and had its own set of cards. All sets were linked by the same call number, and "with" notes were placed on each set to acknowledge the existence of the other composer/title entries. But only one card for each call number was placed in the shelf list. Thus, performers and subject headings for the additional entries would be missing if retrospective conversion were done from the shelf list. In addition, it had long been a policy to place only one card from a card set in the shelf list in order to save space; so any information on second and third cards would be lacking.

Another problem was the large number of name and uniform title changes resulting from AACR2. Because of a lack of time and manpower, Fondren Library staff had decided to cover the old headings in the public catalog with pressure sensitive labels printed with the new name headings. Then, later, when the project was finished, "global" name changes could be made on the archive tapes. As a result, changes were not made on the shelf list cards.

Input from the Music Card Catalog

The Music Library at Fondren is located two floors up from Technical Services, so it is somewhat inconvenient for the cataloging staff. Using the portable inputting device, this cataloger input the first twenty main entry cards from the music card catalog, then transferred the data into the word processor for editing. This took approximately 100 minutes.

Unfortunately, while working in the Music Library, there were a few interruptions from patrons seeking information. The time away from the project was not counted, but it did take a little time to settle back into the routine. If time were not at a premium, the involvement with patrons would be a good link between cataloging and reference work. It is helpful for the cataloger to become more aware of the actual searching techniques of the patron and of the most necessary access points.

The advantages of working with the music card catalog far outweighed this slight inconvenience. All the "with" sets and all the cards in a set are available. An extra benefit is the presence of numerous information cards — "see" and "see also" references. These cross references could be input along with the cards with which they would normally be associated. This, in turn, would cut down on sorting time for the computer.

Input from Recordings

A third group was input directly from the sound recordings themselves. Twenty recordings were input using the portable device in the closed stacks. This took 133 minutes, including time for transferring data into the word processor, editing, and checking name headings on the online Library of Congress Name Authority file and in our name authority file.

Of course, this procedure is essentially recataloging and requires too much time to be considered seriously. However, it would ensure that earlier cataloging errors would not be duplicated in the database (but wouldn't prevent new errors from being made).

A great advantage would be the possibility of analyzing previously unanalyzed recordings, such as collections of opera arias, anthologies of early music, etc. But a firm decision had been made, while planning our new system, to limit entries from any one sound recording to six. This could be up to six compositions (which allows three to a side) or a title entry and five representative composer/title entries. These items are coded in the database, so that at a later date when more time and money are available, the recordings can be fully analyzed. Meanwhile, sound recordings are made available more quickly to the library user. This same principle would be applied to any retrospective conversion project.

Comparison of Inputting Devices

A fourth group of twenty cards from the shelf list was input directly into the word processor, in order to compare that method with the use of the portable inputting device. This group required only 44 minutes, as compared to the first group from the shelf list, which took 91 minutes with the portable device. The longer time interval included transferral of data from the portable device into the word processor and unavoidable editing. A further comparison was done using the larger terminal to input data from the music card catalog, resulting in a time used of 49 minutes as opposed to 100 minutes with the portable device. This ratio of about two to one shows clearly that it is much more time-effective to input directly into the intelligent terminal, despite the convenience and portability of the smaller device.

Proposal

Our conclusions are that cards from the music card catalog should be brought to the word processor during the times when the music library is closed. Capable students could be hired to do the actual inputting. They would not need to know much about music or music cataloging; they would only have to be able to read the card accurately and input certain elements into the appropriate columns as instructed. The resulting database would be revised by the cataloging staff for typographical errors and for whatever updating of name and subject headings was needed.

A training manual is being developed for these students. Actual catalog cards (using both AACR1 and AACR2) are shown, with the necessary elements outlined in various colors. Each color indicates an element, such as blue for label, yellow for label number, green for call number, etc.

Estimated Duration of Project

The time study indicated a possible 2.5 to 3 minutes per sound recording, or 20 to 24 cards per hour, to convert the data from the cards in the music card catalog. Scores could be converted a little faster, since there is usually less information on the catalog card. Fondren Library has approximately 10,160 sound recordings and 6,640 scores already cataloged. It would take about 508 hours to convert all sound recordings and 277 hours to convert the scores.

Additional time would be needed for training, but that could be kept to a minimum. The total time needed would be approximately 800 hours.

This is considerably faster than the 15 to 20 minutes per score needed by the team using OCLC for retrospective conversion. It is only possible using a streamlined procedure and the Micom Word Processor.

A. Example of matrix format used for automated list of music materials

COMPOSER	TITLE	DATE	PERFORMER	LABEL	NUMBER	CALL NO.	NOTES	SUBJECT
	Accordion	1974?	Bugala / Rauch / Messner-Graf / Maihoefer / TrossAccdEns / Wuerthner	MHS	1807	LP.A246 1 SR	ANTHOL	
	Age of bel canto	1964	Sutherland / Horne / Conrad / LonSO / NewSOLon / Bonynge	Lon	A-4257 (S834-5)	LP.A35 1	ANTHOL	
Abraham	Flower of Hawaii	1961	WienStOp / Gruber	West	XWN 18965	LP.A24 1		Ger
Abraham	[Viktoria. Sel]	1961	WienStOp / Gruber	West	XWN 18965	LP.A24 1		Ger
Adam	[Giselle]	1965	ConNatMus / Martinon	Lon	STS 15010	LP.A255 2 S		BAL
Adam	[Giselle]	1958	CovGdnO / Fayer	Angel	35838	LP.A255 4	ANG.35659-ANG.35660	BAL
Adam	[Giselle]	19--	WienPO / Karajan	Lon	CS 6251	LP.A255 1 SR		BAL
Adam	[Giselle]	19--	LonSO / Fistoulari	MercGl	SRI 2-77003	LP.A255 3 SR	SRI 75042-SRI 75043	BAL
Addinsell	Warsaw concerto	nd	LonSO / Mathieson	Col	ML 2092	LP.A3 1	10 in	
Adler	[Dialogues]	1978	Bowman / Stout	Crys	S 393	LP.A33 1 SR	Ed: C.Fischer	EUPH MAR
Aitken	[Canta,no.1]	1976	Bressler / NYChSolo	CRI	SD 365	LP.A36 1	text: Eng	SOLO CANTAsec HIvo / Eng
Aitken	[Canta,no.3]	1976	Bressler / NYChSolo	CRI	SD 365	LP.A36 1	text: Eng	SOLO CANTAsec HIvo / Eng
Aitken	From this white island	SEE	Canta,no.3					
Aitken	[Canta,no.4]	1976	NYChSolo	CRI	SD 365	LP.A36 1	text: Spa Eng	SOLO CANTAsec HIvo / Spa
Aitken	[Fant,pf]	1976	Kirkpatrick	CRI	SD 365	LP.A36 1		PF
Albeniz	[Iberia]	1960	Larrocha	Col	M2L 268	LP.A386 2	ML 5466-ML 5467	SUIT PF
Albeniz	[Piano music. Sel]	19--	Echaniz	West	XWN 18431	LP.A386 1		PF / DANCmus SPANISH
Bath	Cornish rhapsody	nd	LonSO / Mathieson	Col	ML 2092	LP.A3 1	10 in.	
Bax	Oliver Twist	nd	LonSO / Mathieson	Col	ML 2092	LP.A3 1	10 in.	
BodaJ	Sonatina,euph	1978	Bowman / Stout	Crys	S 393	LP.A33 1 SR		
CapuzziGA	Conc,db,D maj	1978	Bowman / Stout	Crys	S 393	LP.A33 1 SR		
Hindemith	[Qt,str,no.3,op.22]	1979	AlardQt	ColdCr	CRS 4184	LP.A37 1		STRqt / vn2 va vc
Janacek	[Qt,str,no.1]	1979	AlardQt	ColdCr	CRS 4184	LP.A37 1		
RossW	Partita,euph,pf	1978	Bowman / Stout	Crys	S 393	LP.A33 1 SR		STRqt / vn2 va vc

B.1. Example of composer list, showing abbreviated forms of name used in automated list
   - Underlined form of name is form found in Library of Congress Name Authority File (LCNA)
   - Other forms are variants or are not listed in LCNA

Abraham, Pal, 1892-1960.	Abraham
Adam, Adolphe Charles	Adam
Adam, Adolphe, 1803-1856.	Adam
Addinsell, Richard, 1904-	Addinsell
Adler, Samuel, 1928-	Adler
Aitken, Hugh	Aitken
Albeniz, Isaac Manuel Francisco	Albeniz
Albeniz, Isaac, 1860-1909.	Albeniz
Bath, Hubert.	Bath
Bath, John	Bath
Bath, John Hubert	Bath
Bax, Arnold Edward Trevor, Sir	Bax
Bax, Arnold, 1883-1953.	Bax
Depres, Josquin	Josquin
Des Prez, Josquin	Josquin
Despres, Josquin	Josquin
Jodocus, Pratensis	Josquin
Josquin, des Prez, d. 1521.	Josquin
Josquin, Desprez	Josquin
Josse, des Pres	Josquin

B.2. List of abbreviated forms of name used for composers

Abraham	Abraham, Pal, 1892-1960.
Adam	Adam, Adolphe Charles
Adam	<u>Adam, Adolphe, 1803-1856.</u>
Addinsell	Addinsell, Richard, 1904-
Adler	<u>Adler, Samuel, 1928-</u>
Aitken	Aitken, Hugh
Albeniz	Albeniz, Isaac Manuel Francisco
Albeniz	<u>Albeniz, Isaac, 1860-1909.</u>
Bath	<u>Bath, Hubert.</u>
Bath	Bath, John
Bath	Bath, John Hubert
Bax	Bax, Arnold Edward Trevor, Sir
Bax	<u>Bax, Arnold, 1883-1953.</u>
Josquin	Depres, Josquin
Josquin	Des Prez, Josquin
Josquin	Despres, Josquin
Josquin	Jodocus, Pratensis
Josquin	<u>Josquin, des Prez, d. 1521.</u>
Josquin	Josquin, Desprez
Josquin	Josse, des Pres

C.1. Example of list of performing groups, showing abbreviated forms of name used in automated list - Underlined form of name is form found in LCNA

```
Aarhus (Denmark)   Universitet   Institute of Musicology      AarUMusI
Alard Quartet.                                                 AlardQt
Alard String Quartet                                          AlardQt
Concertgebouw-Orkest, Amsterdam                               Congebouw
Concertgebouworkest.                                          Congebouw
Conservatoire de Paris                                        ConNatMus
Conservatoire national de musique et d'art dramatique          ConNatMus
Conservatoire national de musique et declamation, Paris        ConNatMus
Conservatoire national de musique.                            ConNatMus
Conservatoire national de musique.  Orchestre                 ConNatMusO
Conservatoire national superieur de musique                   ConNatMus
Consortium Classicum.                                         ConsClas
France  Conservatoire national de musique.  Orchestre         ConNatMusO
France.  Conservatoire national de musique                     ConNatMus
London (England).  Philharmonic Orchestra                     LonPO
London Philharmonic Orchestra.                                LonPO
London Sinfonietta.                                           LonSinf
London Symphony Orchestra.                                    LonSO
Orchestra filarmonica di Vienna                               WienPO
Orchestra of the Royal Opera House, Covent Gardens            CovGdnO
Paris (France).  Conservatoire national de musique            ConNatMus
Paris (France).  Conservatoire national de musique. Orchestre ConNatMusO
Paris Conservatory Orchestra                                  ConNatMusO
Philharmonic Orchestra, London                                LonPO
Philharmoniker (Vienna. Austria)                              WienPO
Vienna Philharmonic Orchestra                                 WienPO
Wiener Philharmoniker.                                        WienPO
```

C.2. List of abbreviations used for performing groups

AarUMusI	Aarhus (Denmark). Universitet. Institute of Musicology
AlardQt	Alard Quartet.
AlardQt	Alard String Quartet
Congebouw	Concertgebouw-Orkest, Amsterdam
Congebouw	Concertgebouworkest.
ConNatMus	Conservatoire de Paris
ConNatMus	Conservatoire national de musique et d'art dramatique
ConNatMus	Conservatoire national de musique et declamation, Paris
ConNatMus	Conservatoire national de musique.
ConNatMus	Conservatoire national superieur de musique
ConNatMus	France. Conservatoire national de musique
ConNatMus	Paris (France). Conservatoire national de musique
ConNatMusO	Conservatoire national de musique. Orchestre
ConNatMusO	France. Conservatoire national de musique. Orchestre
ConNatMusO	Paris (France). Conservatoire national de musique. Orchestre
ConNatMusO	Paris Conservatory Orchestra
ConsClas	Consortium Classicum.
CovGdnO	Orchestra of the Royal Opera House, Covent Gardens
LonPO	London (England). Philharmonic Orchestra
LonPO	London Philharmonic Orchestra.
LonPO	Philharmonic Orchestra, London
LonSinf	London Sinfonietta.
LonSO	London Symphony Orchestra.
WienPO	Orchestra filarmonica di Vienna
WienPO	Philharmoniker (Vienna, Austria)
WienPO	Vienna Philharmonic Orchestra
WienPO	Wiener Philharmoniker.

302

RETROSPECTIVE CONVERSION OF AUTHORITY RECORDS

Elisabeth Janakiev
and
William Garrison

As the online catalog becomes a reality in more libraries each year and is the object of lively interest throughout the library community, the issue of authority control is ever present in discussion and examination of the new environment. Increasingly, the most widely accepted means toward authority control is through machine-readable authority records, which today may be obtained in various ways. The method we shall examine here, and the one Northwestern University Library chose as the foundation of its online authority file, is the retrospective conversion of manual authority records. This paper will focus on Northwestern's own experience in authority conversion. We hope to show that libraries which now have or plan to introduce an online catalog also have the capability to convert their manual authorities. These files are already tailored to the libraries' own catalogs; they can be converted in a simple operation and at a reasonable cost. (Our library employs student assistants in this project.)

Certain aspects of Northwestern's conversion project, such as systems and programming requirements, overall staff needs, etc., are not covered in this paper. Also excluded are detailed project costs, both direct — such as expenditures for equipment, systems activities, project staff, supervision, etc. — and indirect — such as time spent in one way or another by other Catalog Department staff.

Development of NOTIS and the Online Catalog

First, it seems desirable to show the technological setting in which our library operates and to provide a brief history of NOTIS, our computer-based system. NOTIS (Northwestern Online Total Integrated System) not only enabled us to convert our authorities but, since one of its major features is an online catalog, virtually made it mandatory that we do so.

NOTIS is a locally developed computer system. Development of the system was begun in the late 1960s; circulation was brought online in 1970. The year 1971 saw the automation of technical services, including most functions in acquisitions, serials control, and cataloging. In 1977 a major system revision brought extensive improvements. NOTIS 3, as we call it now, is a powerful and flexible support system for a full range of library operations.

One of its features, which is a major benefit to us in Technical Services, is its ability to provide access to records in the database via a flexible index system. Although we did not in 1977 bestow the name "Online Catalog" on our database of bibliographic records, it was evident that we had the necessary structure for such a tool. When, in the late 1970s, our library had to decide on a way to accommodate AACR2 headings and the large body of old, revised LC headings into its catalogs, the library committee charged with the study of the problem had no difficulty in recommending that, as a first step, we close the old author/title card catalog and designate as its successor an online catalog. This online catalog would make use of the machine-readable cataloging and in-process records which had been created over the past decade.

Authority Structure of Online Catalog

That committee, the library administration, and other groups and key individuals also addressed the fundamental question of what, in our setting, would constitute an online catalog. A consensus soon emerged from the public service, technical services, and administrative sectors of the library regarding an acceptable standard. We, at Northwestern University, believe that an online catalog should do more than just provide patrons with a machine-readable list of items held in the library. To achieve the status and usefulness of a catalog, even if the records were to be made accessible through automatic computer search techniques, the system also required an effective reference structure. It needed some mechanism to take the place of the types of references, guides, and searching aids which traditionally have assisted users of our library catalogs.

Our choice for providing such a structure for the bibliographic database was a file of machine-readable authority records which, in addition to generating general and catalog-specific references, would also store other information, such as decisions about heading use. Moreover, and very importantly, the authority records would also serve as the main instrument for heading validation and control. The public access component of NOTIS has been available to patrons for author and title searches since June 1981. Subject access was introduced in March 1982. Although the author/title card catalog and the manual name authority file were both closed in January 1981,

until June 1982 we continued to maintain both a subject card catalog and a manual subject authority file.

Conversion of Manual Files vs. Use of LC Name Headings Tapes

In the Catalog Department, it had been realized for some time
that an online catalog would include cross references and other user
aids. A number of options for securing authority records, such as
taking records directly off the Library of Congress tapes, were explored.

We initially assumed we would use the Library of Congress Name
Headings tapes extensively, and several studies were conducted to
determine what advantages there might be in using them. A comparison of headings in the manual name authority file against the LC
authority file yielded a disappointing hit rate of 10% or less. Among
records found, many LC records were unevaluated and also needed
to be tailored to our files. This occurred particularly with authority
records containing information history references. Frequently, all of
the *see also* references appearing in these records could not be used,
or the information simply did not apply to the Northwestern files.

Given the scope of the MARC authority tapes and the number of
records on them, we came to the conclusion, as recently as 1981,
that the least costly method for us would be to convert our own
manual authority files. These records had the significant advantage
of already being tailored to our catalogs and would need virtually
no editing.

We were fortunate that our manual name and series authority
files were begun in 1969, slightly in advance of our bibliographic
database. Thus, they provided — at least in theory — complete
coverage for all headings used in the database which required cross
references.

MARC Authorities Format

As early as 1978, the Information Systems Development Office
and the Catalog Department had begun planning for the creation and
maintenance of machine authority records. The preliminary version
of the MARC format, which was available at the time, was adopted,
with the assumption that it would determine national standards for
authority records, just as other MARC formats had become the
standard for bibliographic records. Even in its preliminary form, the
MARC authorities format also offered immense capabilities for
generating all types of references, messages, searching aids, and bibliographic instruction; and its structure permitted the exploration of
many options in planning for authority control. Introduction of the

format, both technologically and in application by our staff, presented no major problems. The most serious difficulty was encountered with the 24-character control subfield, called the "w" subfield, which we restructured for internal use to four characters only.

Our expectations for the MARC format proved to be justified, and today our records are formulated in accordance with "Authorities; a MARC format," published by the Library of Congress in 1981. Our older machine records have been revised by machine processes to be compatible with the newly created records.

The Conversion Project

The retrospective conversion project which began in May 1979 has gone through several stages, both procedurally and through the application of different standards. The project is not complete, but most of our name and series records are now in machine-readable form. Although references from authority records are not yet displayed in the public online catalog, they will display after the upcoming NOTIS revision, which is currently in its final design stages. In the meantime, the authority file, with all its references, is available online to the staff throughout the Library. The Catalog Department has conducted a continuing series of orientation sessions to acquaint library staff from non-technical services areas with the construction and coding of these records, so that they may be used in patron assistance.

Initially, a decision was made to perform full conversion, i.e., all appropriate data from the manual authority card was to be converted, at least until some experience of the problems encountered had been gained. Our machine authority records thus included both full fixed field coding and full content designation of variable fields.

This initial phase of the conversion project was headed by one person, without previous professional experience, but with significant experience with authority work. Given the qualifications of our "converter," no pretagging or prescreening of the manual authority cards was performed. This proved to be a very labor-intensive way of converting, but it did enable us to see what types of problems would be encountered in an enlarged project and afforded us an opportunity to look at other methods of conversion that might be used. Between May 1979 and December 1979, our single project member, working approximately thirty hours a week, converted just over 5,000 manual name authority records.

Second Phase of Project

In the second phase of authority conversion, we hired six students.

These students worked 15–20 hours a week and were supervised by professional staff.

Based on the experience of full conversion, it was decided to speed up the conversion project by creating partial machine-readable authority records that contained only selected fixed field elements and the established heading with cross references. All other data on the manual authority card was omitted from the machine-readable authority record.

The students selected for this project were required to have typing skills of 30 words per minute and some foreign language familiarity. An abbreviated authorities tag chart was devised to answer students' tagging and content designation questions. After initial training and revision, the students input authority records with no pretagging and edited their own work, with only selected spot checks performed by the professionals.

We did not expect our students to handle all headings in our files. Instead, they performed a first pass through the manual name authority file, in which they were instructed to convert only personal names with simple "see" references. A second pass picked up more complicated headings. This method of multiple passes through the manual authority file proved to be quite profitable. First, students were able to gain competence and confidence by inputting the easier records and were then able to move on to more complex record conversion. Secondly, the students were not faced with the use of the "w" subfield until a second pass through the name authority file was performed.

The productivity of our six students was remarkable. They converted 20 to 25 records per hour and had completed two passes through the name authority file by the end of August 1980, leaving mainly headings that required higher-level attention. By the end of September 1980, approximately 22,700 authority records had been created.

Serials Authority File

The student project had been so successful that, although funds were significantly reduced at summer's end, conversion of the series authority file was begun. Two students were retained during the regular academic year and continued with the conversion of the manual series authority file.

The conversion of the series authority file was trickier than the name conversion had been. There was, for instance, no LC pattern to follow, since LC was inputting only name authority records. Format problems were encountered, as fields pertaining to series authority records had to be constructed from the draft version of

307

the authorities format. The professional librarians supervising the project screened the manual series authority cards which were to be converted to uncover problems and to select records to be converted. Again, several passes of increasing complexity were made through the file. The first pass converted untraced, unanalyzed series. The students searched the bibliographic file and hoped not to find a series tracing. If a tracing were found, either the professional librarians had to resolve the problem, or the record was not converted, since the students could skip any record that posed a problem. (In theory any conflict noticed was referred.)

Catalogers' Role

Catalogers also played a role in the conversion project and process. Beginning in 1981, professional and then copy catalogers began to be phased into machine-readable authority record creation. Provisional records, as well as existing full records, were searched and upgraded as appropriate and as encountered. However, until all catalogers were fully trained in the creation of machine authority records, Catalog Management continued to convert newly created manual authority cards. By March 1982, all authority work for both original and copy catalogers was being done online. Training, of course, was necessary, and as a result well-documented training materials and written procedures exist.

Types of Conversion

Several different methods of conversion were tried, sometimes spurred by the type and amount of money available, sometimes inspired by a new technological capability. A discussion of the pros and cons of each method follows.

Full conversion, that is, conversion of all appropriate data from a manual authority card and full coding of all fields, has the advantage of resulting in a complete machine-readable authority record. It may be possible to disband an existing manual file. This method of conversion is quite costly, since it requires higher level paraprofessional or professional staff to do the conversion. It also takes a greater period of time to perform full conversion. Online bibliographic files have to be very thoroughly searched for coding purposes.

Partial conversion has the advantage of speed of input and provides in a "skeleton" record the established heading and any references that are needed. Although these data may not be sufficient for all cataloging purposes, the references are made available for the online catalog. The staff required to perform partial conversion is of a lower level than that required for full conversion. Partial records can be upgraded and evaluated on an "as encountered" basis.

308

Although AACR2 was not responsible for our authorities conversion, it was certainly a catalyst, and it had its own "corner" of the conversion project as well. In order to make information about heading changes as obvious as possible to all catalogers, provisional records were created or existing records were updated with the AACR2 form of heading, as published in the *Cataloging Service Bulletins.*

AACR2 headings caused a large problem during the conversion. For example, we had to decide who would be responsible for evaluating every affected authority record when a university heading changed. We had committed ourselves to maintain hierarchical consistency in our files and decided that all of our bibliographic headings and authority file headings needed to agree. When, for example, "Florida. University, Gainseville" changed to "University of Florida," all of the headings in our database were "flipped" to "University of Florida." Because of the continued need for cataloging production, the individual cataloger was not made responsible for evaluating each occurrence of "Florida. University, Gainesville" in the authority file. This meant that someone (eventually Catalog Management) had to flip the records in the authority file.

In addition, the criterion that an authority heading must appear in a cataloged record in the bibliographic file caused quite a few problems to be bounced back to the librarians for resolution. These problems were of several types: 1) an authority record for an untraced series, with a record in the bibliographic file with series traced; 2) an authority record for a traced series, with a record in the bibliographic file with the series not traced; 3) an established heading with a *see also* reference, with the heading for the *see also* reference not in the online bibliographic file; 4) a *see* reference from a heading that appeared in the bibliographic file. Needless to say, with six students unearthing problems, the librarians were kept quite busy during that summer. Some of these problems were solved simply by changing a tag in the bibliographic record, e.g., 490 to 440, or by requesting that a bibliographic record be retrospectively converted, so that a *see also* heading appeared in the online bibliographic file.

Conclusion

We have spent many hours working on this conversion project. We have coped with limited resources and lack of terminal time, and we have converted authority records in several different ways. We have learned many valuable lessons from this process, and we hope that our experience may be beneficial to other libraries embarking on a retrospective conversion of authority records.

NOTES ON CONTRIBUTORS

Anne G. Adler is Head of Bibliographic Processing at Fondren Library, Rice University.

Nancy E. Douglas was the Head of Copy Cataloging at Texas A&M University during the retrospective conversion project. She is currently the Head of Cataloging at the University of California, Riverside.

Elizabeth A. Baber is Principal Cataloger at Fondren Library, Rice University. She has been closely associated with Rice's conversion project from the start, helping to plan the project and training the original staff. She continues to act as consultant on problems and, when necessary, as supervisor.

Kathleen L. Jackson was Retrospective Conversion Supervisor at Fondren Library, Rice University. She is currently Head, Copy Cataloging Section, Monographs Cataloging Department, Duke University.

Gary M. Pitkin is Associate University Librarian of the Belk Library at Appalachian State University, Boone, North Carolina. He was formerly head of the conversion project at Illinois Sangamon State University.

Lois E. Shumaker is Deputy Director for Automation and Technical Services at Sacramento Public Library.

David M. Woodburn is Director of the Mississippi Library Commission.

Gerald Buchanan is Assistant Director for Operations of the Mississippi Library Commission.

Ruby E. Miller is Associate Director for Technical Services at Trinity University in San Antonio. She was Project Director for the conversion of seven libraries in the Council of Research and Academic Libraries (CORAL).

Patricia L. John is Head of the Cataloging Section at the National Agricultural Library. She supervised the library's conversion project.

Andrew Lisowski is Head of the Catalog Department at the Gelman Library, George Washington University. He served as Director of the retrospective conversion project.

Hank Epstein spent eight years as Director of the Ballot Center at Stanford University and developed the Ballot Network there. He is president of Information Transform, Inc., and has recently designed the MITINET/retro System.

Sandra Card is Head of the Serials Automation Service of the University of California, Los Angeles.

Donald T. Green was Music Cataloger at Fondren Library, Rice University at the time of the conversion. He is currently Music Cataloger at Sibley Music Library, Eastman School of Music.

Dean W. Corwin was Assistant Music Librarian, Fondren Library, Rice University at the time of the conversion. He is currently Music and Listening Services Librarian at Trenton State College.

Margaret C. Ford is Music Cataloger at Fondren Library, Rice University.

Elisabeth Janakiev is Assistant Head of the Catalog Department at Northwestern University Library. She has been involved in the conversion project there from its beginning, planning and directing it until its absorption into the Catalog Management Section.

William Garrison is Head of Catalog Management and Marking at Northwestern University Library. He has been involved in the conversion project there as "converter" and Authorities Librarian and, in his current job, is in charge of the project.